Alpha Omega

Alpha

Omega

Markus Ray

Immortal Ray Productions
Nashville   Washington D.C.

Copyright 2020 by Markus Ray and Sondra Ray

IMMORTAL RAY PRODUCTIONS
301 TINGEY STREET, SE
WASHINGTON D.C. 20003

Immortal Ray Productions
Nashville   Washington D.C.

No part of this book may be reproduced by any mechanical, photographic, or electronic process, or in the form of a phonographic recording, nor may it be stored in a retrieval system, transmitted, or otherwise copied for public or private use without the written permission of the publisher.

Library of Congress Cataloging in Publication Data

Ray, Markus; Alpha Omega / by Markus Ray, and Sondra Ray

1. Life Wisdom. 2. Self-Mastery. 3. Philosophy.
4. Meditation/Spirituality

Cover Design: Markus Ray
Back Cover Image: Judy Totton Photography of London.

Quotes from '*I*' *am the* '*I*' and *Peace of* '*I*' Prayers
are with permission from
The Foundation of I, Inc. Freedom of the Cosmos and IZI LLC

ISBN 13: Paperback 978-1-950684-02-1

ISBN 13: E-Book 978-1-950684-03-8

Other Books by Markus Ray

Miracles with My Master, Tara Singh:
Applications of A Course in Miracles

Odes to the Divine Mother

Little Ganesh Book

The Master Is Beautiful

Co-Authored with Sondra Ray

Liberation Breathing:
The Divine Mother's Gift

Spiritual Intimacy:
What You Really Want with a Mate

Babaji:
My Miraculous Meetings with a Maha Avatar

Physical Immortality:
How to Overcome Death

Liberation:
Freedom from Your Biggest Block to Pure Joy

Right perception is necessary before God can communicate directly to His altars, which He established in His Sons. There He can communicate His certainty, and His knowledge will bring peace without question. God is not a stranger to His Sons, and His Sons are not strangers to each other. Knowledge preceded both perception and time, and will ultimately replace them. That is the real meaning of "Alpha and Omega, the beginning and the end" and "Before Abraham was I am." Perception can and must be stabilized, but knowledge is stable. "Fear God and keep His commandments" becomes "Know God and accept His certainty."

(ACIM; TEXT; CHAPTER 3; SECTION III, ¶ 6)

Table of Contents

Other Books by Markus Ray —v
Epigraph —vi
Table of Contents —vii
Foreword —xxi
Preface —xxiv
Acknowledgements —xxvii
Introduction —xxviii

Alpha Omega

1. A journal is a verbal window —1
2. Anger must come from judgment —2
3. Writing in a book in order to understand —3
4. All things in life seem to have a beginning —4
5. Listening to HH Dalai Lama speak —5
6. What are the deeper levels of reverence —6
7. Something impersonal, yet a joining of the heart —7
8. I have no cause for anger or for fear —8
9. By grace I live. —9
10. There are subjects that can be verified —10
11. Am I angry? —11
12. What is pain? —12
13. Judgment, attack, guilt, etc. —13
14. A living stream of insight is never planned —14
15. What dies? —15
16. Today I let Christ's vision rest upon all things —16

17. The last vestiges of judgment linger —17
18. In the end I am responsible —18
19. Brother, forgive me now —19
20. The "home" of the lesson —20
21. What we forgive becomes a part of us —21
22. A beginning and an end —22
23. What am I ? —23
24. I am God's Son —24
25. My sinless brother is my guide to peace —25
26. Joy is the natural state —26
27. It is essential that I end the separation —27
28. I have yet to face my most demanding challenge —28
29. Fear of death —29
30. Judgment and Love are opposites —30
31. You have a role in the Atonement —31
32. Spirit is in a state of grace forever —32
33. Only God's plan for salvation will work —33
34. Sleep is necessary to rejuvenate the body —34
35. A Course in Miracles gives mankind a new mind —35
36. I who am host to God —36
37. The last judgment declares the innocence —37
38. Purpose in life is greater than career —38
39. Old age and the decrepitude of the body —39
40. Taraji has been hospitalized —40
41. Back in Kansas —41
42. K.C. airport. Flight delay —42
43. Accepting that Christ and I stand together —43
44. There is no end to all the peace and joy —44
45. The weekend was spent in leisure —45
46. Sickness is but another name for sin —46
47. More critical is the way I view myself —47
48. Without the Christ (teacher) it is not possible —48
49. My savior is the one with whom I end separation —49
50. No call to God can be unheard —50

51. I resign as my own teacher —51
52. What exactly is karma —52
53. Conversation with KR —53
54. Father, let me remember all I do not know —54
55. The permanent is hosted by the physical —55
56. Spirit am I, a holy Son of God —56
57. The Self does not need attention from outside —57
58. I am responsible for what I see —58
59. It is impossible the Son of God be merely driven —59
60. Do I desire a world I rule —60
61. Upcoming trips: KC to aid parents —61
62. The plans are made to Hawaii —62
63. God's answer is some form of peace —63
64. I suspect the joy ACIM describes —64
65. Discipline is essential —65
66. Why is there unwillingness —66
67. The scriptures —67
68. I rule my mind —68
69. Most of the day was spent —69
70. The responsibility of the student —70
71. Work is only to be my Self —71
72. One revolution of the earth produces one day —72
73. Peace be to me, the holy Son of God —73
74. Father, it is Your peace that I would give —74
75. Who takes a breath —75
76. No one can know —76
77. A supernatural event occurred —77
78. The end of pain and sorrow —78
79. This holy instant would I give to You —79
80. Taraji told me the art of living —80
81. The mind is made open to God —81
82. God in His mercy wills that I be saved —82
83. The real religious person —83
84. What can there be in me —84

85. The Holy Spirit looks through me today —85
86. For all of us must be redeemed together —86
87. The subject of change in our life —87
88. Mother and Dad moved into a new environment —88
89. How many teachers of God are needed —89
90. The human brain believes in limitation —90
91. KC to Philadelphia —91
92. There is a desire to fulfill my function —92
93. The work of the day —93
94. I bowed my head once —94
95. The personal life has problems —95
96. I write to myself —96
97. There is no death —97
98. We are mesmerized by form —98
99. Attachment is a force in life —99
100. There is a meeting with the Unknown —100
101. Laziness and unwillingness are related —101
102. Our life will be assessed —102
103. At the end of the day —103
104. The body has its appetites —104
105. The way I see another —105
106. Obviously, there are disappointments —106
107. The rules of conventional life —107
108. We are forced by the repetitions of the past —108
109. The body appears to wear out —109
110. I feel the love of God —110
111. A person could live his whole life not knowing —111
112. In the end, there is nothing to say —112
113. On route to Los Angeles —113
114. I am the light of the world —114
115. Some encounters in life —115
116. Your goal is to find out who you are —116
117. The Source of Energy —117
118. The Self is bestowed on everyone —118

119. You have not lost your innocence —119
120. What is certainty —120
121. Fear not to recognize the whole —121
122. To give up in order to get —122
123. I am en route to Hawaii —123
124. Life of the body —124
125. Thought is memory —125
126. There is a simple way —126
127. Beyond this world —127
128. The cleaning, or purification of Self —128
129. The peace of God is shining in me now —129
130. I do not know my Self —130
131. A meeting with the wise —131
132. Is memory finite or infinite —132
133. I am as God created me —133
134. The process of forgiveness —134
135. The other's error is my own as well —135
136. The embracing of "evil" —136
137. A being incarnates for a particular reason —137
138. One accumulates in his life many things —138
139. Two friends meet —139
140. My mind holds only what I think with God —140
141. The patterns of memory —141
142. The people in our lives —142
143. I offer only miracles today —143
144. A point in time—another chance —144
145. I walk with God —145
146. The walk I walk is one of mediocrity —146
147. With life comes a great responsibility —147
148. A simple act, done totally in the present —148
149. A person can read the scriptures —149
150. God is the strength in which I trust —150
151. Errors have been made —151
152. A day of giving myself —152

153. A meeting with a friend —153
154. A low life. What is meant by that? —154
155. The physical world is riddled —155
156. The day is given —156
157. There is a pleasure in the senses —157
158. Having knowledge of the truth —158
159. A person can be inspired —159
160. Memory is the culprit of problems —160
161. I am not my memory —161
162. Relationships are the main reason for life —162
163. Few can say they betrayed the faith —163
164. The poet observes nature —164
165. Characters have traits —165
166. I am. Probably the shortest sentence —166
167. A sound is sacred —167
168. There is a revolution in life —168
169. The future is unknown —169
170. We are spiritual beings —170
171. Each day is ever new —171
172. Productivity involves relationships —172
173. I am not a victim of the world I see —173
174. A relationship is sharing and giving —174
175. I am God's Son —175
176. Within thought is the tendency —176
177. Standard religion promotes an ideal —177
178. Learning is touted as a necessity —178
179. Family patterns of relationships —179
180. The wise take birth to liberate —180
181. What is a true action —181
182. To challenge my own status quo —182
183. My mind holds only what I think with God —183
184. Love holds no grievances —184
185. Stillness is the gift of God —185
186. The good and the pleasurable —186

187. The day is given —187
188. The truth needs to be rediscovered —188
189. Art and music, at their highest level —189
190. Attachment to the body —190
191. What is health? —191
192. Spirit am I —192
193. Making contact with the Absolute —193
194. Practicality is a paradox —194
195. Once a man has reached a fearless state —195
196. I do not know —196
197. One must reach a point where he sees —197
198. Let me behold my savior —198
199. I am saved when I realize I am —199
200. To speak of principles —200
201. There must be space —201
202. Having something to give —202
203. What dies? —203
204. A teacher comes to teach —204
205. Every instant is new —205
206. An independence bestowed on me —206
207. There is a great suffering in the world —207
208. A brother with whom I have ended separation —208
209. The tools of any trade —209
210. To simplify life —210
211. What can there be in us —211
212. Thoreau said most men lead lives —212
213. Salvation is my only function here —213
214. What is shared with a brother —214
215. Most encounters in life are given —215
216. Gratefulness must face the nagging doubt —216
217. Lord, may my mistakes be brought to light —217
218. The mystic, if he would write —218
219. Life, Liberty, and the pursuit of happiness —219
220. Within the human brain —220

221. What is a body —221
222. A peace beyond understanding —222
223. We base our trust on the ephemeral —223
224. Conventionally a book is a stream —224
225. To simplify life I must pare it down —225
226. Truth is something beyond our thinking —226
227. Basically, the mass of mankind —227
228. Silence, a state of being with no words —228
229. To read the words of great men —229
230. A productive day begins with gratefulness —230
231. When true words touch the planet —231
232. I am responsible for my unhappiness —232
233. Man takes delight in the world —233
234. At the end of the day before bed —234
235. Light and joy and peace abide in me —235
236. My friend is one who can see —236
237. Depression results from the thought —237
238. Within the day are the physical tasks —238
239. A prayer of prayers —239
240. Certainty is not of thought —240
241. The power of decision is my own —241
242. The call to God has been heard —242
243. A new day begins with a prayer —243
244. Great artists, painters in particular —244
245. When I use the word God —245
246. There are people with whom I have grievances —246
247. Gratefulness to life for all my past —247
248. Today our theme is our defenselessness —248
249. I cannot be my Self by an act of will —249
250. Miracles remove the blocks —250
251. There is quiet and there is light —251
252. A conversation I have with myself —252
253. I must forgive myself —253
254. We must be clear —254

255. Stillness is a state in which thought slows down —255
256. Reverence for the teacher —256
257. I desire to speak somewhere without bounds —257
258. There is a space in life —258
259. A problem is persistent —259
260. To accept my world as it is —260
261. A person can excel in an art form —261
262. Student: Does life take care? —262
263. A meal was shared —263
264. Who is most dead —264
265. What is valued in the world —265
266. Know Thyself —266
267. The times I have heard wisdom —267
268. With every inspiration —268
269. Is my life being guided by God —269
270. Mysticism begins with the admission —270
271. The Chinese sages refer to the way of life —271
272. We know God through our fellow humans —272
273. My salvation comes from me —273
274. The undoing of what is in me —274
275. Man, to perceive his world —275
276. Having the energy to face myself —276
277. Having a body —277
278. We have become a society of robots —278
279. What can one say regarding silence —279
280. What am I giving to life? —280
281. Why does the human being fall into depression —281
282. When I say, I feel, who feels —282
283. There is nothing greater in life —283
284. To be with the emptiness —284
285. What exactly is my body —285
286. Dreams are fantastic —286
287. Self-centeredness of the ego —287
288. Mysticism begins when I honestly say —288

289. A real poet, a mystic, is in touch —289
290. Writing about fictional characters —290
291. Beauty is only the first touch —291

Elegies Between Heaven and Earth

1. Where have you gone? —293
2. There is a point —294
3. I hover over a query —296
4. Inundation of words —297
5. It is night, and I am still —298
6. Speak not about things —299
7. I, on a seat somewhere between heaven —300
8. There is a space inside me —301
9. Isolation's error is just a yearning —302
10. A fasting of my whole Self —303
11. He passed today, 4/7/2006 —304
12. Accountable to my own conscience —305
13. Having my own voice is not that easy —306
14. What would my muse be but myself —307
15. Flat on earth I am —308
16. Hands are the portal into the soul —309
17. Who are angles but the dead returned —310
18. The senses of myself —311
19. What could time be —312
20. Do I want to see what I denied —313
21. Standing on my own —314
22. Patterns of personality —315
23. To lift myself out of conditioned thought —316
24. Worship is an adoration of the Unknown —317

25. A conscious life is attention —318
26. Who am I talking to in the end? —319
27. What used to be called melancholia —320
28. There are missed opportunities —321
29. A person takes on certain things —322
30. Rilke writes of a future happening —323
31. One can corner himself —324
32. I will always have some aspect of my past —325
33. A word comes forth out of me —326
34. How can it be that I write anything —327
35. Once killing, war, and violence are justified —328
36. Without a doubt —329
37. God's peace and joy are mine —330
38. April 7, 2006, 8:05 PM Tara Singh passed —331
39. In the holy light of these words —332
40. To the extent that I am not happy —333
41. The purpose of the Holy Spirit —334
42. We use the word Love —335
43. How do we know a truth? —336
44. What is the source of fear —337
45. The wise say there is a state of being —338
46. A day is given to be harmonious —339
47. What is written in the moment —340
48. Being willing to die for a cause is not courage —341
49. One is either liberated from thought or not —342
50. A religious life —343
51. There is only stillness —344
52. Tableside conversation —345
53. My Self is beyond thought —346
54. It is high time to grow up —347
55. A problem is a memory replaying —348
56. A problem is a memory replaying —349
57. What are the discoveries of each day? —350
58. Rest is in being Awake —351

59. D. H. Lawrence brings me back —352
60. The holy instant —353
61. Something compels me to write —354
62. After a day of physical labor —355
63. I am not a writer of fiction —356
64. The power of forgiveness —357
65. An action of grace has no judgment —358
66. Your task is not to seek for love —359
67. The wise do not seek what is a priori —360
68. Think once of Arunachala —361
69. In India emphasis is placed on liberation —362
70. A novelist writes about people's lives —363
71. A writer describes life —364
72. A novelist is a lover of people —365
73. What are the aspects of the novel —366
74. There is only one end —367
75. There are numerous branches in the road —368
76. I have a wonderful room —369
77. There is a blessing —370
78. There seems to be a great struggle —371
79. Why do people feel that paradise —372
80. A action which brings joy —373
81. There is a vast universe —374
82. My teacher, Tara Singh, has left these planes —375
83. A Course in Miracles has something to say —376
84. Beauty is inside of me first —377
85. Many stories are told —378
86. A day is given —379
87. The rain has finally arrived —380
88. A soul evolves —381
89. When still and quiet, there is little to say —382
90. To be free of memory —383
91. A friend can bear another's pain —384
92. The impact that a person has —385

93. To the degree that what I write is true —386
94. A person is influenced by those around him —387
95. Philadelphia, or City of Brotherly Love —388
96. The human brain holds all the goodness —389
97. The man who stands alone —390
98. The world has its own ways —391
99. Repentance, Forgiveness, Transmutation —392
100. Notebooks are thoughts —393
101. Nature is always new —394
102. An action of life produces something —395
103. Action and activity are two distinct movements —396
104. I am not one to shun physical work —397
105. To be with the day —398
106. The times contain solutions —399
107. Usually what one learns from another —400
108. The empty mind is enlightened —401
109. Vigilance is watching the mind —402
110. Memory is unwilling —403
111. Memory is the fact —404
112. Discouragement is lack of courage —405
113. We are so conditioned by our upbringing —406
114. Water is the second most essential element —407
115. Earth is the progenitor of food —408
116. I have a concept of myself —409
117. Man strives for perfection —410
118. What has death and a thick body —411
119. I am the Alpha and the Omega—412
120. The mind, having been introduced —413
121. My first spiritual Love —414
122. I came from a long way down —415

Epilogue —417
Resources —418
About the Author —420

Foreword

One of the reasons I totally surrendered to Markus when we met again after twenty years was this: He handed me a book of his writings. I started reading that and I was totally blown away. My thought was, "This man is VERY deep." I could not resist him after reading that. Even now there are many books of his writings in long hand that have never been published and they are next to me right now on our book shelf. I kept saying he should get them published and so he is starting to do that. I wrote a book recently called **Lately I've Been Thinking** which contains all my posts for two years from Facebook. I even have another two years of Posts that will be Volume II. This book he has here is kind of like that.

I am always amazed to see how he does this writing in long hand. He starts at the top of the page, and it flows through him to the bottom of the page. Of course he is also a poet and I love his poetry (See **Odes to the Divine Mother**). This book of prose in your hands now really shows who he is and it is very enlightening. I feel privileged to live with such a man who has these high thoughts. I think this book, **Alpha Omega**, is very inspiring and you will get a lot out of it.

His last book is called **The Master is Beautiful** in which he writes about Masters who have inspired him. Because he is tuned in to these Masters and surrenders to them, he can down load something beautiful. I have seen him sit and write in all kinds of places. I might be shopping at Nordstrom's. He sits in a chair and writes while I am shopping. Or he might take out the pen at Starbucks. Sometimes he writes in airports while we are waiting for our flight to wherever. He can write literally anywhere. Because he is a devoted student of ***A Course in Miracles***, much of his writing is quite spiritual and it will make you feel high. It is very exciting that we are both writers. Another reason he can write so well is because he is constantly clearing himself through Liberation Breathing. It helps him become a clear channel. This book was totally written in long hand. That is how he writes, which I find amazing. I tend to type things out. I don't know if I could write like he does. It is so raw.

I have looked at his manuscripts and rarely are there any corrections. The words just flow out of him, and he writes them down. It is kind of like the movie I saw years ago about Mozart called ***Amadeus***. The young Mozart would hear the music in his head, and as the notes descended like falling leaves into his mind he would just write them down on his parchment, without fussing too much—no corrections or edits. Maybe one word here and there Markus will "white out" and put in a better one. But generally, the words are written directly how he hears them. They come from a place of Silence within himself.

I really know that one can definitely increase one's enlightenment by reading this book. It is important to read high thoughts that expand your mind. That is what this book will do for you. You can open it anywhere and just read one page. It is like "drinking the Divine," which is a Holy Nectar that will nourish you in ways that nothing else can. Wouldn't you like to be nourished by God?
For me there is only before I met my Master Babaji in my life, and after I met Babaji. Yet, joining with my husband

ALPHA OMEGA

Markus Ray over 30 years after that meeting infused a new Energy of Spiritual Intimacy into my life and Relationships.

The Holy Relationship is the boon of the Divine Mother given to us. I consider myself lucky to be spending my days, 24/7/365 with someone as creative and serious about his evolution as a soul, as Markus Ray.

Love,

His Wife,

Sondra Ray

Preface

"Truth is a pathless land." So said Krishnamurti, my teacher's teacher. "When you don't want anything, you realize you have everything." So said my teacher, Tara Singh. These two statements of truth were worth my whole Life to receive.

Alpha Omega, like much of my writing, begins and ends without a path, a "direction," except to be honest with myself about what I may be attending to in the moment. I have been trained to question my thoughts. The very nature of memory and the brain is to divide, judge, analyze, and be ever discontented with what it has—resulting from its accumulation of all kinds of "thoughts." Hence, there is a lot in the brain to "undo." Whatever does not result in inner clarity, and with that, more Pure Joy, is questionable.

The purpose of *Alpha Omega* is to begin with Pure Joy, and end with Pure Joy. Each entry is written like that. I try to put my mind in a kind of "silence," which for me is intensely Joyful. Then I explore what flows into me in terms of observations and intimations, follow the beads of meditation to the end of the mental rosary of written words on the page, then end with the same Pure Joy in which I started. This is *Alpha Omega* to me. This process of touching and maintaining something Divine throughout is how I write—be it a one page entry such as these meditations, or a whole chapter, or a poem, or even an entire book. The process is the same. Start in Silence and end in Silence. Joy begets Joy, then everything in between is Joy.

What could be a better way to write—to live—to BE? Krishna Das sings, "I have found a way to live, in the Presence of the Lord." And what could be better than that Presence? I am blessed by the Presence of Silence, of Pure Joy. Tara Singh cleared my mind enough of its dross and drivel that I could then get a glimpse of its true potential. Sondra Ray completed the clearing. And in that Presence they imparted to me—I choose now to live my days.

Recently I have been committing to memory some of my *Odes to the Divine Mother.* These lines stand out, from **Ode # 57—*Vessel of Your Love*:**

> *Open my mind to receive the gift of all-pervasive Presence that is the essence of You everywhere. In all situations and places I can turn my attentions to You and surrender my senses to a different perception—one of gentleness and peace, one of beauty and grace, one of harmony and aliveness. I am but the container of what cannot be contained.*

Who can empty themselves is ever closer to receiving the outpouring of grace—that which is bestowed upon us from a loving Creator. Call that the Divine Mother, or the Divine Father, or call it just the Omnipresent Life Force. All are the same. These meditations in ***Alpha Omega*** are also, like the ***Odes***, the "containers of what cannot be contained." They are clearly "containers," yet the subject they serve is Boundless. What limits could I lay upon myself, upon these meditations, upon you my reader, upon a truth of which we may only explore its most distant edges as it comes closer to our pulsing, living core? From the beginning of time to the ending of time, this boundlessness is a fact. It *cannot be contained.*

I make no apologies for being misguided. In fact, I would rather be admitting this inherent "misguidedness" than assuming I know what I do not know, or saying I see what I do not see—yet. **Alpha Omega** was my process for three years—after Tara Singh made his transition and before I was fully joined with Sondra Ray. It was a "period of transition" for me as well. After Taraji passed I was wayward, in the sense of feeling "captainless on my own ship." Thrown into this dilemma by the vitality of his "passing," I had to pilot my own ship after that. This handwritten Journal was my way of doing what he and the Masters had prepared me to do.

Alpha Omega implies a "first and a last." As I mentioned before, it is more indicative of a Cycle of Immortal Refrain. That which "ends" has a new "resurrection" in the spring of a burgeoning life. I stepped into that spring. And the blossoming looked like my meeting with Sondra Ray in the winter of my discontent, in 2007-2008. By March of 2008 we were together permanently. I never looked back, having left my old life totally behind. I left with two suitcases.

The writing was on the wall—or in this case in the book I called **Alpha Omega**. I knew my old life was over, but I did not yet have a grasp on my new life to come. Left to Faith, feeling somewhat misguided, as I said, I received the Guidance I needed—Babaji, Jesus of *A Course in Miracles,* and the Divine Mother took over my life completely, in the loving and dynamic form of Sondra Ray.

"I came from a long way down, " as Bob Dylan said once. I did too. But fortunately God did not leave me there—and through **Alpha Omega** I have most certainly been redeemed.

The Author

Acknowledgements

My foremost acknowledgment is highly due to Barbara Milbourn. She has taken this handwritten manuscript of over 400 pages and typed it up with the editorial prowess generally reserved for "higher ups." The fact that she revelled in the task, and took in the writings themselves, beyond mere transcription, speaks of who she is—a total human being well tuned in her craft—from the bottom up, so to speak. What could have been a mundane task of "nuts and bolts" became her action of editorial expertise. It is as though she "took me on" under her wing of genius to make sure the work was entrusted with equally astute eyes and ears, to see and hear a truth spoken. In this case written—for her to type and surmise.

My second acknowledgment is to everyone else. There are a lot of people who "shaped me." I cannot name them all here. You know who you are, living or passed on, and also what influence you had over me for which I am gratefully and eternally indebted. The newness of our ALPHA is leading us onward to the the fullness of our OMEGA. This Cycle will continually play out in our perpetual manifestation of Life. ALPHA and OMEGA, thus, are not so much the "Beginning and the End," but rather the perpetual and Immortal Cycles of Divine Life. There is always yet another Heaven to realize. The Seventh Heaven is just a metaphor for the perpetual evolution of our souls to achieve absolute perfection. This *journey* is the real *Acknowledgement*, for which we took shape from the ethers to undergo.

Introduction

In a short moment of "self doubt" I was floundering in the doldrums of disbelief that this manuscript would be completed. And beyond that, it would be going into the pipeline of publishing, and may or may not be well received. Barbara Milbourn wasted no time to draw me out of it, and was sure to cite a passage from **Alpha Omega** itself when I was questioning my motives and my future audience for this work. These following letters of exchange provide the best Introduction to **Alpha Omega**. In this way you, my readers, get to see first hand the creative process through which these "baser works of lead" are "transmuted to gold."

SEPTEMBER 30, 2019:

>Hi Markus,
>
>It's September 30 and I had hoped to finish typing **Alpha Omega** by today, however, see there are approximately 80 pages yet to go.
>I'm getting there.
>Things are looking neat and crisp.
>And your writing is compelling and reaching.
>I'll reach out again when only 5 pages remain.
>
>Love from Arizona
>
>B.

ALPHA OMEGA

OCTOBER 1, 2019:

Hi Barbara,

THANK YOU for you update. There is absolutely no rush.

Perhaps you can "lift up my spirits," as sometimes I feel like I am writing somewhat "into the wind," or scribing in a "little closet to myself."

I read a few passages today in Walden to infuse myself with some new JOY. Thoreau always speaks to the truth inside of himself, and is not so concerned if his readership hears him or not. He hears himself, and makes sure what he is saying is 100% consistent with his heart and head combined, in the most distilled expression of his own inspiration. He could go above the common thoughts, and face the fact the atmosphere is more rarified there, and his readership more discerning, and therefore—well, "smaller." But he always starts with a fact—either one of nature, or the nature of the mind itself. That wisdom endures, though not many may have read his work in his own day. Along with Whitman, I think he Self-published.

Alpha—Omega was written in the space between Tara Singh's passing in April of 2006, and my reunion with Sondra Ray in 2007-9.

I have almost no recollection of what I was saying or writing about back then. Probably a lot about coming to a "still mind," a kind of inner emptiness.

That was the great gift of Taraji to me. I do remember I had a meditation room in which I mostly "lived" after Taraji's passing, and it was in there I scribed the thing.
So reading the new Alpha—Omega will be as much a surprise to me, as probably it was to you.

We are in DC for the moment, but do a 10 day "tour of duty" in the UK leaving next Wednesday. Then back to DC for a couple weeks before going Down Under and to Thailand and Bali.

So all is good in our world, even when I feel a bit "down."

HUGS,

MARKUS

Barbara wasted no time in her response to me, as I heard back the next day, in our very well-tuned epistolary relationship.

OCTOBER 2, 2019

Good Wednesday morning, Markus

Thanks for the reprieve on Alpha and Omega.
I look forward to you re-discovering it and will give you a little taste below.

First, through these pages you have re-affirmed my decision to return to Tennessee to better be available and loving and caring to my family. We are looking and have zeroed in on a Del Webb community east of Nashville. Our house is not on the market here, but was previewed by an interested party yesterday so the wheels have begun turning.

About your writing and feeling the need for a little spirit lifting to address your concerns about writing into the wind from a little closet to yourself…Well, dear, I'm always happy if I can lift your spirits with my own truth which you have helped me find.

Writing "into the wind" or scribing in a "little closet to myself" is something you wouldn't find Thoreau saying to himself and I consider you pretty much up there with him—so pitch those thoughts and remember what you recently reread in Walden, and then take a look at this from **Alpha Omega** concerning your process of writing:

34.

A

How can it be that I write anything that is my own and not an echo of another whose greater thought has born upon me in some circumstantial way? I was not educated in writing, and though holding a Masters of Fine Arts degree from Temple University I have come to distrust the academic impetus of any work of art. Life is the impetus, and a life which has its difficulties. I have felt the pangs of isolation and obscurity but only now see the benefits of my solitude, and for better or worse, my lack of formal education when it comes to writing. After all is said and done, writing is speaking what is on my mind in the form of the written word. Seems obvious. Yet it is also something deeper. It is a question one poses to himself and the discipline to withhold conclusions and opinions so as to discover a here-to-fore unknown truth. To the extent I can discover and speak a truth is the extent my writing is Self-honest. Writing then becomes a process of Self-inquiry, or the means for something new to be revealed or something old to be better understood. I am a late bloomer. It has taken fifty-one years for me to feel remotely on the verge of possessing my own voice. I am compelled to write to uncover a truth in me. A solitude of unlimited possibilities is my most valued possession. Yet, being in the world is necessary as well. Solitude within a crowd; that is an art well worth developing.

Ω

So, there you were then and here you are now. All is well, is it not?

Signing off for the moment. We have a new family member: Anders, a 3-year-old male whippet, recently adopted.

Joy to you and Sondra,

Barbara

ALPHA OMEGA

I was very moved, not only by Barbara's depth of understanding into who I am and what it is I am writing, but her ability to put her finger on the pulse of my malaise and feed me back my own literary remedy, of the homeopathic kind. Immediately I wrote this back to her on the same day, after receiving her heartfelt response.

OCTOBER 2, 2019

>Dear Barbara,
>
>Your uplifting letter made me cry.
>
>The truth is such, as you say. I am so grateful to hear it.
>
>You know me better than me, it seems sometimes, through your most intimate relationship with my words to myself.
>
>THANK YOU.
>
>The move back to Nashville for you seems good timing, for whatever reasons of familial closeness, and also because it is just a plain great place to be.
>
>Ken Burns just did a series on Country Western Music. We watched the whole thing (16+ hours) and thought of our dear Nashville ourselves, and pondered our "easy life" there. And how we missed our ambulation around the Parthenon, so close to us as an actual "Divine Mother Temple" (with 40 foot tall gold Athena inside).

THANK YOU hardly does it. You got me out of my little doldrum, and challenges in our network around the world are receiving the "light of day." Though sometimes we feel some "hurt"(such as when a key organizer leaves our work) our hearts are healing around it day by day. "Letting go" gracefully, and still maintaining our truth, is the lesson on the table. And giving up any "attack thoughts" about the whole matter.

"I can be hurt by nothing but my thoughts." Lesson 281—and in this case thoughts of attachment and expectations not met. So we are "processing" and forgiving ourselves for that. And any organizer for activating it in us.

Whew, this inner work of relationships is never really "done," is it?

I am grateful for you in my life—and having been through little fires that now seem only to be brightening our days. I pray for this kind of "campfire" to be the one we and all our organizers sit around one day. It will come in time, I reckon.

HUGS,

MARKUS

PS. YES, ALL IS WELL. And that Anders is a lucky critter, he is.

And a PPS:

ALPHA OMEGA

> I have scarcely ever received a letter with so much compassion in it.
>
> Only letters from Tara Singh moved me as much. Great gratitude over here.
>
> M.R.

Soon Barbara's reply was thus:

OCTOBER 2, 2019

> WOW, thank you Markus.
> Now you have lifted me mightily too.
> I treasure our relationship and the mutual gratification in it.
>
> Happy day my friend,
>
> B.

A few weeks later I heard back from my Barbara that the transcription of the manuscript was finished:

OCTOBER 31, 2019

> Good morning Markus,
>
> Alpha & Omega is finished and available for review in Drop Box.
> I am packaging your precious notebook (with little surprises inside) and sending if off to you via Federal Express today.

In the package I will include a brief sheet of notes FYI.
It has been my good pleasure to transcribe this for you and to hear your heart.
I always think you have much worthwhile to say, and that it is an amazing beacon to others.
And it's a privilege to be inside someone's innermost journey . . . quest for truth and gift to humanity.

On the morning of the 17th of November Jeff and I and our new family member, Anders, will head east with our cars packed with a few things we will need upon arrival in our new home near Nashville.

We have bought a home in Mt. Juliet (east of Nashville on I-40).

I will miss Arizona very much.
I love the West; its beauty, its intelligent and extending people, all.
One must look harder in Tennessee to see beauty all around, but it is there.

Jeff misses the four seasons.
He tires of the constant blue sky, sunshine, and warmth.
He says he does not want to die in the desert.
Frankly, I think it would be a swell place: the TVs (turkey vultures) and coyotes can pick our bones clean and they can bleach in the sun.
I digress. . .

Thank you Markus.

ALPHA OMEGA

Hoping all is well and swell with you.
Sending love from Arizona,

Barbara

After these exchanges I had a chance to review some of the transcription, as I had forgotten just how extensive the manuscript was. To my surprise it transcribed into over 430 pages, and this could possibly be considered a major work. I came back to Barbara with this:

OCTOBER 31, 2019

HI B.

I am duly impressed. Duly and Truly.

I assume we will receive the original MS package no later than Monday from FED EX, as we leave for 2 months on Tuesday to AU, THAILAND, and beloved BALI. We will not return until DEC 23, just before Christmas.

(Would not be good for that precious package to sit around for 2 months.)

THANK YOU for your kind words about my writings. They serve as a "dialogue with myself," and as I could possibly represent my readers minds as well, I am a good litmus test as to what another might hear. Sondra oft' jokes about how I like to "read my own writings," yet, it is I who most need what I am saying to myself in the first place.

I am indebted, in a good way, for our relationship. If Conrad had his "secret sharer," I have my "inner most sanctum" sharer. Such a rarity to have that in this life. First with Sondra, then Gurus, then my literary Friend.

I think your move, for the time being, is in the Divine Order of things. And because of that, you will receive unexpected Divine Blessings along the way, and GOD will show you that Grace and Beauty are everywhere. Someone from India who was jaded about the West asked Tara Singh how he coped with "being in America." Expecting a negative critique from someone so well versed in the "Indian Ways," Taraji responded to the critical mass of this man with the following; *"The dawn is beautiful everywhere."* So there you have it. It shut the guy up totally and brought him to a "new dawn" within himself.

Nashville rises large in our fond memories of an easy and sacred life. We still have that here, but for "more money." HA HA ! (Our rent literally doubled; but our aesthetic surroundings quadrupled.)

Your family will be happy again to have you nearby.

Maybe you can plummet yourself here and there to go on "desert jaunts" with your Arizona friends—here and there. GOD wants his children to be "mobile," (and most of all—happy). So have a base in Nashville and do jaunts to the South West desert (in the proper proportion).

ALPHA OMEGA

As for the parched bones picked clean by the TV's—well, I would rather prefer you get a flock of them together and "give them a lecture" on the virtues of finding other meat. You are gonna master Physical Immortality. Or at least "GO FOR IT," as the saying goes. They can find dead snakes or road kill or some other source of nutrition. And maybe a couple of them would be interested in Physical Immortality themselves, and the virtues of becoming "Breatharians." Invite a few armadillos too.

LIFE is certainly Swell. I look forward to perusing the *Alpha Omega* file.

HUGS for certain,

MARKUS with a small but steady RAY.

This can give you an idea of what it is like communing with my editor. More than that, it is a Holy Relationship that is nurtured along the road to discovering an inner truth. It also gives you, my reader, a window into the soul of a deeper communication. When we interviewed people as to what they really wanted in a Relationship with friends, family or lovers, they said first and foremost "Deeper Connection."

Alpha Omega is just this "Deeper Connection" forged over a period of years with my innermost Self. These "conversations with God" are realized in this dialogue from within. Everyone has this accessibility, yet, who is quiet enough in their day to listen to the silent inner voice of wisdom constantly whispering gentle intimations? We are too abreast of our computer games, Netflix menus, CNN diatribes, and Fox Sports spectacles to practice the Presence. The Presence is always there, but we are absent. The Presence is always speaking to us, but we do not have "the ears to hear."

Alpha Omega may slow you down to listen to this voice. You will inevitably hear your own—and this is a good thing. Wisdom flows freely without bounds, nor specified directions. It responds to the moment in the moment. You will invariably have your own dramas going on, yet, I pray these beginnings and endings are divinely applicable to them.

—MARKUS RAY—
Washington DC, November 2, 2019

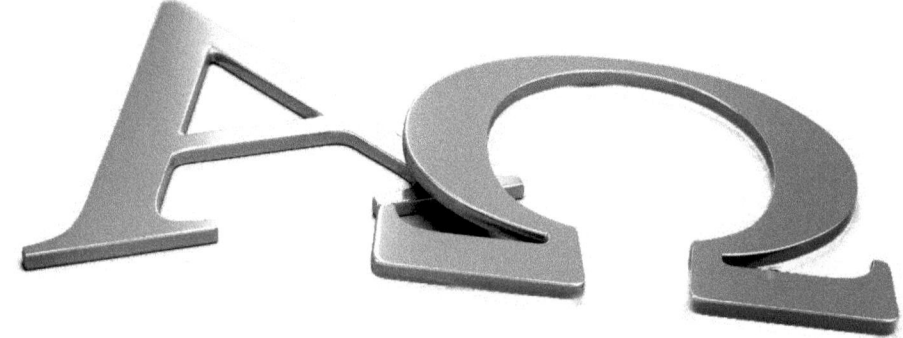

1.

A

A journal is a verbal window into those deeper-most thoughts that spring not from experience alone, but from the space of silence left open when experience is done. Experience is a memory, tainted at best by a personal perspective. When that perspective broadens to view the whole, I come closer to the silence, unattached, without a judgment of good vs. bad. It is possible to be neutral and empty; but a relationship with the wise is necessary. I judge without even the awareness I am judging. The wise point out my judgments, and the falseness of my thought; in so observing this falseness, I have the opportunity to let go of it. Emptiness is a virtue: a state of mind which does not judge. For observations to be true they must come from a still mind that does not judge. I am grateful to be vigilant of my judgments, and to accept the Atonement which sets me free of them. The Mind, my Mind, can return to peace, its natural state of being.

Ω

2.

Anger must come from judgment. Judgment is a weapon I would use against myself to keep the miracle away from me. ACIM, Lesson #347 My brain is poised to attack by its very nature: I like and dislike. Its duality keeps me in constant conflict. The nature of thought, at its very root, is judgment. Judgment leads to conflict. Conflict implies guilt. Guilt demands punishment: the observer of guilt and the guilty are the same. I can step out of the whole mess of judgments if I allow myself to give them up and admit I was wrong. Judgment, good or bad, is equally binding of the one who judges. There is no separation between the attacker and the attacked. The miracle is in seeing my judgment as unreal, and accepting God's *judgment* which is only JOY. He who is JOYOUS does not judge, because he values JOY more than sorrow, and accepts equal responsibility for both. Happiness is a function of innocence, not guilt. Who is guilty? The world is based on expectations, motives, and advantages—the seedbeds of falling short. What meaning do my motives have? All is provided to the one who wants nothing. Only he knows **perfect happiness. *ACIM, Lesson #101***

Ω

3.

A

Writing in a book in order to understand a truth is no substitute for how I live my life. The encounters of everyday living are no accident, and the relationships that come out of them are the test of application. "What do I have to give?" is always the concern. This is determined by the qualities I have inside. Have I overcome greed? Am I angry? Do I judge? Do I put myself first? Am I attached to things? There are impurities that must be overcome. Observation is of myself. Leaving the other alone, I can observe my motivations and forgive them. They are common to the human condition. Once the inner impurities are understood and overcome (and this takes an ongoing vigilance), then I might discover something pure and still within myself that is peaceful, joyful, and happy. This can be extended, and its action is to bring me together with others in an embrace of the common good. It is natural to extend according to my own temperament. To accept myself, forgiven, is the beginning of extending my Self. There is no real Love outside of this acceptance; I love myself first by forgiving. In forgiveness is the end of all judgment. When judgment ends, Love awakens, and I am free just *to be*. Identity is a priori, needing no explanation because it is beyond thought.

Ω

4.

All things in life seem to have a beginning, middle, and end. We think laterally. Physical forms are born, live, and die. But the great men and women of the spirit see the temporal nature of physicality and ask is there something more, something beyond mortality, something unaffected by time, decay and death—*something vertical*. The wisest ones do not rely on a belief, on a projection of some Nirvana to be attained after the body is gone. Their question concerns only what is now. Is it possible to have contact with that changeless, timeless, immortal state while living in the present? Can man know the truth of the changeless within the everyday experience of a world in which there is an endless flow of change? Joy is sought in the field of change—which turns into sorrow. Why? Is it possible, as Krishnamurti asks, for man to empty his consciousness totally, to step out of the "stream" of changing ideas, emotions, experience, thoughts and be in the vast stillness and silence of the Unknown; and do this in the present? Heaven is a state of mind now, free of conflict, when all "becoming" has come to an end. I do not want an unfulfilled pleasure, and I do not cause myself or others pain. There is a relationship with the *present as it is*. The quality of my own inner peace is more valuable than any acquisitions. It's unaffected by time. It is immortal.

Ω

5.

A

Listening to HH Dalai Lama speak on the four noble truths: suffering, cause of suffering, cessation of suffering, path that leads to the cessation of suffering. Thought is the cause of suffering, especially attack thoughts. The desire to "become" is a cause of suffering, because I do not accept who I am now. *Seeking* presupposes *not having*; not having is a form of suffering. Taraji said, "When you want nothing, you have everything." This is a truth so swift, requiring no time, no long practice, just the ears to hear. But who has the ears to hear, to be free of wanting? Desire to have things different than they are is a form of suffering. The sensations and appetites of the body are strong. Denial is not necessary, but indulgence is detrimental as well. The body has needs for air, water, food, shelter, clothing, etc. Once these are fulfilled, what is the function of my mind? To know its own emptiness, its own holiness, its own peace, its own nothingness is to know the cessation of suffering. Experience is transcended; a state beyond the senses and one of a pure and silent mind is the nature of the Self. Buddha realized Himself. Jesus and other enlightened beings did as well.

Ω

6.

A

What are the deeper levels of reverence and the action of life that ensues from them? My thought does not know reverence. It knows authority of one over another. Reverence, the act of revering, is a form of intense gratefulness for Life providing the one who is wise, compassionate, aware of my suffering and able to help me to remove it. For this one there is reverence. I come to Him or Her with a burden, and I leave without it. The wise free mankind from the burdens of thought. They help make one empty, yet with an emptiness that contains everything. There is no lack in the boundlessness of the empty. I am safe wherever I go. There is nothing to fear. God's voice speaks to me in the bird, the tree, the sound of the traffic on the expressway. ***All things are echoes of the Voice for God. ACIM, Lesson #151*** The world of appearances contains sickness, sorrow, despair and death. The miracle questions these appearances. Even within the most abject circumstances, there is a chance to deny their effects. What I see is a mirror image of my thought which is often in a state of conflict and anxiety. But I can change my mind to look on duress as a cover for the call for help; the plea for forgiveness that the world so desperately needs.

Ω

7.

A

Something impersonal, yet a joining of the heart, in which two human beings have decided their interests are not separate, is the purpose of *Alpha Omega.* Can I step out of the personal world of "separation" into the impersonal world of universal principles? I am challenged. ***ACIM*** points out a higher truth: ***I am under no laws but God's. ACIM, Lesson #76*** Yet, I am conditioned by the laws of medicine, economics, governments of the state and the laws of family patterns and psychological entrapments. I am conditioned by my own thought. To step out of this is next to impossible. The human brain sticks to what it knows; even in that knowledge, it is suffering. Why do I accept suffering? What sacrifice do I make, and to what gain? An old person comes to a point in which he cannot care for himself. He is moved around, shuttled from place to place. Friends have not taken him in, out of the joy in their hearts. We do not have the space. The best we can do is to place him in managed care. Is there an Action born out of the Impersonal in which the heart is ready to receive through its own giving? To project a plan is a mistake, yet to be indifferent, accepting the limits of the status quo feels like a graver mistake. I am challenged to find within that Divine Self I have to give.

Ω

8.

A

I have no cause for anger or for fear, for You surround me. And in every need that I perceive, Your grace suffices me. ACIM, Lesson #348 I can do nothing of myself. Without the Grace of God behind my actions, they are a paltry substitute for the Will of my Father. The Father always stands ready to extend help when I have removed my agenda and am open enough to ask my innermost being, my sub-conscious mind, about its memories and concerns. In this prayer I am always asking my sub-conscious mind to invoke the Spirit, the superconscious mind, for solutions to any problem. This is the true meaning of the trinity: consciousness joins the sub-consciousness and asks my super consciousness to be the guide of my thoughts, words, deeds, and actions. The Divine Mother asks the Divine Child, the Divine Child invokes the Divine Father, and the Divine Father connects with the Divine Source—which is the right order. It is a constant state of reverence, of a bowed head which can receive the Joyous Will of the Divine Source. What is not totally Joyous is a memory in need of undoing. All error is a call for Love. Forgiveness, the Love of correction, is an attitude of admitting, "I am wrong in my judgments. Father, forgive me, I know not what I do. You are the light I would follow. Let every voice but Yours be still in me." I ask for Your words, **Requesting only what You offer me; receiving only thoughts You share with me.** ACIM, Lesson #339 Prayer is then an unbroken chain of asking for guidance.

Ω

9.

A

By grace I live. Every breath I take is given to me. I did not create the air; out of the Great Void it came, as I did as well. The Great Void and God are one and the same. Out of this Unknown sprang the Self of Love. *Love created me like itself. ACIM, Lesson #67* Therefore, all problems are projections, attempts to be other than who I am as the Void created me. The natural state of happiness and joy are my inheritance, yet purification has become necessary. Repentance, forgiveness, and release are now necessities, because I live in a world of Self-made illusions. Thank God for creating the uncontaminated Self, and the Christ who fully remembers His Identity as this Self. *He is the Self we share, uniting us with one another and with God as well. ACIM, What is the Christ? Preamble to Lessons #271-280* And then it is confirmed again: *"I" come forth from the void into light. Ho'oponopono, "I" Am The "I" Prayer.* Surrounded by the Love of God, which He is, He has no fear, no anger. His Action is to forgive, to love in the form of correction. He is in me, as well, as my Self. He is the part of me who is the whole; the stillness and the peace of God are His qualities. Responsibility is only to be my Self—to return to the emptiness of Love. I may witness my impurities, but by grace I may release them. This is the function of the Christ, to release me from the hell of sorrow that I made. It is an act of Will that I come to know my Self, The Christ.

Ω

10.

A

There are subjects that can be verified by the senses, or by the logic of a pre-conditioned thought system, or by the historic account of events. I do not write about these. I write after a principle transcendent of the senses and thought. Because I am open the subject is seldom preconceived, forming out of a trust that what is clear is revealed to me as I am present to write. It is not channeled, in the sense that I pretend the words come from some special entity, or envoy from the Spirit World. This is nonsense. Any words come obviously from me. But who is this "me"? As broadly and as deeply as I can, I look toward a thought that would form a new subject, one which has never been described in such a way before. Something new is spontaneous. The yearning of a man to know himself, to be Happy in this knowledge, and to share this Absolute Knowledge with his world – that is the highest aspiration. Unbound by the body and the senses, the Mind is free to be the Self. To forget the body, just for a second, and to identify with the Infinite – that is the noblest endeavor of man. For in that identification with the Spirit–that reality beyond the senses–I am safe and immortal, not subject to the decay of time, nor limited by the box of space. These are the fetters of conditioned thought that I need but cast away; remaining with the Self.

Ω

11.

Am I angry? What is anger? A judgment of loss, a situation not according to my plan, a lashing out from pent up frustration? An underlying sense of entrapment? All the facets of thought are symptomatic of one problem, for which there is only one solution. Denial of my Identity (or separation) is the one problem. Atonement, which occurred immediately with the problem, is the One Solution offered by the Christ. Forgiveness is a denial of the "denial of Love." But something so all pervasive, so essential to all of Creation itself, cannot be denied except in dreams. Realizing the truth will take one's full attention to accept the One Solution. *I am the Holy Son of God Himself. I cannot suffer, cannot be in pain; I cannot suffer loss, nor fail to do all that salvation asks. ACIM, Lesson #191* And based on this, the nature of my Self-Identity becomes clear: *There is no Love but God's. ACIM, Lesson #127* and, *Love, which created me, is what I am. ACIM, Lesson #229* The awakening of the heart is total. Suffering, the cause of suffering, the cessation of suffering, the path (which is vertical, not lateral) that leads to the cessation of suffering – The Miracle – is a meeting with the Great Void of Forgiveness. Only the truly compassionate can forgive. Am I? Have I fully accepted the Atonement for myself? I must.

Ω

12.

A

What is pain? *Pain is the thought of evil taking form and working havoc in your holy mind. Pain is the ransom you have gladly paid not to be free. ACIM, Lesson #190* In this world it is next to impossible not to experience pain. It is associated with the body, but equally involves the mind. Sensation, by itself, is neutral. But what are those sensations to which we ascribe pain? Broken limbs, severe injuries, and sickness give me the experiences of pain. Do I judge them and myself, because I have pain? Pain is the status quo of some experience. *I choose the joy of God instead of pain. ACIM, Lesson #190* Experience is the realm of pain, being mostly of the thought/body. Identification with Spirit, my Father, puts me in touch with a Higher Reality in which pain is recognized to have no meaning. Pain and suffering buys no salvation of any kind; in fact salvation is the end of pain. Pain is the sure sign I am mistaken. So, what do I do with pain I experience now? The Lesson, in essence, says to choose the "Joy of God." What does it mean to choose? To what extent am I choosing? Intellectually I can choose, which makes little difference, because it is partial. Can I choose with my whole Being? The total correction of mistakes would amount to "Choosing Joy." Forgiveness allows me to choose Joy in the midst of the experience of pain. Herein lies the miracle.

Ω

13.

A

Judgment, attack, guilt, etc. are functions of my thought. These will manifest pain. Therefore choosing **the Joy of God** begins with the ending of guilt and attack. When I remove the cause, the effects are ended as well. The dharma is a practice, a discipline, whereby the conditions for pain are eliminated. It is a code of conduct that will steer clear of guilt, usury, taking advantage, waste, indulgences, bribery, etc. Stillness and silence are preferred to activity and stimulation. The meditation of everyday living is a process of observing every action of the day, not taking any small movement for granted. I am lost in my thought most of the time. Yet, with a pause, a reminder, I can come to the present and observe what is: my action and its motive. There is so much memory, much of it negative; how could I possibly empty it all without the grace of God's forgiveness? I do not write to be religious. I labor to find my own truth, where I am not fooling myself again. Lincoln said, "I must disenthrall myself," and usually he spoke for the many, because he saw his moral dilemmas were common to the many. "As I would not be a slave, I would not be a master." The deeper implications show a man who would not, could not, ever take advantage of another. A man such as Lincoln is vulnerable, accessible, a man of the people and for the people. He is our greatest statesman.

Ω

14.

A living stream of insight is never planned because the brain does not dream it up. If it did, the stream would not be insight, as if burbling up from an inexhaustible well, but rather a recurrent flow of thought tainted by the conventions of memory, and ongoing indefinitely with the possible repeat of a self-imposed hell. Thought can manufacture a nirvana, but it is mostly short lived. Things of time are subject to the impermanence of time. Death is a "reality" to the treasures left in store where "moth and rust corrupts." Yet, I am more than the mere corruptible. My Identity is not dependent on a corporeal body. The body seems to have a birth, a life and a death. What about the ego self, made up around the body? Can that die as well? The duality of life and death is inevitable until I see the whole fallacy of thought itself. *My thoughts do not mean anything. ACIM, Lesson #10* So, I write to free myself from the authority of my thought, even of the thought "death is inevitable." This ending of thought's authority is a death, a living death that leads to the resurrection of the Self. **Lest ye die (to thought) you cannot be born again, said Jesus in the Bible.** Yet, all those calling themselves "born again" have not first fulfilled the prerequisite death of their own thought; they merely tuck a tidy feel-good package of *salvation* into their briefcases and make-up bags of thought. It is not so easy to die to thought. My ego clings desperately to its illusions.

Ω

15.

A

What dies? Physical form may disintegrate, and we call this death. We have come to believe the end of our life as a body is death, and there is great doubt about the life of our soul after this transition out of the body. ACIM came to restore man's awareness of his Identity as Spirit. *I am spirit. ACIM, Lesson #97* Identity is only that. *I am not a body. ACIM, Lesson #199* This is the ultimate denial of physical limitation. Who knows these truths completely? Who is so certain of these facts that he lives by them? Intellectual knowing is a block to application. My unwillingness to accept my Identity is almost involuntary, it seems. This is why determination is necessary. *I am determined to see things differently. ACIM, Lesson #21* What is different? I see myself as God created me instead of what I made of myself. Freedom is an attribute of God, therefore of His Son. It is my responsibility to accept this freedom by undoing all that is in my life which imprisons me. The body is just a vehicle. It can be used in the service of Spirit, of Love, of extension—or in some sort of personal striving based on lack and fear. Do I lack anything? Answering with anything but "no" is a sign that undoing is still necessary, and I have not yet accepted my Identity. To die to the sense of lack is the real death. There is abundance in the Universe, and nothing but abundance. It is only a matter of asking and I shall receive it.

Ω

16.

A

Today I let Christ's Vision look upon all things for me and judge them not, but give each one a miracle of love instead. ACIM Lesson #349 At the personal level any one of us can have many "flaws" or "defects" according to the judgments of the world. But at the higher level of Love, where Christ's vision abides, I release my brother from these "flaws." By releasing him I release myself. No one can "cast the first stone" because no one is free from their own error; yet forgiveness releases *all* from the bondage of "guilt and punishment." I cannot judge. Christ judges only with love and forgiveness. Then there is only the peace and stillness prevalent in a forgiven world, seen through the eyes of Christ's vision. All the raucous sounds and conflicts recede, as God's peace envelops everything. I am glad to see my own thought undone. What need have I for judgment? How can I judge the mess I have made with anything but forgiveness as I begin to restore order to my life through my Self who knows only order? Christ's vision is forgiveness. Christ's vision looks upon devastation but is not fooled by appearances. He sees the order beyond the chaos, the Love amidst the hate, the compassion in the middle of indifference. It is my sole responsibility to use the eyes of Christ, my eyes, to see clearly.

Ω

17.

A

The last vestiges of judgment linger in a form of resentment, disagreement, non-harmony, a sense of imprisonment. What is this lingering form of unforgiveness but a "replayed memory," a "fore bemoaned moan?" I am sorry, I say to myself mostly, for enslaving myself to this memory of separation. What do I really want to do with my life? Do I want to go on being a "victim" of circumstances or step into the Life Action in which my energy is given in the service of a Higher Power; victim vs. the master of my destiny, not in a controlling, assertive way, but in a manner attentive and responsive to the will of God, which is also my will. The Islamic extremists believe they are doing the "will of God" by killing themselves along with killing hundreds and thousands of others, non-Muslim and Muslim alike. "Jihad" or "holy war" is justified. What insanity! The intelligent person would be very wary of someone who claims to be directed by the "will of God." There is only One Will of God and that is Love, not hate. There must be hate before there can be violence and killing. The Will of God cannot be found by following the dogmas of religion. The action of forgiveness is its only means in a world gone mad by hate, ideologies of conflict, separation by custom, language, politics, and divisions of nationality. Judgments linger; it is next to impossible to forgive; therefore, the Grace of God is a necessity.

Ω

18.

A

In the end I am responsible for what I do, think, and say; no one else, because there is no one else. The "other" is just a reflection of me in the "mirror" of relationships. I am responsible for my life energy and to what purpose and function I give that energy. Do I give that energy toward the enhancement of the "me" or to the realization of my Self. An Impersonal Action can only begin when the smaller personal activities have ceased. Have I adequately brought these activities to a close? Do the domestic entanglements remain a block? Are they a block? I yearn to be Free, which must indicate I feel I am not. Atonement is an "acceptance." It is offered, yet what is that small "gap" I maintain between myself and full acceptance? I am helpless to really come to full acceptance. My thought says I want it, I can do it, I've done it. None of it is true. I have not accepted the Atonement. This is why vigilance is necessary. Had I accepted it, there would be no need for vigilance. When Taraji, as a young man, went to the saint with his friend and asked him if he would like to go to the birthplace of Guru Nanak with them to bow, the saint paused a long moment and said, "I bowed my head once and never lifted it." That is real vigilance, real "acceptance of Atonement." Knowing this in a deep way, in a reverent way for life having shared it, I am grateful.

Ω

19.

Brother, *forgive me now. I come to you to take you home with me. And as we go, the world goes with us on our way to God. ACIM, Lesson #342* Forgiveness is an interpersonal action involving two or more people. I hold grievances toward others. Even a small irritation is a separation device. The miracle is a release from these grievances. Life is a movement of forgiveness. My thought failure is replaced by the memory of God. What I think determines what I see. Who I am is unaffected by what I think, but what I see is a direct result of "thought." To "think" with God is to be empty of my own thought. Then the world I see is a forgiven world. The thoughts I think with God are my real thoughts. "Brother, forgive me now." The only real invocation here on earth. Repentance is interpersonal because it is impossible to know God without knowing God in the brother. He is worthy of my reverence, because he is God's Son as much as I am. We go home to God together or not at all. Am I preoccupied? In the world there are things to "do." In the realm of the Spirit, there is nothing to "do." Just to "be" is sufficient. The "way to God" appears as a journey we call "life," yet who was I before birth, and who will I be after death, and who am I now? Identity is unaffected by time and the body.

Ω

20.

A

The "home" of the lesson is the place of total forgiveness. Perfect peace of mind is the closest thing to home in this world. It is the end of all grievances. Simplifying my life gives me more space to be with my own Reality, my own peace that includes all the people I know. Liberation from strife, struggle, sorrow, disappointment is the quality of home. Why would I linger in a place not my home? The child of God's created innocence within me is my only guide to home. He is the Christ child, born into my mind to restore it to peace and sanity. Home in this peace, the child is the connection I have to the Father, from whom he comes willingly to take me home with him. Home is the awakening of the heart, a place where Love abides in all its glory, the blazing light of total forgiveness. **Let my forgiveness be complete and let the memory of You return to me. ACIM, Lesson #291** My vigilance is to forgive; that is my function. To be in the world, but not of it, is to forgive. It is a moment-to-moment function requiring tremendous patience, perseverance, and dedication. The tendency of my thought is to judge; yet no judgment is true, each posing an obstacle to Self-Realization. I cannot judge rightly, but the Christ Child can judge my innocence, and all innocence of everyone. Misperception keeps us away from home. Forgiveness sets us on the sure and rightful road home, to the Identity we share with God.

Ω

21.

A

What we forgive becomes a part of us as we perceive ourselves. *ACIM, Lesson #350* The work is always to forgive. First, I must see how I judge, and then be willing to let it go. Self-judgment is the most difficult to detect—the limitations I impose on myself. Do I fear consequences from my actions? What is an action born out of the will of God? God is Love. I am created in the image of Love. God's will, the only real will, which is also my real will, is Love and its extension. Muslim extremists feel they are doing a great act of God's will, for which they are "loved" in the eyes of Allah, by killing the "non-believers." Killing is condoned as a mighty act of faith, especially when Self-sacrifice is part of it. This thought system represents a vengeful "God." **The world I see is a form of vengeance.** *ACIM, Lesson 22* "Attack thoughts" are the roots of violence and hate; these are the very thoughts in need of the miracle of forgiveness. What are my attack thoughts? I cannot separate myself from the Muslim extremists; I am not free of error, of thoughts of hate. Killing is wrong, yet how many brothers have I "killed" in my mind by considering them lowly or unworthy? The world I see is a result of my thoughts. Have I given up my thoughts? Can I say with absolute certainty: **My thoughts do not mean anything?** *ACIM Lesson #10*

Ω

22.

A beginning and an end; from start to finish, there must already be perfection. Perfection is not something attained, in the sense of "practice makes perfect." In the higher realms of being, perfection already is. A tree does not need to practice to be more of a tree. A seedling is just as whole as the 2,000-year-old sequoia. Man, in his essence, is perfect already. Education is a myth of "perfecting" the human being by teaching him skills and refinement. These are alright to learn, but they do not "improve" the essence of what is already there. If education did its most responsible role, it would awaken the individual to that perfection which is God-given and intrinsic. Each have their own gifts and talents to express; already these gifts are present, perfect, and intrinsic, the greatest of these being love, compassion, caring for another. The saint is merely the one who cares for another as much as himself, maybe even more than himself. This caring is a beginning and an ending: I care for another—beginning to recognize the end of separation. This is why Jesus could say I am Alpha and Omega, the first and the last; the beginning and the end. Contained in the Christ is the promise that man will awaken to his perfection—Love—and live to be as he was created by Love. Love at the beginning and Love at the end.

Ω

23.

A

What am I? I am God's son, complete and healed and whole, shining in the reflection of His Love. In me is His creation sanctified and guaranteed eternal life. In me is love perfected, fear impossible, and joy established without opposite. I am the holy home of God Himself. I am the Heaven where His Love resides. I am His holy Sinlessness Itself, for in my purity abides His Own. ACIM, Preamble to Lessons 351-360 It is a lofty reality of my Self given to me. I have one of two choices: I can accept this as the truth, or I can reject it with a grievance or denial. Why would I reject it, knowing in that rejection is the harbinger of pain and suffering? Who do I think "fathered" me? Why would God create His Son to be sick? I have done this to myself, and now I can cease to do myself harm. Healing is in the beginning a declaration to be well, accepted on faith. Forgiveness is the means to healing. I release my brothers and myself from the hell I made by accepting my Identity in the Christ, the Self we share. He is "in charge of the process of Atonement." I can release the past from what I thought it was. Nothing but a memory, it can touch me not; and any repetition I can cleanse and let go. In the present I am God's Holy Son. In the present I am healed and whole regardless of the body's contrary witnesses.

Ω

24.

A

"I am God's Son." That is a demanding statement of the truth. Have I realized it? I have projected all kinds of other small "identities" onto myself and others, but have I really accepted the fact of this statement? "I am God's Son." An awareness of my origins is unique—the ability of man to reflect on the nature of his being—apart from animals that do not consider themselves in the scheme of a whole universe. Because man can ponder the transcendental questions of reality beyond the physical, he is open to receive insight into higher truth. "I am God's Son" which is to say the Effect of a Cause Unknown. Being aware of the vastness of this Unknown; being aware that I sprang out of this Great Void; being aware that my Origin is unthreatenable, unaffected by the changes of time and space; I can be happy that my Identity is that of my Creator's. "I am the I" is another way of putting it. "I come forth from the Void, into Light." (Ho'oponopono; the "I's Prayer") Physicality need not be a limitation when viewed as merely a manifestation of my Identity on these planes. "I am God's Son." One who is in touch with that has no problem in life. The Mind is joined with Love. It has no needs. It has something of its own to give. Love meets the needs of those who still perceive needs.

Ω

25.

A

My sinless brother is my guide to peace. My sinful brother is my guide to pain. And which I choose to see I will behold. *ACIM, Lesson #351* Judgement makes projection; guilt of any kind demands "punishment," leading inevitably to pain. To see my brother *and myself* as sinless, I am removing all judgments of guilt, and choosing to see our innocence in the eyes of God in Christ. The eyes of Christ see only innocence. These eyes are wise and well aware of the world's view: vengeance is the nature of thought's projections. Jealousy, envy, control are all the subtle modes of attack the ego employs to deny sinlessness. The brain (thought) cannot help it. Intrinsic to thought is some form of attack and vengeance. Self-condemnation, "I'm not good enough," is a form of vengeance. The necessity to step totally out of the field of thought, of the "known," is necessary to be free of attack, vengeance, threat, fear, death, etc. Krishnamurti made this crystal clear. "Thought" is Pandora's box, the forbidden fruit, the knowledge of good and evil. Prior to thought of separation, there was only the One Thought of God, which enveloped everything. That One Thought was Pure Joy, without an opposite. Differences were not perceived as divisions, but merely the multiplicity and diversity of one life. Out of the One (OM) came the many— out of the Void came the "I" into the Light. Man was there from the beginning of creation. Now would he be restored to the rightful place of co-creator.

Ω

26.

Joy is the natural state of the Mind. Happiness is the will of God. Sorrow is an attack on reality. Attachment to the body and to things of physicality may lead to sorrow. Therefore, it is best to observe the impermanence of things. Bodies come and bodies go, so are the ways of changing forms. Yet, what does not change are states of being. Love is a state beyond thought but has its impact in the world of thought. Judgments have no meaning; they divide what is whole into irreconcilable parts. Separation, the result of judgment, is a function of thought. Joy comes from joining. What was never different is seen as the same. What was seen as a "threat" is seen as having no consequence. What was seen as vulnerable is seen as absolutely safe and unassailable. I can choose joy instead of pain and sorrow. This is my only choice to make, being mostly a choice to deny the "reality" of pain. Pain is felt, recognized, forgiven in the sense of not judged, released and transmuted by my Creator in the right time and place. Enduring pain may occur, yet I cannot allow its endurance to fortify a belief that pain has any virtue, or that I have failed because I experience pain. Your Love is mine, Father, regardless of my pain experience. Joy is a reality even in the midst of a seemingly ever-present pain.

Ω

27.

A

It is essential that I end my belief in separation between my brother and me. I have been given a savior, very specifically, in Tara Singh, with whom I may join. What is required for this joining to be accomplished? Neither of us are "without error," having made some mistakes in our life; yet the opportunity forgiveness brings releases us together from the consequences of these mistakes. The Christ in us, together, can wash away all error from our minds. In Him are we healed and whole; in Him our function is fulfilled. All have someone in their life with whom joining is essential. To this one these words may be spoken in silence. ***Let me behold my savior in this one You have appointed as the one for me to ask to lead me to the holy light in which he stands, that I may join with him.*** ACIM, Lesson #78 I must get along with this work of joining. It has already happened, yet it must be made manifest as the teaching device for others' (and my) learning. For me to withhold this final step would be to deny future generations the demonstration of the miracles. A miracle undoes the past and future in the present. It maintains the law of the masters, the Law of Love: "There are no problems in Life." Therefore, the mind is empty. Its natural state is emptiness. This is Love's domain—silence—peace—unlimited spaciousness—Pure Joy.

Ω

28.

A

I have yet to face my most demanding challenge. Once this joining has taken place, I am now responsible for my savior's body. He is the crossroad whereby I may take the branch toward Truth, toward Love, toward Freedom, by seeing no separation between my interests and his. To make sure his body is cared for is my concern, like a mother cares for the child, because he is the Child. Without the help of the Christ in me this will not be possible. He is my holiness, my Divine Connection, my Energy, my Love. With Him all acts of Love are possible. Do I still want things to be my own way? For Him, would I serve my brothers? Am I diligent to end the separation, to remove the sorrow of existence by finding within me His Pure Joy. I cannot have without giving all away. The miracle is thus stated, **To have, give all to all. ACIM, Text** Love is not partial, it is whole. It is not reserved for some and withheld from others. But the wise will not "throw pearls unto swine." What is of God's belongs to everyone, but not everyone will have the capacity to receive. The true words are made available to the masses, then to the few. Even amongst the few, will there be fewer who really "have the ears to hear," who will know his God given Self? He must first die to thought. Who has done this? Virtually no one. One could count them on one hand.

Ω

29.

Fear of death permeates the thought system of the ego. But "death" is a release, an ending by which something new takes place. There is no death in the sense of one's being Love; but *death* of illusions—all not of Love—is necessary to identify wholly with Love. **There is no death. The Son of God is free. ACIM Lesson #163** The end of sorrow is the real death, the stepping out of pain into the peace and joy of God. An end is possible when I do not perpetuate the conditions that bring about pain and sorrow. Attachment, desire, wanting to become are the conditions that give rise to sorrow. To end these conditions is a living *death*. The end of the body, which we call "death," is not the end of the Self. A transition of my Being from "in a body" to "not in a body" is often called death. But it is more of a passing: Like ice melts into water and water evaporates into the air. Each step, the essence is still water. Life, in all its changing forms, is Life forever. Death is not the opposite of Life, because Life has no opposite. Death is just a small part of Life, not a "proof" against it. There is no death in the sense that Life never ends. Even if the planet and mankind were blown to bits, a vast universe would still prevail, pulsing and vibrating into a new vitality. Life has no sympathy for death; it merely marches on.

Ω

30.

A

Judgement and Love are opposites. ACIM Lesson #352 There are many obstacles to peace that I have placed, knowingly and unknowingly, in the way of my own awakening into my Self. The statement of the lesson is a miracle designed to reverse my thinking. The obvious block to Love is judgment, which leads to attack, defense, conflict. The Christ does not judge in the face of these mistakes; He forgives, which is to say He looks beyond the devastation toward the One Reality of God's Peace. **Nothing real can be threatened. ACIM, Text, Introduction** Therefore, Reality, Love, is unaffected by the appearances of hate, conflict, suffering of the body, etc. All the ills of the world are a result of judgment of some kind. "Sickness" is a self-judgment, a guilt held onto, that has manifested in the body. Correction of sickness must be in the mind, since the mind is the source of the error. Clearing the mind to empty is the task of the student. He has the help of the Christ, who will always transmute illusions to the truth. But the student must be willing to bring all thought into the charge of the Christ. Readiness is a function beyond thought, therefore not in the field of the known. "Accepting Atonement" has nothing to do with conscious "choice." It is a recognition that conscious choice is limited by a reversion to its opposite. A choice which cannot be undone is a decision. This is made with the Power of God behind it.

Ω

31.

Α

You have a role in the Atonement which I will dictate to you. Ask me which miracles you should perform. This spares you needless effort, because you will be acting under direct communication. ACIM, Chapter 1, Section III The miracle being a correction, is therefore a release from error. Error is brought to truth by *admitting the error*. I even admit to errors, the full nature of which I am not even aware. This invokes the Christ who is the Atonement. An older brother, Jesus, played his part perfectly in establishing His place in charge of the Atonement. Therefore, I invoke His presence in clarifying forgiveness—that I may perceive it accurately and benefit along with all from its release. The incidents of release, or the miracles, yet in store for me, in my charge, are already placed in my trust. I need but ask the Christ, my guide, what they are. They will always produce Joy in the sense of Freedom for all parties involved. I need to be absolutely clear on this. I do not choose the miracle—I cannot—but the Christ will choose for me, pre-arranging all the elements of people, places, things for me. My attentiveness to the thought system in need of reversal is my responsibility. Once it is identified, I invoke the help of the Christ to make the correction and erasure. The error is always *in me*; therefore, the correction occurs *in me* first, then extends to my brother. I am the beginning and the end. I am the *Alpha Omega*.

Ω

32.

A

*S*pirit *is in a state of grace forever. Your reality is only spirit; therefore, you are in a state of grace forever. ACIM, Chapter 1, Section III* While home in a body, I need not concern myself with my Identity. I am fully saved in a state of grace. What concerns me is my denial of truth; the ways my thoughts have separated me from my Identity. Undoing these is the work of miracles. Thoughts manifest form; therefore, the forms of forgiving thoughts come as close as I can to my Identity. Within the known, whose action comes from a place outside the known, the miracle re-establishes divine order so that what is made manifest is totally consistent with Love, with Wholeness, with Eternity. A snowflake forms, unique in its microcosmic order then melts into a water droplet then evaporates into thin air. Beauty at all stages is present, but each form is born, then "dies." Love, Beauty, Order is ever present, immortal, not the physical forms of their expressions. Spirit, or the non-physical aspect of Identity, is in constant communion with the "I" (God). This is what is meant by grace; something given freely. Forgiveness is the closest thing to grace in the realm of the physical. Personalities are illusions, yet forgiven, they are happy illusions. I need only remember my reality is totally unaffected by any event, incident, happening in this physical world of thought. I am in a state of grace. Therefore, I have no problems.

Ω

33.

A

Only God's plan for salvation will work. Where would You have me go? What would You have me do? What would You have me say and to whom? *ACIM, Lesson #71* To the degree I can accept this lesson as wholly true is the degree of certainty that what I am told inwardly is the daily direction I must take. First, I must come to humility—that my plan without God's direction is meaningless. I admit I have been wrong so that the Holy Spirit may enter my mind and serve as God's messenger to His Son. Next, it is okay to ask: "Where, etc." Now, with a clear direction, I can go about my day with a different purpose— the realization of the Peace of God—my inner Peace which God Himself has given me. My salvation depends on listening to God's voice which is my own real voice. It is the utterance of my mind when my own thought has been silenced. My plans for happiness, therefore salvation, have not worked. Why do I blame God for this? He has a plan for me when I have given over mine for His, totally. Allegiance to two different plans cannot work, producing endless conflict. Therefore, I must drop all plans for my salvation. What then remains would have to be God's plan. Today I will make no decisions alone, because I am not alone. And I will check frequently with my directions to make sure of "in-flight adjustments."

Ω

34.

A

Sleep is necessary to rejuvenate the body. Too much sleep is not good; too little is also harmful. The *Course* refers to the "sleep of forgetfulness" as the state of unawareness of my Identity. It says, **The sleep of forgetfulness is only my unwillingness to remember Your forgiveness and Your Love. ACIM Text; Chapter 16; Section VII** Forgiveness, the principle action of my remembrance of God and my Identity, is the means of waking up. God's forgiveness and love are offered; I need only awaken into them. This is the sleep which keeps me in the throngs of sorrow. Accepting the Atonement is the beginning of awakening. Thought is deceptive. Thought says, "I have accepted it," but that is a false acceptance. My thought does not mean anything. I am aware I am asleep, and forgiveness can wake me up. What would be true acceptance—complete forgiveness? Without the grace of my Creator, the true acceptance of Atonement would not be possible. My will, joined with God's will, is that I be fully aware of my Identity—Love , Peace, Joy. I must be grateful that life has led me to this juncture, this moment of clarity. In touch with the futility of thought which perpetuates unwillingness (sleep), I am for an instant helpless. But then I am assured the Christ will help me wake up. He is fully awake, and He can help me to awaken. He is *in me*, my real Identity beyond thought; abiding in the home of God, which is my Self.

Ω

35.

A *Course in Miracles* gives mankind a new mind. Having come out of the New World, it is the first scripture to originate in English. Because we are a "Christian-based" nation, its language deals with the issues of inner transformation within the context of the Christ. It never proposes it is the only way to truth, but it does establish that Love, and its full realization, is the one and only goal of any true teaching. Though it does not profess to teach Love, it does attempt to "remove the blocks" that the human ego has placed before Love's awareness. A miracle, thus, is a teaching device which undoes the notion that the mind can be used for anything but in the service of Love. Grievances, attack thoughts, a sense of lack, are common misperceptions in need of correction. The miracle, whose action is true forgiveness, undoes the mistakes by showing they have no real consequences in reality. When the mind is then freed from the fear of punishment, guilt is dissolved, and fear of wrathful retribution is no longer a concern. Innocence is the natural domain of my Self. I can be glad for miracles that erase my thought—my memory of pain and suffering. Then living in the present is more and more a blessing. I can be free as I am created by the "I."

Ω

36.

A

I who am host to God am worthy of Him. He who established His dwelling place in me established it as He would have it be. It is not needful that I make it ready for Him, but only that I do not interfere with His plan to restore to me my own awareness of my readiness, which is eternal. I need add nothing to His plan, but to receive it, I must be willing not to substitute my own in place of it. **ACIM, Chapter 18, Section IV** The capacity to receive is the end of my own projections. "Doing" is a block. "Following" is closer to real action. The plan of God vs. my plan; how do I discern the difference? Everyone has a unique part to play in God's plan for salvation; each has particular relationships that lead to awakening the whole Sonship. These are not by chance. I am worthy to receive guidance from my Creator and disciplined enough to follow it. I need not know the whole reason for my action, other than the fact it is part of God's plan, the essential part entrusted to me. The question of substituting a "false plan" arises, yet stillness and silence cleanses me of my projections. I can always check with my Source and make adjustments according to these checks. I do not *know* God's plan, yet through these frequent checks it will be revealed to me.

Ω

37.

A

The Last Judgment declares the innocence of all of God's children and creation. The predator is as innocent as the prey. Nature has its own ways. I do not know what anything is for; yet I trust there is an order, a perfection into which all things play a part, down to every particle of dust. A day is full of opportunities to forgive, to release the world from my judgments, to release myself from my judgments. From judgment comes all the sorrow of the world, which is to say all my sorrow. My sorrow *is* the sorrow of the world. Forgiveness is the only meaningful action in a mind/world of grievances, attack, guilt, conflict, deceit. It is a total responsibility, therefore humbling. Who cannot judge—a Hitler, an Islamic "terrorist," a self-righteous president? Who knows he is a killer, a rapist, a thief, by his own thought? I must take responsibility for not loving. I deny my own Identity, and maroon myself in an exile of judgment. I may find those who would "accompany" me on this exile, but separation is still maintained. Forgiveness releases me from the exile of judgements. To say, "I don't know" and really mean it is a most intelligent admission. There is no judgment in it. It is a declaration of my own innocence. The child does not "know," nor does he need to, as he is whole without the burden of acquiring "knowledge."

Ω

38.

A

Purpose in life is greater than career. Who wants to rise to a purpose? Most are preoccupied with the personal domain of their life. Few are concerned with the Impersonal. The Impersonal is a principle which applies to the greater whole. A principle is a Truth—Absolute and unalterable by time or conditions. The particulars of daily living are guided by the quality of mind. What is the quality of my mind? The dynamics of life, of love, are governed by certain laws. Parents have children and protect them when they are helpless. When the parents are old the children must protect the parents when they become helpless. These laws of love are true in any culture, any place, any time in human history. To the degree I can be consistent with these laws, is the extent that I live by love in peace. Parents are old, in need of help. Will I see it as a burden or an opportunity to *give back?* Love would be glad and have something real of the heart to give. I need to ask: "What would the Christ do in this situation,"—not in a sentimental way, but dealing with the facts. The Christ was on fire; he lived only by the Will of God—healing the sick and loving the disenfranchised. Now the challenge is caring for aging parents. Mary was old when Christ performed his miracles. What did he think about her welfare? Were there sisters or brothers with whom she lived? Now, what is the plight of the old? Are they abandoned?

Ω

39.

A

Old age and the decrepitude of the body is not a tragedy when accepted as a process of healing and the call for forgiveness. Forgiveness looks on the ailment of the body with compassionate eyes; not to judge the pain is the first step in relieving it. I accept whatever pain as a lesson and a call to forgive. Then forgiveness can be applied. So much correction is needed. "I come to mend." Most of the responsibility of life is reparative. Every person is fragile and precious inside. So much hurt is carried within, in need of release. The gifts of God are healing drops of living rain, lightly falling as forgiveness upon the inner hurt of a separated existence. To bring this separation to an end is the function of wisdom. Naturally, on the human scale, this may involve an extension that touches the lives of many, because artificial boundaries have been overcome. Ending separation from an awareness of Love is to be joined fully with a brother. No one can teach this lesson; it cannot be sought, but life can provide the opportunity to end separation. A matter of life or death is the demand of this joining. To mend is to release and be released. As I release another, I release myself. My father and mother are aging and becoming more and more dependent upon help from their children. What will Love do? Love would make sure they have no anxiety about their care and possess tranquility in their final days.

Ω

40.

A

Taraji has been hospitalized. Science cannot solve the deeper problems of man. Only Love can overcome fear and judgment. Science can't. A chemical is no substitute for the healing action of Divine Love. The Christ can invoke this power to cancel out the effects of fear and separation. Making contact with the Christ in me is my only *real need*. He is my Self. He is the Self who connects me with all humanity. He is the Self who is the Master of all forgiveness. Father, I come to You to know my Self, to know that I am the Christ, as He is in me, and You are in Him. My only home is in this Self. It is not a place, but a state of being. To know this Self fully requires I see It in my brother. It is a gift in which my brother's past is overlooked and released. I must see the Christ in him in order to see it in myself. The Son of God is my fellow human being; by acknowledging his Divine Self I acknowledge my own. Self-realization is the liberty that mankind seeks. Love is the Self. Love has no problems, needs, incompletions. *It is perfection itself.* God and Love are virtually the same; both are beyond the knowing of thought, beyond the definition or limitation of any kind. Giving all to all, Love permeates everything, even the bars of the jail cell, even the hangman's noose. Yet my mind cannot fathom It.

Ω

41.

A

Back in Kansas, having visited Melanie and Marvin Coulter in Redfield, Iowa. Everyone is on some level of evolution on the spiral upward toward total Self-realization. The Coulters are fairly well along, having outgrown reactions. It is a matter of undoing, having gone through many disillusionments and come out the other side with an acceptance of what is. A life is lived with very little loose baggage from the past, brought forward into the present. The present is new and clean, dedicated to the Will of God. This Will is only for the good of all. It cannot deprive nor rebuke any for a "wrong." It can only forgive and provide what is needed. This Will is always giving, thus It is charitable—not in an artificial way, but in the sense of responding to Life with one's fullness of heart. Charity begins at home, with family first. Specifically, now with parents the challenge is to care for them in a dignified way, putting the past behind and not slipping into the negative patterns of reaction, insecurity, and avoidance. My Self which can respond is certain and Self-contained. From the strength of this stalwart holiness I can deal with any thoughts of fear. Life is giving me opportunities to respond. Will I respond rightly? Cleanse, erase, erase. Only an empty mind can Love.

Ω

42.

A

K.C. airport. Flight delay. Sitting, watching, waiting. People with laptops, people reading newspapers, two young ladies playing cards. Spacious concrete and glass structure on a curve with coffered ceiling, poured and formed concrete triangular grid of support beams and pylons—very interesting. High ceiling makes the space expansive. People feel comfortable waiting—not cramped or crowded. Plenty of seats. The young ladies playing cards are happy, smiling, bright. A man talks on his cell phone; business most likely. The modern-day embarkation is very clean and streamlined. People are relaxed and certain of their travel and arrival. Though the flight is delayed for one-half hour, there is little concern on the part of the passengers. A man reads a book. The attendants behind the desk offer 1st class upgrades for $100. It is tempting, but the additional expense is not necessary. A young man drinks a large beverage through a straw; his hair is short and spiked with mousse. He looks like a porcupine. The ladies continue to play cards in casual clothing that accentuates their shapely bodies. A blonde teenage girl in blue reads the most recent Harry Potter novel. A thin, middle-aged woman with long blonde hair past her waist exits the waiting area. Few women have hair that long. A gray-haired gentleman with a briefcase sits down in the middle row of seats facing the tall, floor-to-ceiling windows.

Ω

43.

Accepting that Christ and I stand together, as Lesson #354 suggests, is a remarkable change of mind. *We stand together, Christ and I, in peace and certainty of purpose.* All of organized religion projects a "savior" outside of myself. *ACIM* brings this projection to an end. "You are the Christ," says Jesus of *A Course in Miracles* to His brothers and sisters, through my teacher, Tara Singh. The undoing of a false identity, a body identified personality, is the main purpose of the miracle—to erase the memory of a false self of sorrow. What is left then is the open space of the real Self, bound by nothing, forever free in God. I am God's Son. Who else could I be? Created, not made. The Christ in me is my only Identity, Christ being the fully God-realized Self. When I have fully realized the Self, it has its own Action; I need but follow toward greater avenues of Joy. But Joy is not only in pleasure—the two are vastly different. There is Joy in seeing the holiness of creation, my own holiness; there is Joy in stillness; there is Joy in freedom from the known. There is Joy in seeing the innocence of another. When I am not in a state of Joy, I am in thought of lack or insecurity. Joy is an inner state not dependent on externals: The nature of my being is to be free. Freedom from guilt, sadness, lack, is the only real freedom. This is Joy—accepting who I am as God created me.

Ω

44.

A

There is no end to all the peace and joy and all the miracles that I will give when I accept God's word. Why not today? *ACIM, Lesson #355* A truth is that I am as God created me, unaffected by my mistakes, redeemed through forgiveness, and fully worthy of Love, my Identity; this is the Word of God made clear in *A Course in Miracles*—the words of the Christ. Acceptance of the truth is a matter of my will. Free will is the freedom to choose heaven or hell, hell being separation from Joy and Love. To be at Peace is dependent only on this choice. It is the only choice in life to make—all others are diversions from this one choice. What I accept I extend, so I need to be aware of what I accept. If I am sad, depressed, guilty, these are indications I have chosen wrongly. I can choose again, rightly, with the Christ as my guide. Why would I delay? My Identity is always intact, regardless of my awareness of It. Yet to be fully aware of It, is the beginning of my experience of Peace and Joy. This awareness is the Kingdom of God on Earth as it is in Heaven. Invoking those Divine forces to help me to undo, to "remove the blocks to the awareness of Love's presence" is the only real prayer. I cannot come to this awareness without the help of the Christ in me. Christ is not a person, but a state of being totally free in God, as God's Son. He is my Self. He is the Self that binds me to God and all my fellow human beings.

Ω

45.

A

The weekend was spent in leisure. I drove to the New Jersey shore to visit Mary Anne and Bob Norton. Mary Anne, a long-time friend through Ho'oponopono, is the one with insight—a different vision from deep within. This kind of vision is not based on the known, the past, the physical conditions that prevail. It is based on an ability to empty the mind of thoughts, so it is open to receive. What the mind then receives is shared. The Source is the Unknown; one prepares to meet It through forgiveness, repentance, invocation, etc. Once this state of emptiness and stillness is reached, the mind is free to receive and give. This is the dynamic that constitutes insight; it is a witness to a truth beyond our thought, beyond our memory. Mary Anne has this gift. Perhaps she had it from birth; perhaps it was developed from her own process of forgiveness and letting go. But she can see things differently with the all-pervasive acceptance of non-judgment. So, a visit to see Mary Anne is often what is needed to help show a new direction. A kind of "confession" takes place between two friends. It is spontaneous, usually occurring on a long walk on the beach in front of the vastness of the Atlantic. What better place is there to empty oneself? It is as if the vast space can absorb and transmute any "problem" to nothingness. And it is within the Void the human being experiences profound Peace.

Ω

46.

A

Sickness is but another name for sin. Healing is but another name for God. The miracle is thus a call to Him. *ACIM, Lesson #356* In any situation I perceive a lack, I need but call on Him to supply what I may need, in the way He sees fit. Father, in the situation involving Tara Singh, I invoke Your Presence in coming to right Action involving His care. If I perceive him as "sick," then I have condemned him as a "sinner." If I perceive him as healed, then it is Your care that can restore my health and his. The opportunity to join with my brother would lead me to an action of Life in which he and I are One. I need but call upon Your help and it will be given. A call to God is a call for healing. As a man, I am imperfect like other men, but as a Son of God I am entitled to know my own perfection as God created me. That knowledge is absolute, not affected by the past mistakes of my personality. I am not a "sinner." Redemption is a return to my original state of wholeness with Love, with Spirit, with God and Self. What is preventing me from accepting the release of redemption? I am as God created me. Would I substitute for my Self-Identity an insecure self I made up?

Ω

47.

A

More critical is the way I view myself. Do I see myself as "sick" and full of sin? Healing is offered, but it is I who must accept the Atonement for myself. This is not a matter of "if," but more a matter of "when." I made time and I can undo time as well. The Christ awaits my decision to join my brother—the one who awakened me to my function. In Him are "all decisions already made." *It is but the first few steps along the right way that seem hard, for you have chosen, although you still may think you can go back and make the other choice. This is not so. A choice with the power of Heaven to uphold it cannot be undone. Your way is decided. There will be nothing you will not be told, if you acknowledge this. ACIM, Chapter 22; Section IV* Charity begins at home. Family, relatives, and ancestors are the relationships most in need of healing. Yet the family can be the block to accepting total healing. Their fear and attachment disguised as "love" can perpetuate the illusion of separation. Loyalty to family, although to negative conditions, holds one hostage to sorrow, error, sin. To heal the family, one must heal himself first, then from that space of wholeness extend back into the family (relatives and ancestors). The teacher is of utmost importance. Healing with him is the first healing with my Self.

Ω

48.

A

Without the Christ (Teacher) it is not possible to overcome my illusions inherited from my family, relatives, and ancestors. An "idea" is substituted for the Christ, which has no power to heal because it is a projection of the ego. Organized religion does not produce the Christ or lead one to a meeting with the real teacher. It could not. The fact it is "organized" shows it has been denigrated to an "idea," an illusion of something otherwise quite necessary. Life provides a Teacher. He (or she) is real, authentic, sent by Higher Forces to awaken me to my God-created Self. Family, relatives, and ancestors cannot awaken. They can sometimes allow a freedom by letting go without judging, but usually they do not "let go," therefore, my "problems" are inherited as memory. The Teacher forgives and brings me to a state of mind emptied of past errors and mistakes of my thought, my memory. He is the harbinger of the Present. Family is stuck in the past; therefore, I am stuck as well. The Teacher is not stuck. He offers a holy relationship, which by definition, is totally free, healed, and whole. It does not see any "problem" as real. By freeing me of my problems, the Teacher inspires me to be free, and to set free. Family is forgiven. The whole of humanity is one family. My ancestors are all humans who have lived and died before my current life. No one is left out. My healing begins and ends with everyone.

Ω

49.

A

My savior is the one with whom I end my sense of separation. Life provides many brothers, yet there is one evolved who is my particular savior. *Let me behold my savior in this one You have appointed as the one for me to ask to lead me to the holy light in which he stands that I may join with him. ACIM, Lesson #78* God has appointed the savior, but it is up to me to recognize him. He serves as the bridge between my ego and my Self because he knows the falseness of one and the truth of the other. Because he can impart the clarity to undo the ego, he is the teacher. The grace of God is behind his words and deeds. Now I am at the branching of the road where I must choose which direction to take; stay with the status quo of my past thought or embark on a singular journey to know myself. This is the Self beyond memory, outside of thought, not subject to the past nor projecting future conditions. The savior can aid me in knowing my Self. It is through sharing that this Self is made manifest, therefore made "known." It is through asking that the light of holiness is given and received. "Ask and it shall be given" is the same as "Ask and receive." To know the Christ is to be the Christ. To see my brother's sinlessness is to know the Christ. The forgiven have the privilege to forgive. I and my savior are One in forgiveness.

Ω

50.

A

No *call to God can be unheard nor left unanswered. And of this I can be sure; His answer is the one I really want. ACIM, Lesson #358* My call to God is to know and obey my higher will, which is also His Will. No conflict can be in him who acts according to the Will of God. Not so easy to know, yet it results in Joy. If I am not supremely Joyous, then I have gone against the Will of God and my own. "His answer" is Peace and Joy. What do I want to do that is consistent with Your Will, Father? It would involve the friend, the teacher who has imparted truth to me. Whatever joined in God's Will cannot be un-joined. He and I are joined. Now what? What is His will? To go Home is the will of both of us. We are Home in our holy relationship. Apart from that there may be a journey to India yet to be made together. The Golden Temple, not a place, but a state of being Joined in God together, is significant to Taraji's beginnings. And now would he go there to end his time on the planet in this incarnation. It is my destiny with the Will of God, to accompany Him Home. Either in the realization of our holy relationship, or to his ancestral home in the Golden Temple of the Sikhs, or both. *We stand together, Christ and I, in peace and certainty of purpose. ACIM, Lesson #354*

Ω

51.

A

I resign as my own teacher because what I attempt to "teach" myself has led to failure, uncertainty, and depression. The curriculum I have selected is one of misinterpretation. I fight against real learning because I have rejected the real teacher. "Try to learn but do not succeed," is the motto of my vain attempts to learn peace, joy, and happiness—the certain attributes of Love. Yet, there is a Real Teacher within me who requires and desires my attention to set me free. Even now He stands ready for my undivided attention. *Your learning potential, properly understood, is limitless because it will lead you to God. You can teach the way to Him and learn it, if you follow the Teacher who knows the way to Him and understands His curriculum for learning it. The curriculum is totally unambiguous because the goal is not divided, and the means and the end are in complete accord. You need offer only undivided attention. Everything else will be given you. For you really want to learn aright, and nothing can oppose the decision of God's Son. His learning is as unlimited as he is. ACIM, Chapter 12, Section V* Undivided attention is key. I must be determined to be undivided in my attention to the Voice of God. There is no other Teacher and no other curriculum. Love is all inclusive.

Ω

52.

A

What exactly is karma beyond the conventional notion of the cause and effect of thoughts, deeds, words, and actions? Thought is karma, or the root of it. What one thinks yields the "form" of manifestation. Everything is interpreted by thought; formed by thought. There are seemingly two main results of thought: life or death. In the terms of Identity, either "I am" or "I am not." (To be or not to be.) Beyond the boundaries of thought is the Mind, which holds these opposites as One. The level of form appears to maintain the possibilities of life and death, yet in the realm beyond thought, only life is possible. This is the level of the Spirit—not of the body form. Karma functions in the region of form: bodies and the inter-relationships of minds with matters. Spirit functions in the region of form as well, but its primary function is in the mind. It undoes thought which produces form, especially unloving versions. It harmonizes with thoughts and form at peace, which is to say it remains neutral. Form usually comes with motives, comparisons, choices, and preferences. Spirit has none of these. Its action is to "accept what is, as it is." I am a student of *ACIM*, whose curriculum is designed for my liberation from thought, fear, and belief in death.

Ω

53.

A

Conversation with Kamaililauli'I brought up a sense of guilt and remorse—the incident with T.S. regarding my staying at the Foundation. I went home to family, responsibilities of marriage. I held some guilt around that. A time now to let go. If I was meant to have a more active role in his care I would already be with the power of attorney, etc. With T.S. ready to transition, my work with him is done. Should other JPF board members request I take him to India, that is another matter. He spared me the responsibility of his care. That karma fell on others. Time to let go; not to confuse the messenger with the message. Krishnamurti said the same—not to make him into a "guru." When Taraji asked K. if he should be more active in his Foundation, K. told him, "don't get involved." I was given a tool by Kamaililauli'I: a five-pointed star—like a cookie cutter—to come down upon me like I am the dough; also to eat star cookies—with powdered sugar—let crumbs get everywhere. These tools will dissolve thought, intellectually, so I can be more with inspiration. If I have a "because," then I am not with action. Action has no "because." Inspiration is not premeditated. Miracles are not under "conscious control." Studio sale, not "this or that." Up to me to be inspired. There was a sense of relief, like a burden had been lifted. I can visit Taraji, but need not feel obligated to "rescue" him. A visit may be productive.

Ω

54.

A

Father, let me remember all I do not know and let my voice be still, remembering. But let me not forget Your Love and care, keeping Your promise to Your Son in my awareness always. And by Your Love I would remember: Let me not forget myself is nothing [death], but my Self is all [eternal life]." *ACIM, Lesson #358* And so would I claim my true Identity, my Self, which is one with all things. I am not to doubt my Self, who is beyond all doubt. I move from doubt of the ego, which questions the reality of the spirit, to the divine "doubt" of the Self which rejects the value of impermanent things of time. What was of birth and death is of time. To doubt that as my "realty," the body, is to step into another life in which changing forms has no meaning. Death is just an ending of appearance, but the reality behind appearances, the Will of the Spirit, has no death. That is the Self. I am that Self. All other statements of being are fragments; therefore, partial identities that come to an end. Only the Self is immortal—not affected by time, cause and effect, changing forms. Let the voice of my ego be still and let the Voice of God through my Self be forever heard. And let this Self have its real affect to bring Heaven even to these earthly dimensions.

Ω

55.

A

The permanent is hosted by the physical. Form seems in a constant state of change—birth-life-death; the cycles that revolve are ever changing. Yet, seeing this, I am inclined not to attach myself to the impermanence of changing forms; rather inquire of that which does not change. I am told the Self is immortal; changeless; boundless; unaffected by time, decay and death. Can immortality be applied to the physical? Immortality is my only reality. It is not attainable from thought, by study, by desire, by accomplishment. It is not to be found in success, wealth, worldly possessions. It is akin to Nothing, the Void, the non-physical, unknown by the five senses. I need do nothing to be my Self. Yet would I undo my thought and simply be attentive; live by the essentials. And then there is the space to be silent and still. What better boon in life can there be—to be free of projections and pursuits—to be happy with "what is," as it is. The residuals of past mistakes may linger in the form of pain, but so what? Even pain will pass away with right mindedness. Don't make it a problem. It is part of physical existence—the pleasure/pain syndrome. To not seek pleasure nor avoid pain is to be present. In this present moment I can identify with the transcendental Self, not of my thought's making.

Ω

56.

A

Spirit am I, a holy Son of God free of all limits, safe and healed and whole. Free to forgive and free to save the world. Prayer from ACIM, Lesson #97 I, who am as God created me, need but tell my mind these facts, and would these words serve as a constant reminder that whatever body/problem I perceive is nothing in the light of my true Identity. Now would I simplify my life and let go of the non-essentials. Father, help me to let go and to forgive myself and others. Who do I forgive? It would be my ego because the Self needs no forgiveness. I cut my ties to my illusions of thought—this is the work of forgiveness (Ho'oponopono). The mental "tools" of forgiveness are the "thoughts" that neutralize the non-loving thoughts in my mind. These are miracles. Mind is subtle, containing the physical and the non-physical. Yet must I decide to whom my affiliations are given—to death or to life, to that which can perish or to that which cannot die. Let me not doubt Your ways, unbeknownst to me. Yet, I need not "know" Your certain plan for my salvation, but rather trust I follow it by accepting it is so. I am Spirit (Immortal Love).

Ω

57.

A

The Self does not need attention from outside; it needs my inner attention, irrespective of thought. Peace arises from within, from the Source in me of all peace. It is not arrogance to accept that I am the Son of God. I accept a truth. But to accept with certainty, I must "see" with Christ's vision that *all* human beings are part of this Sonship. I am not "special" in being a Son of God, yet I may be in a rare minority who recognizes this fact. What is the action of the Son of God? ***Forgiveness is my function as the light of the world. ACIM Lesson #62*** The Son of God has a function to forgive. Forgiveness is to see that mistakes have no effect on reality. A mistake, an error, does not alter the facts. "Two plus two is four." To say "two plus two is six" is an error, yet the error does not render "two plus two is four" untrue. To view myself as an ego does not alter the reality of my Self. Self am I, unaffected by the time and changes of the personality. At some point I must "die" to the personal Self, see it as meaningless, in order to be aware of my Real Self. The brain is limited to thought and memory; the mind of the Self is not limited. The Self is my Identity in the Spirit—free of all limits—safe and healed and whole.

Ω

58.

A

I am responsible for what I see. I choose the feelings I experience, and I decide upon the goal I would achieve. And everything that seems to happen to me I ask for and receive as I have asked. And then: **Deceive yourself no longer that you are helpless in the face of what is done to you. Acknowledge but that you have been mistaken and all effects of your mistakes will disappear.** *ACIM, Chapter 21, Section II, Responsibility for Sight* It is therefore impossible to be a "victim" of outside circumstances. I choose my experience to coincide with my thought projections. It contains pain, sorrow, and death. Why am I so self-destructive? The lesson begins to question the iron grip of my thought and its "results." I begin to see my thought is the culprit of all problems. Thought is the mistake. The miracle, a stepping out of the stream of thought, is the solution. I am as God created me in reality, not as my thought made me. My Self is free. Only my ego is not (thought)—at least it "thinks" it is not. But everything is free in Reality, even the illusions of the ego. What has no reality will pass away, "and all effects of [my] mistakes will disappear." Just by seeing I am the only one responsible for my mistakes, and all those I witness, I open the door to freedom (full awareness).

Ω

59.

It is impossible the Son of God be merely driven by events outside of him. It is impossible that happenings that come to him were not his choice. His power of decision is the determiner of every situation in which he seems to find himself by chance or accident. ACIM, Chapter 21, Section II, Responsibility for Sight* *I choose all my experience either joyous or sad. *No accident or chance is possible within the universe as God created it, outside of which is nothing. Suffer, and you decided sin was your goal. Be happy, and you gave the power of decision to Him who must decide for God for You.* "Him who would decide" is my Self, the Christ. He is in me, as God is in Him. He is the liaison between my awareness and Reality. He is the one I invoke to bring me happiness. He is the Child God loves. *This is the little gift You offer to the Holy Spirit, and even this He gives to you to give yourself. For by this gift is given you the power to release your savior, that he may give salvation unto you.* The power of decision is to let the Christ decide in all that I do. Inspiration is the promise of release. I would release my brother and myself from all I thought we were. Father, forgive us both that we may be saved.

Ω

60.

A

Do I desire a world I rule instead of one that rules me?—Do I desire a world where I am powerful instead of helpless?—Do I desire a world in which I have no enemies and cannot sin?—And do I want to see what I denied because it is the truth? ACIM, Chapter 21, Section VII* Happiness, God's will for me in perfection, has eluded me because I have "denied it." I have actively vacillated between my own versions of happiness and sorrow. I am not a victim of the world, yet I have projected a world "beyond my control." Therefore, it can "attack" me at any time. **There is nothing my holiness cannot do. ACIM, Lesson #38** Yet, I have denied my holiness and made a belief system based on limitation. *I bless the world because I bless myself, ACIM, Lesson #187,* yet there are some with whom I still hold grievances. So, therefore, my *denial* of the truth has kept me in a state of uncertainty. It is a very subtle denial. At the idea level I would "agree" with the first three "desires." But at the "results" level I see I have also denied them. "Yes" and "no" is my status quo. So now I would like to admit to my denial of the truth. *I want to see what I denied because it is the truth.*

Ω

61.

Α

Upcoming trips: KC to aid parents in their move to retirement community; LA to see Taraji and Kiki; Hawaii to participate in Basic I and II Ho'oponopono. Meanwhile to complete the jobs on the books. The challenge is always to do the cleansing no matter what the externals look like. All this traveling will be very costly; yet life provides for the necessary. None of the above trips are for "pleasure," rather to be doing what is right and divinely purposeful. This has its own pleasure and fulfillment. I am concerned about the money. Selling the studio may be the answer to relieving financial pressure. But what to do with all the artwork. Is it even "art" or just my ego's preoccupation? Not for me to judge. I have a responsibility to forgive and preserve the good. That I will do—a daunting task when it comes to 30 years of painting and drawing. Long in terms of a lifetime; short in terms of eternity. To the degree the art relates to the eternal, to that degree it is worthy of salvation. It will be a process to preserve the good and not to be attached to things which should be released. "I release the world from all I thought it was." This could be the "mantra" of sorting out the studio. It is time to lighten up and "simplify."

Ω

62.

The plans are made to Hawaii and LA. Next is to make the plans for KC. This will depend on work schedule. The travel arrangements took much attention. By using dividend miles to LA then a cheap flight to Honolulu, I saved over $700.00. Now the internal trip, inter-island hop, still to be booked. And the trip to KC is very important. Parents are making the transition to a retirement "home." It seems difficult for me more than them. I need to let go. Seeing them age then pass away from the body—this is what I am witnessing; a process of ending this lifetime. Human emotions feel a "loss," but death is not possible to the spirit. Spirit is deathless. But we do not live our daily lives so aware of spirit, and then when the body "dies" we expect to be in touch with "higher" realms, not having given them attention all along. The work of the day in the real sense is to transcend the physical experience for a spiritual experience. Perhaps experience is the wrong word. "Insight" would be better used to describe the daily practice of looking toward a higher knowledge, beyond the limitations of the physical. Insight places the mind, not the body, at the center of being—even in the physical world. Spirit is made manifest through the mind. Reality proceeds from the non-manifest of spirit to the incarnation of matter.

Ω

63.

A

God's answer is some form of peace. All pain is healed, all misery replaced with joy. All prison doors are opened. And all sin is understood as merely a mistake. **ACIM, Lesson #359** No real difference exists between what we call life and death. One seems to hinge on the body, the other on the body-less state of the spirit. One could say the Christ, not incarnate, is still affecting the affairs of humanity. He has influence over the events of the mind, manifested in the body. Now, because we are similar to Him, we, as well, can rise to the reality of the Christ, and while seemingly being in bodies, come to realize our being is just as real without the body. In fact, our being in not a body, though it may "inhabit" one. The transition from incarnate to not incarnate need not make any difference. Before – Christ maneuvering about in physical form, essentially out of pure Love. After – maneuvering about in the Mind of God in the boundless, timeless, all-inclusive Spirit—also out of Love—affecting the minds of men and women who have the capacity to receive. What they receive they already possess. They receive an awareness of the Christ *in them*. Each time a child takes form, the Christ is made manifest. That Child need but know the Self.

Ω

64.

A

I suspect the joy *A Course in Miracles* describes does not depend on the body, the fulfillment of desires, the happiness attained through pleasure. Peace, as well, has very little to do with external conditions. I am responsible for my internal affairs, first and foremost. Peace comes when the external is forgiven and left alone and the internal is examined and emptied. The difference between "thought" and "objects" is one of degrees. Thought is the physical "seed" for the more gross forms of manifested things. In this world thought "makes things." Yet, contained in thought is the manifestation. Likened to the acorn and the live and massive oak, thought is the acorn. Contained within the kernel is the life force which generates the large tree. The tree, fully grown, is contained within the acorn, if only potentially. But metaphysically, the great tree is already in the seed. Peace and joy abide in another world, a parallel universe, in which the seed is my Spirit—completely a non-physical entity. It cannot be threatened by physical events because it no longer engages with them. It identifies with the Great Void of Nothing out of which comes Peace and Joy. I am supremely happy to the extent I dismiss attachments to physicality and thought. In a body I bring this Joy into physical realms—which then, in turn, manifests as Heaven on Earth.

Ω

65.

A

Discipline is essential. What is it exactly? A truth is given, yet until one has practiced it diligently, lived it, it remains as an idea only—no real transformation has taken place. I stop short. Why? Unwillingness gets the better of me. Why? Discipline deals with unwillingness. Discipline knows the power of unwillingness. It sees a truth through without wavering or giving up. The strength that makes discipline possible is not personal. It is "in me" but not "of me"—as if the will of God is channeled into me and I can make my will one with It. Then there is real strength to persevere and to follow a practice. Practice means to harness the lower nature of thought and the body to be in the service of the higher nature of the good and spirit. Yoga deals with some basic principles. First, to make my words true—not to lie. That is a discipline. I see the subtle ways I lie to myself. I see the ways I put myself down. The first principle of yoga is to put these false "thoughts" away. I am a Son of God, worthy of His attention just as He is worthy of mine. Attention is the beginning of "know thyself." It is the easiest thing to do, and the hardest thing for "unwillingness." Attention has the space to observe what is—as it is. It could be anything. The sky or someone's words.

Ω

66.

A

Why is there unwillingness? There must be fear in order for unwillingness to thrive. Fear of losing. This is why attachment is an impurity. Without attachment, could there be fear of losing? What can I lose? "Freedom's just another word for nothing left to lose."—Janis Joplin. When I meet death, what can I take with me? What is the point of my attachments? There is also fear of succeeding. Even what we are attached to can be some form of misery, yet the possibility of being free of suffering can be uncertain and frightening. This is why the ego's rule is "seek and don't find." I may seek salvation—freedom—yet would I accept it? I am inclined to perpetuate my particular form of bondage, remaining miserable, but not walking through the door to joy most readily available. My unwillingness wants me dead—sick, then dead. I must stand up to this very common and prevalent tendency. And more, is where the fear comes in: one could fight off the undesirable, yet the very fight is conflict, a major pillar in unwillingness. I can observe my destructive tendencies without condemning myself. It is so. The nature of the human mind and body is to gradually degenerate and decay. So, who am I? Would I degenerate and decay? Or is it my responsibility to "re-generate"?

Ω

67.

A

The scriptures, those writings generally deemed as holy and true, say that the Self is my only reality. It defines itself through timelessness—that which is not subject to the decay of time. I must distinguish between the permanent and the impermanent. The Self is permanent. The ego is not. It comes and goes, subject to birth and death, the cycles of taking on and leaving a body, etc. What would the Self, my permanent being, do in a world of the impermanent in which we live? It would begin by seeing that my small self, the ego, is very unstable and changeable. It would begin to disengage from it, much in the way of detachment, while still paying it attention. Forgiveness of my ego, an essential step in the undoing process, is very deep and subtle. The levels are many, and therefore being clear on all levels, I may see "I am not a body," but I still have to take out the garbage, feed the body, clothe it, and tend to the needs of the body. This having been done, what is my mind? That level requires much more leisure to investigate. First, I find a "wanting creature." Having somewhat overcome "wanting," what is the next level of my mind and its function? To know my Self and everyone's Self is an insight only my mind can fathom.

Ω

68.

A

I *rule my mind, which I alone must rule. ACIM Lesson #236* The last and furthest-most subtle region of the mind is the stepping-stone to the Self. To rule that region requires a Silence, an ability to empty my thought, not to be swayed by the enticements of mental activity. It is not a fixed point, nor will "concentration" get me there. If I am focused on achieving something, which all concentration is, how can I be free of my "wanting?" Obviously, I can't. So, I question any method of concentration as a means to knowing my Self. Plenty of "gurus" claim to have an answer to the "pathway leading to nirvana." But the fact remains not so much a path to it, but rather a path coming from it. Nirvana is a present state of bliss where I have already been. Stopping my distractions, including all "seeking," brings the mind to a kind of discipline which is not based on blind belief. The Self asks that I accept what is true only after I have discovered the fact of it directly for myself. I can say "God is Love" but until my experience reflects this truth, somehow, I am hypocritical. I can talk about the Mind of God, which is Love, but have I stepped into It? *I feel the Love of God within me now. ACIM Lesson #189* This state of mind can only occur when I have transcended all other "feelings" as temporal and fleeting. Yet, I abide within the realm of the permanent Self, which is eternal. This Self lives within the Mind of God.

Ω

69.

A

Most of the day was spent on the computer making travel arrangements. It was exhausting work getting the dates and times correct, at the best price, and "clean." A number of times I thought I had it, but it was not to be. Then it fell into place, but I was by then determined to have things work out and be cleansed. A lesson about Maui was learned. Haleakala National Park has a summit end and a tropical forest end. The two are miles and miles apart. By road one must circumnavigate the island to get to the opposite ends. A person can hike across the park, but that takes a couple days. So, we will begin our stay at the summit, spend a couple days, then go to the waterfalls nearer the coastline. The purpose of the trip is to place myself "in the crater" to be purified. Perhaps I can "let go" of this weight, this ever-present sense of ingratitude that blocks me from accepting my happiness. The "letting go" may not be a "motive" I seek, but an opportunity given. The Given is not projected, yet I must be willing to follow, to "be guided," as I proceed toward deeper levels of purification. A productive day, but I am spent. I am glad to not need any more "plans."

Ω

70.

A

The responsibility of the student to the teacher is to learn the lessons the teacher taught. Stillness and Silence, both states of mind in the present, are lessons that do not require learning; the lessons are given and it is the responsibility of the student to receive them. That is all. They cannot be "learned" in the conventional sense. They are imparted by the teacher—the one who has brought his mind to silence. Tara Singh imparted these lessons to many. Who really received them? Did I? Fully? An action of Love in my life has taken place. How will I extend that? Is my gratitude complete? I would honor the teacher most by learning the lessons. Is my brain still? Is my mind silent? Am I at peace beyond understanding? These are the attributes of happiness—an internal state of joy. The purpose of yoga is to bring myself to that state. Pranayama, which Taraji imparted to me, *must* be practiced in a disciplined way. Its purpose is to bring the mind to stillness and silence. This is given. Can I fully receive it and overcome unwillingness? It is possible. Taking it from potential to actuality is the challenge. I am the one who decides to be "with it." To be lax is to be self-destructive. I have witnessed the ego's self-destructive tendencies. Unwillingness must be overcome. With the help of my Self, I can.

Ω

71.

Α

Work is only to be my Self. All other is dross. Attention given to this work permeates all other. To know Love directly, totally, without exception or distraction, is what the poet Rilke called "day labor." If not for the "fallen man," who is myself of the ego divorced from Love, there would be no need for forgiveness. But this illusion of a "fallen man" is so strong forgiveness is needed to restore my mind to sanity. Sanity is only to be with the fact, the unalterable truth of Love. It is not subject to memory, thought, or the changes of physical phenomena. A Constant Life Force, Love transcends even "God," which man has projected as a creator of the universe. The human being comes closest in his Mind to Love through forgiveness (Ho'oponopono). The Christ is in charge of that process of Atonement because He established it the instant man "fell." Who knows when that was—eons ago, ages and ages, back to the beginning of time. Time, in fact, was a symptom of the fall. Before that only the Present occupied the Mind of God's Son. Only when fear and guilt entered his mind did the past and future assume meaning. Fear was associated with an uncertain future, and guilt was associated with a regrettable past. Neither had meaning but the fall gave them "meaning." Only forgiveness dissolves these pillars of illusions, revealing the true pillar, the "I".

Ω

72.

Α

One revolution of the earth produces one day and one night. Yet would the Self know not day or night or revolutions or cycles. These only have meaning in time, physicality. The day is for attention to work for most people. Even the animals hunt for food. At night there is space for rest. You can't see much in the dark, so the body is laid down. Who sleeps? The body isn't moving, and the brain is not planning, yet the heart beats and the blood flows and the mind is active in dreams. So, who rests? What is real rest? It may not depend on day or night at all. The Self does not plan. It does not pursue a desire for achievement or acquisition. It wants nothing because it has everything already. Seeking "enlightenment" is over. Light is. I am that which has no definition, no boundary, no dichotomy of opposites. I am not attached to anything, yet I am in everything. Everything and nothing, am I reconciled to be my Self, beyond form, yet manifested in all form. Spirit am I, free of all limits. And I can be focused in a body for a spell. Like steam condensing to water, then solidified as a block of ice; before water, mere molecules of gas; before that, pure ideas; before that, just an urge, a Force. And whatever Force that is, my Self is that.

Ω

73.

A

"**P**eace be to me, the holy Son of God. Peace to my brother, who is one with me. Let all the world be blessed with peace through us." *ACIM, Lesson #360* I can be the one who bestows peace to my brother. Yet is my attention required. Who thinks of peace as the main purpose of his day? Much of the day is spent in some sort of activity to "earn bread." But my function is to come to peace and to bestow that peace with my brother, to the world. The brother is the world. My brother and I are the "world." The world I see depends on me. What do I want to see? Peace or war? Freedom or conflict? Conflict to safeguard "freedom" is a gross fallacy that is used to fool the people. Freedom has no cost. It is a natural state of being, created whole and unthreatenable. Governments cannot bestow "freedom." It is God-given. But there is a kind of "freedom," or facility, that comes from affluence. Technological and financial advancement brings a kind of ease in living. Food, clothing, shelter, and transportation are readily available. These give the individual a greater sense of well-being. But the higher freedom of the Spirit does not rely on financial and technological "freedom." It is a reality unaffected by conflict or impermanence. It is the reality of peace, my Self.

Ω

74.

A

"Father, it is Your peace that I would give, receiving it of You. I am Your Son forever just as You created me, for the Great Rays remain forever still and undisturbed within me. I would reach to them in silence and in certainty, for nowhere else can certainty be found. Peace be to me and peace to all the world. In holiness were we created and in holiness do we remain. Your Son is like You in perfect sinlessness. And with this thought we gladly say Amen." ACIM, Lesson #360 The Christ, the Buddha, Yudhisthira, Krishna, Sri Bhagavan, Dr. Schucman, and all the Great Rays are within me. I need but invoke their presence to bring me to peace. Their peace is mine because their sinlessness in mine as well—as it is my brother's too. Peace is therefore already given, coming from the Father. The Child can invoke the Father's love. The Mother initiates, but the Child is the conduit for receiving peace. It is the Mother's job to forgive—the Child is innocent and can bring down the grace from the Father. The Mother protects the innocence of the Child, and lets the Child be the Self, forever free. Then all three, integrated, bestow only Peace—the "Peace of I."

Ω

75.

Α

Who takes a breath? The body moves, the lungs expand and fill with air, and then exhale the spent breath. But who moves the body? When the mover of the body no longer needs a body, the mover departs and the breath ceases. Then the body decays and returns to the basic elements. The mover of the body is not of the body. The Self rules the physical yet is not attached to the physical. Leaving the body behind, the Self is no longer concerned with the breath. The flow of oxygen, which the body needs to function, is the most basic of necessities—of the life of the body. Prana, the most rarified aspect of Life Force, is the focus of the Spirit. Pranayama, the practice of breathing so as to enhance awareness of this Life Force (prana), is given to man to restore his primary state of being—gratitude and stillness. Pranayama is a way of withholding the breath, then releasing the breath, bringing focus to the presence of the mind. The body moves, but through the inhale, hold, exhale, hold process, the mind is brought to stillness. The mind decides to breathe prana, the body moves accordingly, and the mind enters into a state of silence. I have no thoughts worth trumpeting about. My Self is the ruler of my Life.

Ω

76.

No one can know just what his part will mean when God from little lights completes a star from what we give to Him. —*Dr. Helen Schucman, Scribe of A Course in Miracles* Judging from the standpoint of an individual Self, life seems small and insignificant. Time, space, and the body are the limitations imposed by judgment. Yet are they quite meaningless when considered from the standpoint of the Impersonal Self. This Self is not divided from the whole. It does not perceive in terms of an individual, but as the One transcendent of time, space, and the body. It does not analyze through thought; it does not know through understanding. It is happy to realize It does not need to "know," to "understand." Freedom is from the *known*, as Krishnamurti pointed out. The Self observes the limitations of thoughts of time, space, and the body, and sees their passing impermanent nature—and does not identify with them. Renunciation is of all the thoughts of death, all of which result in the impermanence of things. These are not the domain of the Self. Holiness is a Thought of Eternity in an everlasting Pure Joy. All else is but illusion, a passing flicker in an all-pervading light. The light is not a physical "light," but a certainty of that which is eternal is the heart of me.

Ω

77.

A supernatural event occurred. I was at my desk, late, two evenings ago, reviewing the workings of a new camera. I used the small pen knife on my key ring to open a computer card from its package to be inserted into the new digital camera. Having worked hard that day, I was spent. Using the pen knife, I cut out a picture of a man in an early whirlybird machine from a grocery bag to paste in my journal. Having glued up the picture, I went upstairs to stick it in the journal, most likely leaving the keys and penknife on the desk. The next morning when Uncle Lenny met me to go to a job, the keys were nowhere to be found. I looked high and low until finally I gave up and borrowed the truck key off my wife's ring. After work I looked again and again, everywhere. Nowhere to be found. Every possible nook and cranny were searched; anyplace they could have fallen, even in the recycling bin, basement, clothes baskets, and other hideaways. No keys. I had given up, and went to bed dejected, not in the habit of losing such important and symbolic items as keys. This morning I called Uncle Lenny, and said, "I lost my keys." "No, you didn't," he replied, "they're over here on the kitchen counter." Between the desk two nights before and this morning I had not been to Unc's. Go figure. Keys can't walk. Must be a leela.

Ω

78.

A

The experience of pain and sorrow, such prevalent factors in what we call living, can be overcome. Thoughts of God made manifest through the Christ, the liberated soul, speak of a state of being in which happiness and joy are the only real emotions. Yet are these states so unlike what we call happiness and joy in the world. The world of dualism is one in which opposites rule; joy has a sorrow and happiness has an end. The Christ mind is one transcendent of opposites. Joy is not dependent on an object that is changeable, therefore making joy tenable as well. Joy of the Holiness of Divinity has no opposite. It sees opposites as meaningless; and being meaningless, without reality. Illusions of thought manifested for a short while then gone, have no real effect on the Mind of God, Christ's mind. *ACIM* points out this Mind is my only real mind; all other thoughts of sorrow, pain, unhappiness are results of my own false belief, products of my belief in "sin," a thought "I am not." The end of this belief is also the end of its results. Therefore, pain and sorrow come to an end when I accept my inherent innocence. Have I accepted it? Obviously, I haven't because I still experience pain and sorrow. So am I in need of forgiveness still. What other means are there to let go of guilt or remorse? Forgiveness is the only means, in a world of false means, by which I may recognize my innocence and freedom, and transcend pain and sorrow.

Ω

79.

A

"*This holy instant would I give to You. Be You in charge for I would follow You, certain that Your direction brings me peace." ACIM, Lesson #360-365. Amen.* The holy instant is a beginning in which the Christ's voice, the One of Love, directs my actions in all that I do. The day is a gift I give to God by asking for what He would have me do. I can be assured that guidance will be provided in His Name and that only happy outcomes will result. When I go astray, I can return to stillness and ask again, "Father, what would You have me do? Where would You have me go? What would you have me say and to whom?" And in what I hear would be the sound of His voice in me. I can decide for truth—it can be this simple. Direction is the way toward freedom from thought and judgments. All the lessons of *ACIM* have been studied. They are true and reinforce my understanding of my Self. Yet now is the time to Act my Self, by being, not by "seeking." Learning is done. Being is the real step to take. Without taking this step, learning is pointless preoccupation. Now is the time to Love through complete forgiveness. By asking the Christ for my directions, I am accepting who I am as God created me. I am the Christ, and nothing less, by asking to be led by Him. Because to ask of Him is to ask of my Self. The results are Pure Joy only. Amen.

Ω

80.

A

Taraji told me the "art of living" is the only real art, and that would be the art of Loving because Life is Love. How one lives moment to moment is most important and deserving of my attention. To know my Self is the purpose of the art of living. The Self is not "knowable" through thought. At best, thought is just an "image" of the Self. The fact "I do not know" has more vitality than the pretense of "knowledge." Admitting this emptiness (of thought), the truth can be revealed as it is. The honest approach is toward stillness. Stillness is the end of seeking. When seeking ends, "what is" becomes apparent. It is important to know "what is," even if it is negative. How else would I forgive myself except by owning the negative effects in my life as my own making? Yet I hold faith in my Self who is unaffected by the effects of mistakes. My Self forgives by virtue of being unaffected by errors. This is what makes forgiveness possible. Nothing can affect the Self. It is always whole and complete, connected to its Source. Separation from Divinity is not possible to the Self. By definition, it is the Identity shared by All and God together: It is the state of being free of problems. The art of living is living to be my Self. That is the only thing to know—the Self.

Ω

81.

A

The Mind is made open to God or not. Thought's activity is a block to this openness. Even the most "religious" person could be blocked to receiving direct revelation from the Self. It takes vigilance to undo thought, and this vigilance is lacking. The instant I say, "I know," I am blocked. To "know" the Unfathomable through a fragment of understanding is to limit the limitless. Why would I do that and deceive myself? Religion is a meeting with a state beyond thought. Thought is actively manufacturing problems—fear. When the fallacy of thought is fully realized, something else can happen. I am freed from my limited and relative knowledge and connected to the awareness of something Absolute, some reality not dependent on the body and its senses. A state of "not wanting" begins to emerge. It is a state in which I may respond, but I no longer project. The fruit of Life falls to me, but I do not pursue it. "V" is the vector of manna which inflows from on High to the "channel" of Divinity incarnate. The Christ is the Son of God who has the means to receive the given. What does He receive? The certainty of His Identity in God: "I and my Father are One." OM—the most elemental root of the word comes to me, and by my attention, is extended outward as a blessing. OM and Love are similar words. Love is an action of OM; the all-encompassing extends the all-encompassing.

Ω

82.

A

God in His mercy wills that I be saved. ACIM Lesson 235 Without mercy, the gift of God (Love), there is no salvation. But salvation or mercy are not ideas to be given some and not to others. Everyone is given mercy, but it is up to them to accept it through awareness. Intellectuality denies it, blind belief oversimplifies and divides "believers" from "unbelievers." So, mercy must be something not an idea, but a relevant fact. Salvation is an awakening into the present. Mercy is now or not at all—and it is total—not partial. Therefore, salvation is now as well and equally total. Man believes something outside of himself will save him. He has projected a Christ who is not himself who can save him, but who is the Christ? Salvation is simply seeing the Christ in me. I am He. He is the part of me who undoes my illusions; this is forgiveness, the process of Atonement, of which He is "in charge." Undoing illusions is the action of the Christ. Mercy is undoing, or reversal, of thought. Strictly an internal matter. The real action of the Christ, or "mercy," is internal. Dr. Schucman knew it as a "journey without distance." From a mind steeped in judgment, fear, and strife to a mind free of fear—this reversal is the miracle of mercy by which I am saved.

Ω

83.

The real religious person of the age will not be found in a church. "Organized religion" fails in liberating man from the limitations of belief. It does not solve the "problems" of man. In fact, it uses belief to divide mankind into "tribes." Religions of belief are used as justifications for these divisions which produce conflict and lead to war. But the "war" of belief is in my own mind. If "you" do not believe in what I "believe," I can perceive you as adverse, the "enemy." This is mental warfare. Magnified on the larger scale of mass events, this projection of disagreement produces war. Man kills man; man exploits man. But some see the error of belief and seek a world free of psychological, political, and religious divisions. "You may say I'm a dreamer, but I'm not the only one," John Lennon said in his song "Imagine," referring to a world of One Mankind, free of belief. That is a reality transcendent of the status quo of nationalism and politics. It is a matter of priority. Beliefs may not disappear overnight, yet a glimpse of wholeness is all it takes to undo the beliefs that divide humanity. Humanity is One. People are more alike than different. We cannot think that we are "right" and others are "wrong." The truly religious person belongs to no belief of a system.

Ω

84.

A

What can there be in me that needs forgiveness when Yours is perfect? *ACIM, Chapter 16, Section VII* A full acceptance of the Atonement is my only function. *Full* acceptance transcends understanding. Who has forgiven everything? Taraji told the story of going to see the saint as a boy with his friends to ask him if he would like to go with them to the birthplace of Guru Nanak to bow, on Nanak's birthday. The saint sat silently for a long moment, pondering the invitation, and then he said calmly with the certainty only a saint could impart, "No, I bowed my head once and never lifted it." That would be full acceptance of Atonement. A complete action need not be repeated. Atonement is not subject to the conditions of time. The ego makes "time" to evade the real issue. To think it takes time to "become" the Christ is to project an opposite. "I am not he; I will become he." This is the thought illusion of time, of becoming, of active denial of the Christ. Once forgiveness is fully accepted there is only the perfection of God. Even pain is not pain because it is not perceived as the opposite of pleasure. "Pain" is experience. The Self is free from experience. Independent of the body, the Self forgives "pain" completely. The mercy of relief is given.

Ω

85.

Α

The Holy Spirit looks through me today. ACIM, Lesson #295 Christ's vision is mine. What blocks it? Have I given my vision over to Him? To what extent? ***Christ asks that He may use my eyes today and thus redeem the world.*** Does Christ use my eyes? What do I see? Do I see pain and suffering? What do I see? Do I see joy in a forgiven world? Only the Christ can cleanse my vision and remove all "terror and all pain." ***Redemption must be one. As I am saved, the world is saved with me.*** So called born-again Christians are not necessarily "saved." Salvation is something beyond belief. Evangelism does not mean the one preaching is the one "saving." Anyone who divides believers from unbelievers is false. Division of any kind is a Self-projected fallacy. "Redemption must be one" That means it does not rely on belief. My awareness of what is already given, and my acceptance of it, will give my life the energy of salvation; but salvation is still wholly present regardless of my awareness of it. What God has given cannot be taken away. And what God has given has been so since before time began. Salvation is a state remembered in time, but not born of time, nor affected by time.

Ω

86.

For all of us must be redeemed together. ACIM, Lesson #295 And in the mind of Christ, it is so. Redemption has already happened. The decision has already been made. Yet would He wait upon His brothers and sisters to awaken to this fact. Thus is His Presence still upon the planet, 2000 years later, and thousands of years before He walked the earth as Jesus of Nazareth. The Christ has infinite patience for mankind to wake up. He has infinite patience for me to wake up. *My Father, Christ has asked a gift of me, and one I give that it be given me. Help me to use the eyes of Christ today, and thus allow the Holy Spirit's Love to bless all things which I may look upon, that His forgiving Love may rest on me.* ACIM, Lesson #295 A vigilance of my own sight is needed. What do I see? Without Christ's vision my own is meaningless. My thought determines what I see. Is my thought given to the Christ? Conversion is merely the cessation of my thought and the beginning of Christ's thought in me, which is already there! The prayer of the lesson is the "help" I need. "Help me to use the eyes of Christ today." This is the only prayer. What would Christ see? A forgiven world. Help me, Lord, to see only that.

Ω

87.

A

The subject of change in our life is a source of uncertainty and fear. The move from one stage to another seems to come without my control: childhood into adolescence, young adulthood into maturity, middle age into old age. Then there is the final transition—death. Each transition comes like a force of nature governed by the laws of nature. Psychological change accompanies these apparent time/body changes. Does fear subside with maturity or does it increase? Does the final transition we call death come with regret? Disease seems to overtake everyone at some point. Why? Do I fear death or any other transition? What do I really fear? A thought, a projection, is not a reality. Do I have dominion over my thoughts, and even "the thought of death?" The only real experience is Now. Fear is always in the future, which does not exist. The present is where the real choice between fear or love occurs. This is where the denial of love must be corrected. "Thinking" is a problem because it treats the future as if it knows the possibility of disaster is likely. Remembrance of things gone awry is projected into the future and may actually taint the events. Death is seen as inevitable and therefore sorrowful. But who grieves and for what? Most grief is self-pity. So the only change that need occur is that of my mind accepting that Love, happiness, joy, peace, eternal Life form my only reality. All else is illusion.

Ω

88.

Mother and Dad moved into a new environment, one in which elderly people live together in a community of apartments. The place is called Garden Villas. Of course, it would have a name indicative of something far more "romantic" than it actually is. It is more like a hotel for the people who need assistance, but who do not want to live with family (perhaps because they may feel burdensome). Old age, in a culture that worships youth, is a stage in life no longer revered—it is "managed." The elderly need help; but now it is no longer the family members who provide the principle part in that help, but rather the "professionals" who earn their livelihood in the service of these people. So, Mother and Dad have rented a place in Garden Villas. Two meals a day are provided. Their two-bedroom apartment feels spacious and well lit. Do I think it is wise for them to live here? In lieu of living with me, this is the next best thing; maybe even the better thing. I don't know. I pray the people who run the place are authentic and not just doing their jobs to make money. It is the love in my heart that makes a difference. Parents with me could be a disaster—or a blessing. Parents here in Garden Villas could be a blessing as well. Just be grateful for all life provides.

Ω

89.

A

How many teachers of God are needed to save the world? The answer to this question is ONE. One wholly perfect teacher whose learning is complete suffices. This one, sanctified and redeemed, becomes the SELF WHO is the SON of God. He who was always wholly spirit now no longer sees himself as a body or even as in a body. Therefore, he is limitless. And being limitless, his thoughts are joined with God's forever and ever. His perception of himself is based on God's Judgment, not his own. Thus, does he share God's Will and bring his thoughts to still-deluded minds. He is forever one, because he is as God created him. He has accepted Christ and he is saved. ACIM, Manual for Teachers, Section 12 This passage describes the unity of my Self in God—a wholeness I must emblazon in my mind; beyond thought, beyond doubt, beyond blind belief. I must perceive the truth in such a way that does not rely on the reasoning of thought; rather in a way that acknowledges my mistakes, my illusions, but that does not hold on to them. A man who *fully* accepts his innocence in the eyes of God *is* by definition "saved." Innocence is free of conflict. Free of conflict it is peaceful; peaceful, it is the greatest tribute of my Identity, which includes everyone, even the most abject criminal.

Ω

90.

A

The human brain believes in limitation, having identified with the body. And this sense of limitation is one of futility and depression at worst, stoicism at best. What a person does is small and limited. How on earth can he break out of the mind/body paradigm? *ACIM* says, **I am spirit. ACIM, Lesson #97** It does not say I am spirit "in" a body; it says I am only spirit. Therefore, dealing with the physical facts of the body without identifying with the body is the challenge of existence. Life is a force beyond thought. Unlimited in scope and action, Life moves the physical universe in an ever-changing dance of creations and destructions, of births and "deaths." Yet within this movement is the ever-present quest for man to know his Self. This is the nectar of Life, a knowledge that does not rely on memory or thought. Beyond the brain, when thought has been examined and dropped, there is a trust that Identity is unaffected by consequences of any kind. ***Spirit am I, a holy Son of God; free of all limits, safe and healed and whole, free to forgive and free to save the world.*** To know my Self fully, actually, is to offer the world salvation. It is to realize "I am Spirit," which is free of all limitations, and to extend that truth to everyone.

Ω

91.

Α

K.C. to Philadelphia. The responsibility to care for my parents in their old age is primary. One cannot escape this responsibility in life. As one ages, he becomes less able to do the things of everyday necessity. The faculties of the body begin to deteriorate, making simple tasks more difficult. Even walking becomes a chore. Therefore, one's world shrinks. It would have to. Even one's desires diminish to just the very basics: food, clothing, shelter. Memory of the past joys of days gone by becomes more acute. A feeling of "homelessness" can occur. Friends and family have "passed away." Yet, there is always the present, and the qualities of beauty, gratefulness, and appreciation for life are ever available. Each day has the potential for newness; one must be open to receive something beyond the "wanting" of life. To receive what is given, as it is given, that is the way of peace. "Give us this day our daily bread." That bread is more than just what feeds the body. It is a bread of life which provides all the sustenance—physical and non-physical—for a happy existence. Man cannot live on physical "bread" alone. He needs the love of the heart, a real Friend, and the blessings of parents well off in old age.

Ω

92.

There is a desire to fulfill my function as God created me. To outgrow the personal—survival of me and mine—requires miracles. These are quantum shifts in my "thinking." The old thought which is based on insecurity and fear must come to an end. The new thought, which may not be thought at all in the conventional sense of memory and conditions, comes as an inspiration. This is more akin to emptiness of mind. A stillness does not project and pursue, but it does receive. Emptiness does not mean a vacuum, rather a space open, one into which life may freely flow, unencumbered by what I "want." I do not know what I am doing before it is revealed to me, but I do not need to know. What is a real Action of Life that does not originate from my projections of thought? Who can be empty? Who can meet life empty, without fear of any kind? That one is blessed. The universe is given to him who does not want anything. To be free of "wanting"—that would be a virtuous state. To want to be free of "problems" is a deception: the ego manufactures problems then seeks to be "free" of them. One problem may be solved, but in the solution is a new problem. I am not my problems. In reality there are none; only challenges to face and undo.

Ω

93.

Α

The work of the day appears to be a task of physical exertion, yet it stems from a mental exertion first. And this is no less tiring. The mind has many levels. Going up the ladder of these levels, one finds less need for the physical body and experience. He does not seek further enrichment out of future encounters. This is not to say future encounters will cease. It merely means one goes forward with no motives and expectations for desired experience or result. "Don't seek results," the teacher tells the student. An action is therefore not a projection, nor a pursuit; it is a realization of Being. When I am aware who I am, then survival is no longer an issue. The body has certain basic needs—food, clothing, shelter. To serve stillness and silence the dynamics of wanting must be diminished, otherwise one is always busy with some sort of maneuver of "getting." To shift from the activities of "getting" to the certainty of "having" requires renunciation of wanting, of fear, of insecurity. What do I have? Everything is mine which is of value; these things cannot be "bought." Can the sky be acquired; how much is stillness worth? When I am not engaged in seeking something, I am still. Only in that stillness can I be my Self.

Ω

94.

A

"I bowed my head once and never lifted it." Who but a saint could say this and have it be true? The saint lived near Taraji when he was a boy, thus making a lasting impression upon his mind. The one who can still his mind has dominion over himself because his mind is not projecting all kinds of nonsense. A simple man who has fathomed the deeper life issues—love, livelihood, relationships—that man is blessed. He has begun the seemingly arduous journey of "know thyself." A man who does the meaningful thing begins to question his actions and words. He sees he has made mistakes. Bowing the head in reverence for another, or just in reverence for my Self, is the correction. Repentance is just forgiveness— what I was attached to is gone. Mistakes are forgiven because they did not affect reality. The real is not affected by anything; it is unchangeable. **Nothing real can be threatened. Nothing unreal exists. ACIM, Introduction** Bowing the head is to say, "I do not know You, Lord," but nevertheless I trust what I cannot perceive with the body's senses. Leaving behind what is meaningless in the end, I would be transformed. To "renounce" is to renounce illusions. The projections of thought are illusions. I am formlessness amidst the ever-changing forms of physicality.

Ω

95.

A

The personal life has "problems." The impersonal life has undone problems and has something to give of stillness. Who has risen above the personal? The first steps are to bring order and simplicity. What is essential? Is ownership necessary? A householder owns his property. Is this oasis sanctified by the impersonal? What do I have to give? Am I clinging to possessions? I can only question myself. There is no other with whom I need to end conflict. Conflict is within, not without. Who sees it that way? Thought sets up conditions of conflict. My thought is the only "problem." True forgiveness is the only solution. My thought is meaningless, yet the thoughts I "think" with God—inspiration—are not. How do I tell the difference? I can hypnotize myself into thinking I am inspired, but do I know for certain? What is certainty and my source of certainty? Certainty does not deviate from facts. There is the fact of God's care: ***God's healing voice protects all things today. ACIM, Lesson #275*** Do I hear that voice? What is it telling me to do? Am I listening? In the present there are no problems. My concern is only to be in the present. The business of incompletions: more letting go is needed in a responsible way. I fulfill my agreements and responsibilities. I pay all debts. I stay only with the essential. Then I am complete.

Ω

96.

A

I write to myself. Who will read what I am saying? I read it while I write. Who else may read it? Like I am marooned on an island with no one to talk with in my conversations, so I talk to myself. These are conversations I have with my own thought. Who talks with God? Even those who claim divine dialogue may just be self-hypnotized. I can be more honest in saying I'm talking to myself. Is it solipsism? I don't know. Thoreau wrote Walden in the first person, but what he had to say transcended his personal opinions and touched on something universal within. The discovery is always within, though its demonstration may occur in nature, human relationships, words or deeds. I have discovered I am alone. People are around me, but most of the time I spend with myself. The person I must get along with the most, forgive the most, treat well the most, is myself. If I do not love myself, can I love anyone else? To know myself is to discover this love; it does not exclude others, but it begins with an inner conviction that I am okay. I need not condemn myself. God created my perfection; why deviate from that? Problems are illusions that I have projected. A gradual dismantling of my life would reveal I am responsible for all that does not work. I manufactured my problems. I can disassemble them by forgiving myself completely. Toward that end I write to myself.

Ω

97.

A

"There is no death" the *Course* points out in Lesson #163. But in this world in which we identify with bodies, the ego, the personality, there are beginnings and endings. There is another Self to which the *Course* refers which is unaffected by "death." Who is in touch with that Self? *And we would look upon the glorious reflection of Your love that shines in everything. ACIM Lesson #163* Everything has been created by Love. Would I forget that? Physical forms come and go. What does not come and go? Love does not come and go. It is the basis for forgiveness in this world. It is the basis for everything that takes shape and has form. I am as God created me, at one with all creation, in Love. Why would I want anything to be different than "what is"? The Christ, synonymous with the Self, is the full realization of Love—forgiveness in this world—which makes one still. Silence is more pure than ideas. Love is unaffected by opposites of any kind. Death, and the ensuing sorrow which accompanies it, are illusions. I wrongly choose them and ascribe to them a "reality" which is not so. The passing of the body is governed by my consciousness. There is no cause for sorrow or death apart from "thoughts" of sorrow or death. Thoughts of Joy would be more appropriate—then a greater freedom is reached, and the Spirit is realized unattached to form. Now it may soar to new heights hitherto unfathomed. It can imbue form with its immortality. Now would I be my Self.

Ω

98.

We are mesmerized by form. We judge according to form. We have forgotten the Source and worship the body in the form of the 5th Avenue standards. Hollywood determines "beauty" and "glamour." The American dream is to be affluent, beautiful and somewhat famous. Form and appearance is everything. But the human being is more than a body or a belief system or a master of some career. "I am spirit," the Course says in Lesson #97. This is a statement of Identity—it defines who I am. Do I know who I am as spirit? What is the meaning of "I am spirit"? Three words, so simple a statement yet so profound in its implications. All those achievements, desires, pursuits, and personal attributes I think define me, are absolutely meaningless. "I am spirit," something beyond the manifestation of form. What form would my spirit manifest? What must that Being be in the world who has fully realized this Identity? What work would he do? What form would he take at these planes of existence? Most of us are asleep to our Identity. We spend our days preoccupied with concerns of the body and the self-made personality. One who devotes his energy to discovering "I am spirit" may appear "off," or going against the grain of *normal*. But the closer one gets to Absolute Truth, the farther one goes away from convention and tradition. He stands alone who has realized "I am spirit." In that stance he is one with everything.

Ω

99.

Attachment is a force in life. I find myself amidst many things which I think I "need," but perhaps do not. Possessions abound, and I question the necessity of owning so many things. Artwork, tools, books. These are my areas of attachment. The books I cherish most are those which take me beyond attachments into the realm of the spirit—freedom. Artwork, mostly my own, aspires to be that transcendence. Tools, which aid in my work of earning bread are a means to good craft which ultimately is being true to my word—straight and true. There is a joy in making things; tools are needed to make things. The things are very physical, but good craft is not. Good craft is manifested in whatever it is I am making; however, its Source is something far greater. Making something fine out of wood requires a reverence for the tree that supplied the wood. Some kind of Self-giving is necessary. The tree gave of itself; so must I. What do I give? The exactitude of good craft which puts all things in their proper place, serving their particular function in the most clear and precise form. What is square should be square; what is straight should be straight; what is level should be level. Tools which can aid good craft are useful to set me free. Free from error. That is an art. Artwork uses tools to make a form free—something beyond the physical—something of abiding Love.

Ω

100.

A

There is a meeting with the Unknown. But to meet there I must bring my thought to silence. Just knowing this is 99% of the work. All kinds of uncertainties and fears come up to cleanse, and that is where thought usually projects some kind of plan for "self-preservation." My ego thrives on what it "knows" and defines itself through experience. The Self observes the meaninglessness of thought and memory, but in a gentle way. It knows thought is needed at the body level for practical things of the body: food, clothing, shelter, livelihood, etc. It knows that to participate in the world a body is needed and that the brain of the body is conditioned by fear. So, the function of the Self is to undo fear while participating in the world of "bodies." The Self stands apart, yet also affects the parties of people who have forgotten who they are. I have forgotten my Self; but the miracles remind me of my Self, and I am restored. Miracles are thoughts, yet they proceed from the Self, not from the brain. They are put in a language the brain can "understand," but they even eliminate the need for "understanding." Something as simple a statement as "I don't know," is a miracle. What is there to know? Love is a force in life inseparable from Life itself. Who "knows" Love? It transcends understanding. Forgiveness is as close a thought may get to Love. In forgiveness the Unknown is revealed.

Ω

101.

Α

Laziness and unwillingness are related, both void of gratitude. To say "I am tired" is a way of avoiding action. There is the fatigue of the body which is natural; night is given to rest. But the psychological fatigue is from misplaced motives and incompletions. Amidst the effects of this fatigue, disorder comes into the picture—a sense of not wanting "to do." Yet action is necessary for Life. To what ends do I live my life? What do I live for? Certainly not just to feed and maintain the body. Gratitude is essential; without it I am not aware of Love. I am grateful to be still and to look within my mind to question my thought. Am I my thought? Obviously, much is dreaming; I do not ascribe "reality" to dreams. But what of "waking dreams"? My thoughts during waking hours may be just as unreal. Do I question those? My life is the product of my thoughts. To be clear of the "effects" of thought I must question everything in my life. This is very unsettling to the status quo. The ego attempts to "improve" the conditions of the status quo. The Self would undo those conditions. What is left in the Void of undoing is then up to my Creator to fill. I am then grateful most for the undoing process. Who else but one who no longer projects and pursues dreams could be the receptacle for the given?

Ω

102.

A

Our Life will be assessed whether we like it or not. There will be a reckoning, like a final review in which what we have given to life comes to the forefront. Mistakes which may have resulted in pain and sorrow can be observed without "guilt." Circumstances, supposedly "beyond our control," can be seen as our choice—for whatever lesson we were to learn. There is nothing that "happened" to us that we did not ask for on some known or "unknown" level. The purpose of strife is to bring us toward surrender. As long as we feed the fires of conflict, there will be no real and lasting happiness. There may be great substitutes for happiness—wealth, status, power, fame, etc., but these are no guarantees that our life review will be free of regret; hence, free of sorrow of any kind. Something worth saving merits saving. There is the Self beyond thought, and the self of the personality, immersed and defined by thought—the "Higher" Self and the "lower" self. The Higher Self does not need saving from thought; the lower self only exists as a projection of thought. Salvation is the undoing of my identification with the lower self, and the beginning of my acceptance of my real Identity in Spirit. No one can adequately define the "I," the Source, yet there is a pervading sense in human beings that there is something beyond themselves, certainly beyond the body and its perceptions. In the review of our lives only this transcendence will have any real meaning.

Ω

103.

A

At the end of the day before going to bed, there is quiet. Usually this is a time for reflection and a review of the events of the day. The day begins with some sort of work, a task that needs attention to complete. There is usually no ambiguity about this; it is clear what to do, or at least clear where to begin. The first step in work is to *start*. Then the next steps reveal themselves as the work progresses. This is true for any task—start with the most basic elements, then the secondary elements, then the final touches. Often, though, the most important task cannot be done without preparation. The structure underlying the main elements—like the foundation of a house—must be in place first. Often, in the end, the foundation is hidden, submerged, underground, yet nevertheless essential. When the underlying structure is sound, the main features fall into place smoothly, crisp and clean. Then the work as a whole is productive and the fruits of the work a source of joy. When something is made to the best of standards of good craft, it frees one from consequences. Good craft is a way of life. Without the attention to be precise to every detail, Life becomes a meaningless activity. When the day ends and a review of its happenings comes to mind, the fact that I exercise good craft is a relief and a blessing.

Ω

104.

A

The body has its appetites. The senses recognize pain and pleasure. The industry of advertisement is based on eliminating pain and gaining more pleasure and ease. Take this pill to cure an ailment; buy this car and life will be better. The illusions of the body are strong and have all the appearances of reality. The external "good" has taken precedent over the "internal" good. Value is placed on the things of the body, which in this world do not last. The mind is poised between Identity of spirit and identification with the body. Time, birth, and death are major forces which seem beyond control. Yet who is born? Who lives and then dies? Is it not the body? The mind, my "mother," decides what the body—my "child," will do. When it admits it doesn't know, it gives the child space to invoke the Spirit, my "father," for guidance. It is simple to admit "I don't know," yet the world is based on knowing. Those who think they *know* will never admit the one who does not know has any value to them. Knowledge is worshipped. What is known? Conflict is wired into the brain; there are allies and enemies. Who has no enemies? That person would be free to say, "I don't know," and have it be a fact. That person is beyond good and evil, pleasure and pain, right and wrong. He doesn't believe anything. Emptiness is a vital aspect of his being, similar to a great bowl the likes of which could contain everything yet be attached to nothing.

Ω

105.

A

The way I see another—his personality, his traits, his strengths and weaknesses—only builds an illusion of him in my mind. My perception is limited to my assessments and opinions. What would it take for my thought "about him" to cease? Until they do I shall not "see" the Self in him or in me. I may not "know" my Self any more than another, yet I acknowledge there *is* a Self, transcendent and independent of my personal character. We are but players in a drama of Life as Shakespeare said, and our world is our "stage." Everyone has chosen their particular stage, and there are no real accidents. Events are predetermined, like the script was written before we took shape in a body or proceeded along in the drama with the people we have chosen. Lessons are events and relationships, and the main lesson is only one of forgiveness and love which requires I give up, undo, let go of the *self of fear* I made up. What is there to fear? Why should I fear another? Why should I fear life? What I withhold from life is a result of fear. Who has met life without fear and without some self-centered plan for survival? Who are the people on the stage of my life and what is my relationship with them? I can see them in the light of love or in the dark suspicions of fear. I have only that choice. No other choices have any meaning.

Ω

106.

A

Obviously, there are disappointments, unhappiness, grievances in the mind which require forgiveness. "Perfect happiness" is the "elusive fish" of the Self, seemingly unattainable. Yet what I have made, which is not joyous and happy, is my responsibility to undo. I can choose again the life I want to live, one in which my function is to be happy. Today must be dedicated to happiness or I will not be aware of it. The brain is conditioned to "think." Happiness, which is perfect, is a state beyond the duality of thought. It does not have a sad counterpart with which to do battle. Perfect happiness simply is. And because it *is* created, not "made," it cannot be affected by time, decay, change or threat. It is written, "God gives me only happiness." Is that true? Given happiness is from God, and unhappiness is something I made in separation from God, then I am responsible to "unmake" the mistakes of my separation. God's messenger will help me with this, but I must be willing to question and forgive myself. What is the cause of my unhappiness? It is something of my "meaningless thought." Have I accepted my God-given happiness? Only partially. So then I have denied the will of my Creator. Yet I can always change my mind. *My only function is the one God gave me. My happiness and my function are one.* ACIM, Lessons # 65 & #66.

Ω

107.

Α

The rules of conventional life define success as house in suburbs, a couple children, two-car garage, career with six-figure cash flow, etc. What may not be meaningful is given tremendous meaning. To see through the system requires having gone through the system, at least to the degree that any renunciation is clear on exactly what is being renounced. Being a householder has its values; family life can be well-balanced, creative, and good. Yet any member of that family may begin to question: is there something more in life than fulfilling the expectations of success and conventions? What is true freedom? Who am I? Is there identity beyond my personal self I made up? Most do not ask themselves these questions as they strive within the expectations of personal success. But a few, who may appear to be at odds with the status quo, "perennially discontented," question the confines of conventional life. They are the seers and visionaries who transcend thought. They are open to receive something of the Spirit simply because they are not so invested and preoccupied with achieving conventional success. One could say they are empty; receptacles for the given. Mozart would be one of these; Gandhi another, Mother Teresa certainly. All gave something lasting. Now, everyone must eventually ask himself or herself, "what do I have to give?"

Ω

108.

A

We are forced by the repetitions of the past to be "dead" while living. What is new? The patterns of confinement, mental and physical, shape our lives into lowly imitations of something vital, yet bygone. The genius of ancestry does not fulfill the genius needed now. But we have become "dead" and fooled by the amusements of commercialized life. What is cleverness in this age profits by the unnecessary; waste has become normal. "Throw it away" is the mantra of planned obsolescence everywhere. "Toys" are for children yet continue into adulthood. We are diverted away from authoring something original and pure. Fashion, or the focus on the surface appearances of things, floats and flits on a media blitz; the masses are made to buy anything as long as it has been "logo-ized" into popular fame. I buy a "name" on the back pocket of my dungarees and feel current and well-clothed. But there has to be something more meaningful to my life than outward appearances and copied patterns of behavior. The status quo is deadly; a waste of my life. What is it I want to do and how do I want to do it? The slate is wiped clean. Begin now! Anyone can start afresh, not based on the past. The present is potent with a million possibilities. Step into it, which is all there really is or ever will be.

Ω

109.

A

The body appears to wear out, malfunction, and die—it stops breathing air, stops pumping blood, and begins to decay. Now everyone related to that being must deal with the end. Relationship is now strictly inside—in the mind, heart, and memory. A new era begins, one in which life is renewed while old life is completed. Earth to earth; dust to dust, and in the end the body amounts to a few pounds of dust spread to the winds or buried in the earth's crust. Old patterns will continue. Time will have its effects. The young will marry and produce new life as the middle-aged become the elders and move toward their expected meeting with death themselves. Death, or the radical exit from form, is viewed by many as a necessary step in the Spirit's transcendency. Resurrection is the re-entry of the Spirit of Life into a "new body." Yet, this can happen every day. We think of death as the end of the body, but is it ever seen as the end of the content of the mind? Krishnamurti spoke of this empty mind, free from the known. This still and empty mind is free of beliefs and ideologies; therefore, it can meet the present as it is. Embracing the present, I am aware of Love working in my life afresh. So the death, or the ending, is the doorway into the new beginning. "I die, but I do not die," said Saint John of the Cross. A death is always a new start; therefore, in the bigger view of reality there is no death, only the continuity of immortal Being after a cycle which has completed itself.

Ω

110.

A

"I *feel the Love of God within me now." ACIM, Lesson #189* Who does? The world's view prevents this. Can a person be clear of the obscuring effects of the world's view of fear? An action of the will can; mostly it is a determination to give up judgments and fears. Forgiveness is the means toward a vision, one in which the Love of God is the inner core of sight. Do this: *Be still and lay aside all thoughts of what you are and what God is; all concepts you have learned about the world; all images you hold about yourself. Empty your mind of everything it thinks is either true or false or good or bad, of every thought it judges worthy, and all the ideas of which it is ashamed. Hold on to nothing. Do not bring with you one thought the past has taught or one belief you ever learned before from anything. Forget this world, forget this course, and come with wholly empty hands unto your God. ACIM, Lesson #189.* This is the commandment of *A Course in Miracles*; it is the necessary step before I can receive anything of the Will of God. Then it is the Action of Life working through me that is significant. I am not the one "in control." Otherwise I lead a life of thought of the ego—personalized in the "me and mine." *What is*. All that is contained within the Will of God unfolds and is not contrary to that will. How can I judge any situation or event? I am not the judge. To be free, I need no opinion. Then I am unattached.

Ω

111.

A person could live his whole life not knowing the Self. There is a self I made, called my personality, and a Self Whom God created, called the Christ. Everyone has these two. With some, the similarities are great, and the gap between the two are small. With others, the similarities are small, and the gap between great. Yet, when anyone chooses to end the gap, the bridge of forgiveness is provided. I can recognize mistakes have been made and I fell into the "hell" of my own conflict by my own doing. My thought manufactured a body and the belief in "good vs. evil," and I forgot my own inherent goodness which has no opposite. This is what the Christ remembers; an Identity not plagued by the duality of thought. He remembers who I am as God created me, a being totally free of conflict—inner and outer. His Presence is always inside me, but the attention must be given to realize it. It is not difficult to give this attention, but the self I made wants center stage instead, and I forget to *be present*. As *A Course in Miracles* points out, I must empty my mind of thought first, and leave behind all self-concepts. Not so easy for the ego. But the ego will never know the Self. A whole life could go by and the human being would never have contact with the Christ inside his own breast. Without another attention, one of renunciation, the Self is inaccessible.

Ω

112.

A

In the end, there is nothing to say. I would speak of a "problem" amidst a reality in which there are no problems. All problems are manufactured by thought, separated from the Divine Self. But in reality, separation is an illusion; therefore, "problems" are illusions. Need I give attention to illusions? Only to see them as such. Thinking an illusion to be "real," I am trapped by my self-deception. "Mental problems" manifest as "physical problems." The mistake, though, originates in the mind where it must be corrected. My true Mind is Divine, wholly joyous and at peace. Any state of mind "not that" is an illusion I have made. God, or that Great Unknown Force, which Created All Things, had no part in the making of my illusions. I would not be here if I had no mistakes to correct. Furthermore, even witnessing a mistake makes it my responsibility to correct. There is no such thing as "someone else's mistake." "No man is an island" John Donne wrote, as all death tolls for thee. My responsibility is to overcome death, mine and my brother's simultaneously. "Do not ask for whom the bell tolls; it tolls for thee." The "loss" of another is my own "loss." Yet forgiveness is the great Correction. The consequences of illusions are nullified when I recognize them *as* illusions. The horrors of the dream have no effect upon the one awake! The Self does not suffer. It remains forever silent and full of Joy.

Ω

113.

A

On route to Los Angeles. Peace is always a state of mind accessible. Gratefulness invites this Reality into my mind. It has no future and no past. The ever-present Now has all peace within it. Conflict is something perpetuated by thought—thoughts of opposites. Good vs. evil; right vs. wrong. Christ's vision sees neither. Reality is *what is*. *What is,* is only Peace, stillness, silence. "No thought," or the Void, transcends my "understanding." Nevertheless, I may touch upon that state. Perception is whole when it does not judge and divide. Now it is possible to be at peace. My thought "about" anything is meaningless. Yet my thoughts I "think" with God (stillness) result in Peace. Problems are unreal. They have no validity in truth. Peace is all there is; love is all there is. Nothing else exists. Reality is unthreatenable; unchangeable. In that state of Mind, it does not matter "what happens." Whatever "happens" is meant to "happen." Upset is always a choice to react to what "happens," without accepting the perfection of it; therefore, denying the peace of God. Love does not react but responds to the "lack of love" with forgiveness. When something has "gone wrong," anger does not set it right. Rather, admission of responsibility for the error invokes Divinity to aid in a different vision, one of Peace. In this state of Peace, correction is given, and my awareness of a Higher Reality is restored.

Ω

114.

A

I am the light of the world. ACIM, Lesson #61 Who is the light of the world except God's Son? This is merely a statement of the truth about yourself. The question is one of unwillingness; unwillingness to accept who I AM as God created me; my holy Self. The ego sees this statement as "arrogant" or "self-glorification." False "humility" rules the ego. Yet, **true humility requires that you accept today's idea because it is God's Voice which tells you [and me] it is true.** This lesson distills my purpose down to a few essential statements regarding my function. "I am the light of the world. That is my only function. That is why I am here." Unwillingness manufactures all kinds of other "functions." In the world we call these "career decisions." These may have a place in earning our bread, but they are not the primary function of life here on this planet. Mesmerized by the senses of the body and the thoughts of education, the human being pursues a job and money, success, etc. These may divert his attention from his function rather than provide the "stage" on which he may perform his function. Yet the lesson dissolves these secondary concerns by the unequivocal language it imparts. "I am the light of the world. That is my only function." Only means One. Not two or three in addition to the One. A single function is to be *as God created me*. Only that One is true—no ego as a false "self," and no distraction from peace.

Ω

115.

A

Some encounters in life bring powerful alterations in the course of personal events. To meet a person who has freed himself from the conditioning of thought is such an encounter. After it, life is never again as it had been. One cannot lie to himself regarding the internal issues of fear, motives, insecurities, doubts; yet he also sees the light of stillness, peace, and the present which dissolves these issues. An encounter with a teacher will turn life around. Having grown accustomed to the common conflicts in life with relationships, work, etc., a teacher is needed to question them, and hence undo them. Without a teacher of life, complacency sets in, and I grow to accept my limitations. But the encounter with a teacher changes that. I can question the limitations I have imposed on life. When I do this process of Self-inquiry, I then become my own "teacher." The external teacher has done his job and now I can continue on my own. This is the first step in having something to give because now I am not wasting energy on non-essentials. My energy is contained in order to rise to my function: ***Forgiveness is my function as the light of the world. ACIM, Lesson #62*** It will take energy to realize the truth of this; therefore, simplification is necessary, aided by that first encounter with the wise.

Ω

116.

A

"Your goal is to find out who you are, having denied your Identity by attacking creation and its Creator." *ACIM, Lesson #62* Finding out my true Identity and fulfilling my function are one. Through forgiveness I am told, I can discover this Identity. Fulfilling my function and my happiness are integral. I must, therefore, be clear that my function is forgiveness and that I accept this as my only function. Yet, I need not, and cannot, "know" all the particulars forgiveness involves. "Thought" projects what it thinks is needed, but in fact it does not know. Forgiveness, in light of any situation in which all of the factors are not fully known, is best left in the Hands of Divinity. Therefore, my part is only the petition of these Hands to "correct" and wipe clean the slate of my thought. Myself is the one in need of forgiveness, because the world and myself are the same. Therefore, any gift of forgiveness I give to the world I give to myself at once. A continuous chain of forgiveness is formed from my whole attention. When I forget and falter, it is forgiveness itself that sets me straight; it is the "means and the end," the Alpha and the Omega, the beginning and end of existence. I can end my attack upon creation, my Creator, and myself simultaneously. Then my Self emerges into my awareness. I am at peace. My Identity is known to me. This is all I really need to know, who I am as God created me.

Ω

117.

A

The Source of Energy to know the Self is within me. To tap into that Source requires my attention, and to the degree I am attentive, more energy is provided. There seems to be plenty of time to devote to the activities of survival, but what portion of my life is devoted to realizing my Self? The space to be relaxed and well rested is provided. Now, what will I do with that space? Attention to the lesson is free of distractions—do I use this freedom to come closer to my Self? The statement, "I am the light of the world" is sacred and true; but is it my truth? What would a fully realized person do with this light? What would I do with this light which is mine? Extending forgiveness is my function. How would I do that? Is it for me to decide or just my openness is required? I don't know, but my Self does. Not to pursue what my thought projects is a challenge. Equally challenging is following directions when I receive them. Distinguishing between projections of thought and directions from my Source takes discrimination. Following one may turn out to be the other; that is why constant forgiveness is necessary. Even the best intentions may produce a mistake. Therefore, it is important to recognize the strength of the unknown in my decision to do anything. Beyond thought, there is a force of reality which moves my actions.

Ω

118.

A

The Self is bestowed upon everyone from the beginning of creation, yet the awareness of this Self is realized by the very few. Therefore, it is not something I "learn" or accomplish; rather, would I awaken from a "sleep of forgetfulness." Simplicity is the result of knowing my Self. Because the Self has no needs and the body's needs are reduced to the essentials, my physical and mental environments become very simplified. Order is spacious; emptiness is a virtue. Then I can be helpful. Am I helpful? Am I simple? These are questions that require my attention. Why am I engaged in the disorders of the ego? What keeps me attached to the things of the body? Unwillingness to be my Self is destructive. What do I think I gain from this unwillingness? Isolation is impossible; why do I believe in it? What would awaken me fully to be my Self? The process of awakening seems slow and incremental. But is it, in the end? The light is either on or off. Is my light on or off? I have the power to switch it *on*. What prevents me from doing so? What am I afraid of? Do I fear my Self? Do I cling to an ego and fear being without my small self? Have I ever really been helpful to myself or another? Have I ever represented the Christ "who sent me?" I put these questions to myself in order to wake up. Will I ever fully wake up? It would take miracles.

Ω

119.

A

You have not lost your innocence. It is for this you yearn. This is your heart's desire. This is the voice you hear, and this the call which cannot be denied. The holy child remains with you. His home is yours. Today He gives you His defenselessness, and you accept it in exchange for all the toys of battle you have made. And now the way is open, and the journey has an end in sight at last. Be still an instant and go home with Him and be at peace a while. ACIM Lesson #182 Home is within. The Kingdom is within. Renunciation is the recognition that "external beauty" is a result of an internal state of mind. My innocence is all I need to "know." My holy child accompanies me wherever I go. No words are necessary to communicate with him, just an awareness of his presence is all I need. The mistakes of the past are erased; they are gone. Memory is cleansed by forgiveness each moment of the day. My home is always present. It is a stillness, a quiet, an acceptance of *what is*. What responsibility do I have to those Higher Forces that brought this to my attention? Even here, amidst the illusions that are not my home, I am responsible for my mind, and the truth of what is given me this day. I am responsible to accept my Home and to repent for all my wanting and seeking which kept my mind away from Home. I am grateful the lesson gives me clarity and my seeking can cease. This end is a great blessing.

Ω

120.

A

What is certainty? It is certain that people will behave as they did in the past. It is certain that limitations will be justified. It is certain that physical cycles will repeat themselves, like the sun will rise and set, and the body is born then grows to adulthood. It is certain that the Word of God is true and man's unwillingness will not accept it. It is certain that the status quo equates power and money. It is certain that sexual suggestions get men's attention, and this attention can be used to sell things. It is certain that a different view will be rejected. It is certain that a compromise in the favor of the compromiser will be made. It is certain that excrement smells. It is certain that love will prevail over logic. It is certain that practicalities do not preclude miracles. It is certain that survival will bring about fear. It is certain that the brain and its thought are insecure. It is certain that death is an ending of something. It is certain that wanting something will make me do things to get it. It is certain that not wanting anything brings a lot of space. It is certain that a question without an answer has a lot of energy. It is certain that my attention is mine to direct. It is certain that I can change my mind. It is certain that violence does not solve a problem. It is certain that thought cannot answer a real question. It is certain that without air, the body will die. It is certain that without thought the brain is still. It is certain that peace does not judge.

Ω

121.

A

Fear not to recognize the whole idea of sacrifice is solely of your making. And seek not safety by attempting to protect yourself from where it is not. Your brothers and your Father have become very fearful to you. ACIM, Chapter 15, Section IX How do I project the idea of sacrifice in my life? What thoughts do I have that keep sacrifice alive? In order to do "good" I must give up something I value. This is sacrifice. In order to please people, I do things I don't really want to do. I take on a "burden" because I think I must to do the "right thing." All of this is a mental sacrifice. I trade my freedom for some sort of bondage. I go along in order not to rock the boat of the status quo. I have sacrificed my true Identity for one of a lower level. I avoid confrontation when what I am to confront is my own Self-deceptions. I sacrifice honesty for some form of evasive action. The ego sees sacrifice as a means to "correction." But this is not so. Thought of the Holy Spirit of Truth shows the falseness of my dark thoughts of sacrifice. Why dwell on the crucifixion when the resurrection proved there is nothing to sacrifice? Death has no meaning to the Holy Spirit. What is real has no end and no beginning. It is One with the Immortal Source of All that Is. When I open my eyes to see the Source in my Self, the end of sacrifice has taken place and I am reborn in the stillness of the Present.

Ω

122.

A

To "give up" in order to "get," or to "suffer" in order to "save," to "die" for another's "sins" are all erroneous thoughts of "sacrifice." I have made them, not the Christ. The Christ would say "nothing real can be threatened. Nothing unreal exists." To give up what has no reality is giving up nothing. Therefore, it is essential that I recognize what has no reality, and not to value it. Then it fades away. I let go of my attachments to nothing—that is all. The awakening of discrimination which recognizes the valuable from the valueless is a process, usually not without some "struggle" which can feel like sacrifice. But it is the attachment, fear of letting go, which makes sacrifice seem real. Yet I can accept the thought which says sacrifice is an illusion. What is real cannot be threatened. Happiness is in being my Self, free of conflict. I AM the I. My thoughts of separation are meaningless. When there is Love, problems do not exist. What is to be done is clear, and directions are followed. The Self makes known the unknown, and I am free to extend who I am as God created me. I will not accept limitations as real. Who am I to doubt the power of my Creator working through me? To be an instrument in the Hand of God is the greatest function of man. But there would be no conflict in it, no blame, no exclusion, no enmity. I can "love my enemies" because they are really one with me.

Ω

123.

Α

I am *en route* to Hawaii to a luau, to a Kahuna gathering of Ho'oponopono, and to the Haleakala Crater and the Kilauea volcano. It is my intention to leave behind old memories of "sacrifice" in which "pain" is thought of as the price for joy. Joy has no cost. It is in the stillness of the ever-present NOW. I do not know where I am going, but in general I trust I am going in the direction of my Self. The shadows of memory still accompany me, and the "pains" of the body persist, but I would be divorced from any complaint, or wish for things to be different. Forgiveness is a process of "going through" that which is not Love in order to release it. Love brings up anything "not love" in order to be cleansed and released. How long has memory persisted? Freedom from the negativity of memory is given through forgiveness. I do not need to know how long, but rather be willing to petition Divinity for release. Into the Bowl of Divinity's Void would I go to place my "problems" there. It is a sacred journey, one of Atonement, in this lifetime. Can I be my Self? Overcoming unwillingness: I "want" and I "don't want." The duality of opposites is inherent to thought. To step into the place of no-thought is one of grace bestowed by my Creator. I am empty to receive it. To be empty is my only need.

Ω

124.

A life of the body seems to have a beginning, middle, and end. There is much evidence to this dynamic. The body experiences pain and pleasure. The mind vacillates between the emotions of joy and sorrow. What is constant? Spirit, I am told, is my Identity, and death is an illusion. My Self is not a body. And I must choose the "joy of God instead of pain." The denial of death and pain is my responsibility. The mind can identify with the Spirit, though thought will always doubt its reality. At some point I need to surrender to the Word of God which make these facts clear, and *accept* them as the guiding principle in my life. The Word of God is true because it comes from God. Now, I can trust its authenticity or not. That is my first decision to make. Having accepted the first fact, I am now faced with the second: my unwillingness to apply the truth in my life. This is the reason I need the Word in the first place, to make the essential correction of Identity—a reversal of identification with thought and the body (an existence of duality of pain/pleasure) to Identity in the perfection of Spirit that is only peace and joy. Life of the Spirit, my Life, has no birth or death. Do I remain attentive to the freedom this Life offers or do I "fall" into the calculations of thought, survival, body, ego, etc. The determination to see Life differently is essential to realizing who I AM.

Ω

125.

A

Thought is memory. The mind is either the thought of memory or the Thought of God, Inspiration. The Mind which is still, or empty, is open to receive the Inspiration. Cleaning, or repentance, forgiveness, transmutation, is the way of life which clears me of memory. "Cleanse, erase, erase, and return to your port of Self-Identity," is given by my teacher Ihaleakala. What is an error is in need of correction. I have plenty of memory, and therefore errors. Without the process of repentance, forgiveness, and transmutation, I am lost on the road to death. The miracles are given when I take responsibility for my errors. "Don't look an inch beyond your nose or your toes," said Morrnah Simeona, the founder of modern day Ho'oponopono. In other words, what is an error is inside of me, and the correction is there as well. Leave other people alone. Don't blame or separate from "another's problem." If I am seeing it, I am responsible. I must go "down into it" before going up to Divinity for the transmutation (miracle). I am responsible for recognizing the error and then stopping—disengaging from thought. This is a moment-to-moment process. I am grateful to have this insight from the wise that I may discipline myself to use it. Cleanse, erase, erase. Without the "delete" button, my thought becomes memory impacted and dense. Forgiveness is my means of "deleting erroneous thinking."

Ω

126.

There is a simple way to find the door to true forgiveness and perceive that it is open wide in welcome. When you are tempted to accuse someone of sin in any form, do not allow your mind to dwell on what you think he did, for that is Self-deception. Ask instead, "would I accuse myself of doing this?" *ACIM, Lesson #134* Step one is to recognize my accusations. Step two is the question this direction proposes. Obviously, I would not accuse myself of the error. In the event I have made the same mistake, how could I condemn the other without condemning myself as well? Therefore, I either release us both together or destroy us both by accusations of guilt. **In truth is innocence, the only thing there is.** All the memory of thought which is not pure joy is an illusion to be undone. Forgiveness deletes illusions, not the truth. Truth of my innocence needs no defense; any thought of guilt or "I am not" requires undoing; therefore, in this world, forgiveness if necessary. **Forgiveness stands between illusions and the truth; between the world you see and that which lies beyond; between the hell of guilt and heaven's gate.** The gate to my own innocence is open when I see the other's innocence is my own. All states not pure joy are washed away by the awareness they are not real.

Ω

127.

A

Beyond this world there is a world I want. *ACIM, Lesson # 129* The world I see is one of duality; joy is followed by sorrow, pleasure by pain. The world I see can be different when I am in contact with my Divine Creator. The Will of God for me is only happiness, and this would be a world in which duality has been undone. It is not a world of bodies, though it may manifest (inspire) in bodies of physical form. It is a world of the Mind, original and pure. *Today the lights of heaven bend to you, to shine upon your eyelids as you rest beyond the world of darkness. Here is light your eyes cannot behold. And yet your mind can see it plainly and can understand. A day of grace is given you today, and we give thanks. This day we realize that what you feared to lose was only loss. ACIM, Lesson #129* Beyond the world of "loss and gain" that fear has made, there is a world in which loss is impossible. It is one of total trust that my Creator takes *total* care of me, no matter what the situation "looks like." Why should I interpret the situation I am in with thoughts of fear and loss? The lesson puts me in a different mental state, one of *right now* in which all I need or will ever want is totally given. If something passes away and is gone, then I did not need it, and I am free. Therefore, my fear of loss is gone as well. ***Loss is not loss when properly perceived. ACIM Lesson #284***

Ω

128.

A

The cleaning, or purification of Self, will always have thought (memory) to undo. Who is the Self without a blemish of thought? I fool myself by a false identity, feel not at home, and seek improvements. All seeking of improvement is for a lower order of the self. The Self at One with the Divine Creator has a mind/body free of thought. Improvement is a fallacy. The perfection of the Self is like clear water; the impurities of the ego cloud the water, therefore purification, not improvement, is needed. Education seeks to improve; awakening seeks to purify. Both are processes. Education attempts to add knowledge. To awaken, one must "remove what distracts him from his perfection"—the Self. These impurities are anger, envy, hate, gluttony, lust, greed, arrogance, pride, attachment, etc. They must be dealt with, observed, and forgiven. God's promise is to transmute these impurities when His Son is willing to admit them. But as long as the conflict of "good vs. evil" is maintained by thought, forgiveness cannot be fulfilled. Purification is a tedious process of undoing. It questions every thought, word, deed and action that I may be free of memory and live in the Inspiration of my Holy Self as God created. Forgiveness is the means to an empty mind which has the vitality to receive.

Ω

129.

A

"*The peace of God is shining in me now. Let all things shine upon me in that peace and let me bless them with the light in me.*" **ACIM, Lesson #188** The things we do with our day forget the fact that we are holy beings. We do not remember that our function is to be, rather than "to do." To be who we are is effortless in a world steeped in effort. This is why *ACIM* is needed. It is a "mystery" school in the sense that the world does not know it. All that the world purports to be necessary to know is basically tainted with uncertainty. Even science stops short of the Absolute. Relative knowledge is taught and accumulated. Academia as well as the corporate domains operate in a survival of the fittest mode, complete with pecking orders. One is either a "businessman" or an "employee." But these are experiences devoid of Identity. In nature there are predators and prey. In very subtle ways the human being falls into this dualism. "Jobs" are too often for people who are "preyed" upon by corporate systems and organizations. Who has his own work, independent of the corporation? Commercialized life is almost unavoidable. But there is another way to live. The premise of my life is different when I am determined that the God-given peace is in the first place. Peace must be given away to be received, as the giving increases my awareness of it.

Ω

130.

Α

I do not know my Self, though I do not doubt It exists. As an ideal, the "Self" is meaningless. Yet as a fact, even though I may not fully realize it, the Self awaits my awareness. *Yet the essential thing is learning that you do not know.* **ACIM, Chapter 14, Section XI** Working with that fact is more valuable than assuming one has "learned" the truth. God, or Truth, cannot be perceived by my thought body. That's okay as long as I do not doubt that God's awesome results are ample proof of His Power to Create. At a place like Haleakala Crater in Hawaii, the stillness and scale connect with the God-given stillness within. I was there to witness this grandeur, clearly a great offspring of the Unknown. The Unknown is very dynamic. It gives the freedom to Creation, and to me, that I may be the co-creator of my own destiny. By acknowledging I have "errored" and that I do not know what anything means—the correction, given by God, can be accepted. When my peace is "threatened," or at least I think it is, then I must confess: *I do not know what anything, including this, means; and so I do not know how to respond to it. And I will not use my own past learning as the light to guide me now.* **ACIM, Chapter 14, Section XI** Opportunities arise in which I can come to this surrender. Pray I am not so willful in maintaining my false sense of righteousness that I cannot stop to "pause" and ask Divinity for the proper guidance.

Ω

131.

A meeting with the wise requires the mind to be still; not projecting all kinds of "problems." Can I be empty? Is it possible through the grace of God alone without effort on my part; because any effort would be a thought, a memory. Nature is dynamic, yet always in the present. The diversity of Life makes for many remarkable forms of earth, air, sea, plants, and animals. Even human forms are diverse, related to climate and geography. Yet in this diversity there is an ever-present connectedness, a oneness, an inevitable sharing. Without the water in the sea, the plants would die; without the air to evaporate the water, carry it through the sky, and distribute it to the plants, the oceans would not serve their function. So is the Self manifested in a dynamic form. My Self has this dynamism, this Inspiration, yet its Absolute source is emptiness, void, nothingness, nada, nil. And it is in that State I must meet the wise. Incremental dissolution of the ego is meaningless. One is either deceived or not; him Self or not. To relate to form as though it is my Self is to confuse levels. The mind that takes responsibility recognizes the physical form can be determined by memory, and this is an illusion. Mind says to physicality: I'm sorry, please forgive me for confusing levels. You have access to the Source—Love, Emptiness, Clarity. I will stop dictating to you. Just be and ask the Father. I will follow.

Ω

132.

A

Is memory finite or infinite? Being physical, it must be finite. Being finite it must have an end. Who knows when that end would come? The issue then is undoing memory, letting go of all memory. Beyond that is the Infinite—my Identity. The holy family, or Divinity—father, mother, child of my Self—is a unique being, created in Divinity's Image, not my own. See the Self at zero, in the Beginning. Why put any Inspiration into it? That is the work and Will of God. Why should I oppose it? "Unto Thy Will I commend my Spirit." And as long as I have a mind/body, that would be commended to Divinity's Will as well. Who forgives? ***God does not forgive because He has never condemned. God is the Love in which I forgive. As you condemn only yourself, so do you forgive only yourself. Yet, although God does not forgive, His Love is nevertheless the basis of forgiveness. ACIM, Lesson #46*** The practical application of this occurs in day-to-day relationships. Yet I must always remember that error is 100% mine, therefore correction is mine as well. What I witness as error outside of me is actually a manifestation of error *inside* of me. Day to day, this commitment to correct amounts to vigilance of the mind. To correct the errors of the mind requires ceaseless attention to the mind. The process of forgiveness is simple, but the level of attention needed is rigorous.

Ω

133.

A

I *am as God created me. His Son can suffer nothing. And I am His Son. ACIM, Lesson #110* Suffering, primarily noticed in the body, begins in the mind. Separation of mind from Spirit is essentially the mind looking toward the body for guidance instead of from the Spirit. The body cannot guide consistently because it, along with the mind, operates in the relative world of opposites: likes and dislikes, this vs. that, etc. But the mind with the body, turned in the direction of the Spirit, or the Unknown forces of Divine Love, can be guided consistently. There are no opposites in the Kingdom of the Spirit. Guidance is uncontaminated by uncertainty—the mind admits "I don't know" thus letting go of its control by thinking. The body is then in the direction of the Spirit, thus reconnected to the Source. It is the Source that guides, not subject to the understanding of thought. Mind and body are certain of their direction, certain that it is not of them. This integrates the levels and balances the triune of the Self—spirit-mind-body. Direction can then truly be called Free. It is free of suffering because it is in the service of undoing it. The Son looks upon suffering; and not judging it, He is in the position of undoing it. **Forgiveness is my function as the light of the world. *ACIM, Lesson #62*** Acceptance of Who I am, apart from memory, is acceptance of my Life free of suffering.

Ω

134.

A

The process of forgiveness seems ongoing. Is there an end to it, a completion in which a person is fully at peace with nothing to forgive? "Let my forgiveness be complete and let the memory of You (God) return to me." The only "problem" is separation from this remembrance of God, my Source. My Source, in the image of Who created me, is Zero, or the Void. "I come forth out of the Void into light." (The "I's" Prayer, Ho'oponopono) Light is manifested out of Nothing. I am manifested out of nothing. "Where is the Divine Creator"? "Everywhere and nowhere." The nowhere is the Void—Zero; the everywhere is Creation—Inspiration. The problem is thought—memory—which is separated from both the Void and Creation. Erasure of thought is essential for me to know my Self, and this erasure is called Atonement for which the Christ is 100% in charge. It is a process, meaning it exists in time and space, yet its purpose is not bound by these limitations. Its purpose is Freedom of the Creation, which is already Truth, but forgotten by the Sons of God. That is why the older brother, the Christ, is needed, to remind His fellow Sons of God that they are really Free. Only their thoughts bind them, and these are illusions. Atonement erases them, corrects them, forgives them so we can return to Freedom unencumbered by any thoughts of bondage.

Ω

.

135.

A In the other is the error that every human being must correct; therefore, the other's error is my own as well. To give attention to this aspect of memory being repeated is to say, "I see the error, I am sorry, please forgive me." Look within, not without. There is no separation between the "other's error" and my own. This is how healing can occur, because there is no blame; blame being, "I am pure, you are not." The impurity is mine to correct. I can be grateful to witness the error, even if it is "an attack on me." It is another opportunity to affirm my innocence. I'm sorry, please forgive me, my Self is only Love and happiness. I forgive you (myself) for thinking otherwise. We are like children who do not "know" because thought cannot "know" innocence. As little children the duality of "good vs. bad" is not necessary. All is innocence—a state before thought, guilt, attack ever entered the mind. Yet the tendencies brought into this incarnation, be they producers of sorrow, must be undone. Eventually they manifest because they are in memory. That is why it is essential to empty the mind of thought. Get to Zero. Peace is an emptiness. Divine Forces help him who is ready to help himself by 1) only looking at himself, 2) invoking "I'm sorry, please forgive me" to initiate the process of Atonement, and 3) accepting the transmutation Divinity provides, not the results "I want." This is clearly practiced in Ho'oponopono.

Ω

136.

A

The embracing of "evil" as part of my Self is something challenging. There is nothing the Self does not contain. Whitman, the true poet, looks upon the part of the Self which is considered the "dark side," yet through the eyes of complete forgiveness. "I am he who knew what it was to be evil." (Line 74 Crossing Brooklyn Ferry) Yet does he rise above it. Having gone down into the psychological "pit," he is lifted up by the ending of guilt, of conflict between "good and evil." He embraces both and joins with his brother in this integration. "It is not you alone, nor I alone. Not a few races nor a few generations nor a few centuries. It is that each came, or comes, or shall come, from its due admission, from the general center of all, and forming part of all. Everything indicates—the smallest does, and the largest does—a necessary film envelopes all and envelopes the Soul for a proper time." (Lines 95-100) Each comes to these planes to be an essential part of the Self. None are superfluous, even the murderer has a role to play. Neither good nor evil divide the Self. "I AM THE I." Identity contains all, beyond space or time; boundless and eternal. What Whitman says is true forever. What the truly wise say will guide mankind for all generations, that each may come to connect with and "transmit" his God-created Self, free of death, free of duality.

Ω

137.

A being incarnates for a particular reason, and that is to be his God-given Self. One comes with abilities which can be employed in the purpose of the Divine. This can manifest as a talent. A voice given to one by God is humbly used because its power comes from on high. It is an expression of Divine order and beauty, of truth and rightness, of acceptance and gratitude. In the realm of music, the human voice communicates something of the character of who is singing. Even when the music is remarkable, it is the quality of the voice which communicates this Power and Presence beyond the words and even beyond the sound itself. Marian Anderson had such a voice, and her music was like a holy offering to mankind for future generations to come. From very humble beginnings, amidst the prejudices of hate, she rose above it all with a dignity that transcended racial conflict to present to the world her incredible love for music. Her voice—a holy voice—was inspired from on the high, and she knew from whence it came. The voice of the 20th century, she was the one who liberated not only her own race, but every human being from the confines of belief and limitation. She came to these planes to Love through her voice and sing a song of gladness and joy that would undeniably restore the dignity to be human.

Ω

138.

A

One accumulates in his life many things, experiences, beliefs, hurts, joys, disappointments, achievements and the like. These are limited mostly to the personal self. At a higher level, untouched by the accumulations of thought—memory—there is an emptiness, a clarity which is not governed by intellectual understanding. In this state of being, one is complete. He has confessed his innermost secrets of guilt and now he is in the light of true awareness, one in which everything is imbued with the holiness of God's creation. Even the most abject human being is beautiful; there is no high or low, respectable and unrespectable, just what is, as it is. Nothing needs to be other than what it is. Released, the soul is free to be itself. The aspects of Self that are regarded as liabilities are now assets because of their conversion through forgiveness. This state imparts a new energy, one which can act according to the Will of God. Of course, there are myriads of false prophets, ones who claim to be divinely inspired, yet are not. A tree is known by its fruits: what is holy produces that which is joyful and of the light. If there is no joy and only sorrow, one can be certain that the results are repeated memories of separation from God, and not the reflection of God's will. God's will is only happiness. What is not that is only a dream of separation, a memory crying out for forgiveness and release.

Ω

139.

A

Two friends meet. One sees in the other a tendency, a self-effacing gesture. He points it out. That is what a friend will do—help the other see himself. And vice versa. One can go to the friend and confess, "Brother, I've made some mistakes and trying my best to correct them. This is the fact of the matter. How do you see it?" And the friend would probably say, "I see the tendency in you to do such and such. It really does not behoove you. You can change your ways. Rise above it and be dignified." Forgiveness is in seeing the error and invoking correction: the removal of that memory from the mind. All experience is a replayed memory. Unless the mind is emptied of thought, the Mind of God cannot prevail in one's awareness. It is important to realize thought is not real, yet the thoughts I think with God, inspiration, are my real thoughts. **God is the mind with which I think. ACIM, Lesson #45** The Mind of God is my real mind as well—a mind free, and in no need of defense or attack. These are seen as unnecessary. Its nature is silence. Who can silence their thought? There is no technique to it. Attention is necessary. What one attends to is *his own thought*. All reflections of happenings in the world are from the mirror of my One Self. In the end, the body is given up for the direction and immersion in the Spirit.

Ω

140.

A

My mind holds only what I think with God. Only salvation can be said to cure. Speak to us Father that we may be healed. ACIM, Lesson #140 And through the lessons is the Voice of God made known. *Forgiveness is the key to happiness. ACIM, Lesson #121; Forgiveness offers everything I want. ACIM, Lesson #122* We do not fully understand the Power of forgiveness. Thought cannot know it. Yet thought must invoke the process to begin. The conscious mind invokes, having confessed, "I do not know." The subconscious mind is brought in alignment with the Spirit through this act of confession, and together the conscious and the subconscious hold hands in this invocation. Then the Spirit can receive the petition and send it "up" to God. Divinity can give what is needed for Salvation, and the patient is now with the cure, and not the memory of the problem. We, as human beings who have been separated from truth, from pure joy, have the Power of forgiveness at our disposal as the means toward receiving Pure Joy. Happiness is our Natural State of Being as Sons and Daughters of God. Anything "not happy" is a denial of our Identity, and therefore unreal. The real correction occurs only in the Mind. It is a realignment of the Self, in order to truly be the Self. I am grateful to have the facts made clear. Separation is an illusion when I realize, *My mind holds only what I think with God.* My Mind is vast, and contains the whole Universe. My Self and my Mind are the same.

Ω

141.

A

The patterns of memory run deep. "Samskaras" in Sanskrit are those "scars" of mental thought forms which repeat themselves lifetime after lifetime. Grudge begets grudge, just as love begets love. To free the mind from guilt, problems, and repeated horrors of memory, forgiveness is needed. Petitioning the Creator to restore peace and sanity to a mind besieged with thoughts of attack is a process of forgiveness. It is simply seeing the false as the false; the false has no real consequence because it *is* false. But I will think the false does have consequences until I give it up. My interpretations are given so much validity. I have grown to accept the pain of maintaining them. Why? Man is conditioned to bear his suffering rather than to question the real root cause of it. "The time of sacrifice is over," said Morrnah Simeona, but the ego finds many ways to justify suffering. All suffering is self-inflicted. The soldier who is shot and killed by the "enemy" already entered into a destructive relationship regarding this "enemy." To live by the sword, one has accepted the possibility, however strong or weak, that he may possibly die by it. Therefore, it is already decided; he chooses death and all its possibility. This need not be. The body need not be "sacrificed." The mind can serve a transfigured body, one in which the view of the world is forgiven.

Ω

142.

A

The people in our lives are those who we see every day. Some we see infrequently; others, perhaps, once. What is it we give? There are no chance encounters. *Today I learn to give as I receive. ACIM, Lesson #158* What do I give? The lesson speaks of Christ's vision. The experience of holiness cannot be given, but the vision of that experience can be. Vision is "to see." To see the innocence of my Self and of every other Self—that is the vision of Christ—to look upon a forgiven world. Something like a vigilance, the vision of Christ in my life is to be present without a judgement, without a fear or anxiety, without a motive or desire for anything to be different. What can affect the external is a certainty that *inside me* the Peace of God prevails, that nothing external can intrude upon it. A person in this state of being affects the very atmosphere around him. We think that activity alters the externals, and to a degree it does but usually along the repetitive lines of past thinking. What would happen around one who has silenced his thought? He is no longer conditioned by fear, by all the internal impurities, by desires. Having everything of real value already, the wise person wants nothing. He is whole and complete NOW, not sometimes off in the future. One desire is a denial of wholeness. I desire to be desire-less. That is the one and only desire which is the last.

Ω

143.

A

I offer only miracles today. For I would have them be returned to me. ACIM, Lesson #345 A miracle is a change of mind. We seem to be bound to bodies and personalities. Experience, or the accumulation of all our life's encounters, seems to define us. What does experience have to do with miracles? Experience is mostly of the past. The miracle is of this living moment, every one different, always new and alive. A day without the self-imposed pressure of activity is a blessed day, one given by the Creator to the Created. I am with that. Who needs experience to be present? Education is not needed to love. What can the accumulation of more knowledge do for the human being? There is more and more fear and anxiety put into him. Why? Education does not awaken one to be his Self. Real education would take a somewhat "hands-off" approach. The child would have his own creative interests and expressions. Why does he need to be conditioned at all? We are like ants in a colony—conditioned to labor toward some assumed social end. But the "end" is usually the "means" of some few to live at a higher level on the social order, either economic, political, academic, popular, etc. Improving oneself is a fallacy. Who has accepted himself as God created him? Already whole, already perfect as is?

Ω

144.

A point in time—another chance to accept who I am. A decision I make with God; the only real decision, which requires no time. Time ticks on, a man-made construct whose primary purpose is to postpone this one decision. I stand on the "outside" of it, looking inward, toward the final dissolution in which separation ends. Separated by time—the time I think it takes to "wake up," to "become" my Self. Of course, this separation by time is an illusion which the ego maintains. Because it maintains it, all kinds of methods are devised to get me to my holiness, a state of being which already exists in me. Why do I need to go where I already am? Obviously, I need go nowhere; I need practice no device, and I do not need to improve upon what is already perfected in the Eyes of God. But I do need to See through those Eyes. This would be called Christ's Vision. He, not I, has a Vision of Reality. And He, being inside me as my Self, can lead me to the Peace and Joy of God if I but let Him. For Him, time exists only as this Holy Instant—the ever-present Now—moment to moment. I take a step, one which has already been taken, to arrive where I already am. I Am the I. I do not get to be any more than that because that is Everything—timeless, boundless, complete in Love.

Ω

145.

A

I walk with God in perfect holiness. **ACIM, Lesson # 156** Do I walk with thought or with God in my awareness? Thought dominates my life, preventing me from accepting who I am as God created me. Most of the time the mind is preoccupied with some task at hand. The task may be necessary. Yet where is my awareness? Is God my first thought? Any distraction into "thinking" is a choice to "reject" the lesson. Every movement of life is a result of God moving through me. How could creation be otherwise? All that is, is, because God has created it so. Holiness is a natural attribute of the created. All of my movements in life are accompanied by this holiness. How could they not be? What is missing is not the holiness but my awareness of it; and thought blocks awareness. Therefore, the cessation of "thinking" is necessary. This does not mean living in a vacuum doing nothing, but rather approaching every movement, every action, with a new purpose—one in which the holiness of the movement is seen first, and each movement a "link" in the chain of gratefulness for the Given. "I am the I" is a posture of accepting this holiness in everything I "see" and do. Life, then, becomes a blessing, a benediction to my Creator, as "I am His Son." Who am I? I am God's Son, "safe and healed and whole; free to forgive and free to save the world." It is a new vision, not of a new reality, because reality has always been; but now my sight is present.

Ω

146.

A

The walk I walk is one of mediocrity. I am not vigilant enough to be 100% aware of my holiness, therefore my walk is mid-way, mediocre. Discipline, not imposed, yet understood as necessary, is the deciding factor that would determine my fate. Will I remain only partial or take the step to be totally with the truth of the lesson? Discipline amounts to the quality of attention given to something. The lesson is a thought given to me by God which undoes my own thought. I need but give it my full attention, and without denying the truth of it, see how I "fall short" in its application. My thought, my effort, my wanting to be with the lesson is not enough to apply it. The factor of God's grace comes when I admit my utter helplessness. There is a Self in me not contaminated by doubt, by effort, by uncertainty. This is the "I" of the lesson who walks with God in perfect holiness. This is the "I" who can read the lesson and bring it to application immediately without effort of any kind. "I" am He. The little self of the ego, which does all kinds of penances to be holy, diminishes in the light of the Self. In this light there are no penances. Only the recognition of a fact. The Present is the only time there is, and in the Present is my own perfection, my holiness, free of thought. What a blessing to read the lesson with a different mind, one that is not tainted by doubt and opposites.

Ω

147.

A

With life comes a great responsibility to be wholly alive, free, and present as my Self. It is a responsibility to undeceive myself, or rather to be true. What does that mean, *to be true?* Reality is often substituted with appearances. What seems real today may be gone tomorrow—transient things of time come and go—bodies are born and die, personalities are formed and then fade, and are forgotten. Yet Truth by its very nature is definite, unalterable, a thing that is Eternal. Unaffected by time at all, it has no beginning nor ending and is unaffected by the constant play of changing forms. So subtle, so unperceived by the body's senses, and even the mind's intellectual understanding, the Self eludes all but the most determined seeker. He who rejects all other pursuits and endeavors but to know Reality, to know Truth, God or what have you, is the one whose one desire may be granted. Liberation from the ignorance of separation from the Self. The Self is not the personality, though the personality may play a role in its discovery. The teacher who has realized the Self, or at least the one eternal question that leads to this realization: "Who am I"? is the one who can aid others in approaching this profound purpose. He can be free, in the Self, and serve as a beacon to others seeking total Freedom.

Ω

148.

A simple act, done totally in the present, becomes a benediction of the Good Life. A short walk, a particular task of work when taken with all the love of true attention, is a blessing in one's day. I can hear my own steps and appreciate my unencumbered course of no particular direction. I arrive where I am going without the pressure of going there. It is a whole course, not just a trip from A to B. There is time to observe the trees, the houses, the people walking on the sidewalks, the traffic, the construction of new buildings, the lady calling her dog out of her back door. I do not know what to expect, nor do I want to know. The stores along the main street are open. One of them is a bakery. I stop and order a birthday cake for the friend. While there, the leisure for a cup of coffee and a small sweet roll is spacious; a blessing I give myself. Sipping the hot coffee and observing the young woman behind the counter and the lone black man at the adjacent table, I am grateful to be alone and quiet. She looks out the large picture windows onto the street scenes. The man gets up from his table to go to the restroom, then returns to his Styrofoam cup of coffee and newspaper. Finished with the afternoon snack, I head out, onto the main thoroughfare, on my destination home. Gratefulness is upon me to lead a simplified life, one free of strife and struggle. I am glad.

Ω

149.

Α

A person can read the scriptures, the so-called holy books, until his face turns blue, but until he *lives* the life of holiness all his reading is absolutely meaningless. A truth is uttered or written down by one who is actually in a state of holiness. Now someone reads that truth and assumes that now, because he "knows it," it is his. Not so. Unless the life goes with it to back up this "knowing," knowledge becomes self-deception. So why read scriptures, one would ask, if there is no means to applying their truth? The reader must see his shortcoming and live with that. In so doing, the shortcoming begins to fade away by mere virtue of admission. This is not "guilt," but rather a sober, dispassionate look at the status quo. I am told my mind is part of God's; I am very holy. But first I must see my complete and utter denial of this fact. My mind is preoccupied with "past thoughts," with illusions, with projections of my images of thought, not at all focused on my holiness—the aspect of my mind which is part of God's. I can get all sentimental about religion, believe I have "sacrificed" sufficiently to attain some good, but in the end this sentiment falls short of real holiness. To be who I am requires that I uncover and face this kind of self-deception. Only then can I ready my mind to receive the awareness of its real holiness.

Ω

150.

A

God is the strength in which I trust. *ACIM, Lesson #47* To act takes strength. The difference between an action and an activity is the source of strength. Activity employs the "strength" of memory, some reliance on what I "know," which is by its very nature always incomplete and limited. Therefore my "strength" is one riddled with an element of weakness, of doubt, of hesitation. Yet the strength of God, or God who is strength, does not rely on what I "know." Rather, when I trust those Unknown Forces that created me will provide all that I need in any situation, then I can say the lesson is true for me. Abilities I have may be used to serve this strength, but abilities in themselves are not the "strength." Inherent abilities are not so much acquired as already present, just in need of awakening. These abilities, in the service of the strength of God, can be used to liberate me from the false as I discover what I can do, what I have to give. Liberation from my self-imposed problems is of paramount importance in life—not a career. **God's will for me is perfect happiness. *ACIM, Lesson #101*** This would be the fact which dissolves my thinking a problem has any real use—except to show me what I need to let go of in order to be fully with God's will for me. What God has willed must already be. Such is the strength of God. *Will* creates what it wills immediately.

Ω

151.

Α

Errors have been made. Held in memory, the past is a powerful force that repeats itself in the present. Errors are perpetuated in this way, perhaps given different forms, yet still the playing out of memory. Time is thought to be an asset to correction, yet more often it is an excuse to postpone facing the error. One could say, "I am greedy. I need time to become generous, not greedy." This approach seldom leads to the real transformation of an individual. His circumstances may change, they may even "improve," but his internal make-up remains the same. What would erase memory in the sense that all strife and sorrow are a result of it, and would that require memory's full erasure—at least the aspects that produce problems? I am given forgiveness. What is its profound action? Forgiveness is not overlooking something "bad," but seeing that I made up the "bad" before I needed forgiveness. Errors are thoughts of "bad" I hold onto, repeating themselves until I let them go. The process of correction, ultimately, is in the hands of God, but I must choose to go in the direction of this correction. Memory is erased when I recognize its ill effects and no longer hold onto them. Then Divinity can transmute my errors into Miracles.

Ω

152.

A day of giving myself to what is before me. To not "project" is a freedom. Let Life guide. This is rare. Most of our time, my time, is given to commitments and routines. Commitments, or contracts, exist as agreements/promises to do something. Once the commitment is made, work is required to fulfill that word. That is what gives the word meaning. Action is consistent with the word. Then I am true to myself. I am. The word, my words, must reflect this epistemological statement. The word must also transcend my thought in order to be inspired; otherwise, my word is just a recapitulation of memory—mine or another's. Be that as it is, Divinity's word and mine are the same when I am attentive to receive from above. I must first *empty* myself of thought. Go to Zero before my mind can receive inspiration. To not "project" is to bring the mind to Zero, emptiness, nothingness. An empty bowl can be filled; I need but guard against putting memory into it. I may not know I am filling the bowl, so I need to invoke the process of forgiveness to undo my errors. The vulnerability of having no opinion or judgments is a necessary step—no defenses or attacks. Can I say I am that vulnerable? I do have judgments of like and dislike. The brain (memory) has its own involuntary action of dualism. So what! My meaningless thought cannot affect my Identity. "Keep the bowl [of the Mind] empty," Tara Singh said so aptly.

Ω

153.

A

A meeting with a friend is an opportunity to be myself without any particular motive. Self-honesty is shared between two people. I say what I am going through—the friend does likewise—and in the sharing, both become free. Free of what? Judgments and opinions. I may point out my judgments to a friend, but he can gently show me my fallacy of thought. In this mirror I can see my judgments for what they are: meaningless thought that composes my meaningless world. But with the friend, something else takes place; by seeing my judgments as meaningless thoughts that I project, I can instantaneously be free of them. Why project my errors of memory onto the world? With a friend I can be free—free of attachments, free of errors, free of memory itself which contains all the "problems" of man. Any problem is therefore my projection. It is occurring to give me one more opportunity to set it free; to let go of it. The friend is one who can provide the safe haven that I may "expose" myself. What am I exposing? Expose means to bring to the light. The dark thoughts of guilt can come to the surface of the mind to be cleansed and healed. The friend helps me to see who I am in the looking glass of unconditional Love.

Ω

154.

A

A "low life." What is meant by that? Usually a term applied to a genre of human characters engaged in activities contrary to the respectability of conventional society; thieves, prostitutes, murderers, rapists, and criminals of various kinds of infractions. The moral stance is that low life is a bad thing, and that the pilgrim navigating through the snares and mine fields of life should avoid the temptations of lying, sensuality, stealing, killing, etc. Is there another way of looking at the mind of one engaged in those things commonly associated with low life? The brain and the body are physical, sensual things. It is a fact. Sex is a powerful urge. Acquiring the ease associated with wealth is desirable. Pleasure is a pursuit. Inherently these are unalterable conditions of being human. Yet, mankind has perennially questioned the temporal nature of physical life—namely the seemingly inevitable "death" waiting for him at the end; is there life after death? Is there life, even now, living with the fear of it coming to an end? What would happen to the one who no longer fears death of the physical form? For most people, the body is born, lives, and dies. But do I die? Low life identifies with the body, confusing it as the only identity. Since it will "die," it "goes for the gusto" as long as it can. Sensuality is the substitute for transcendence. Transcendence is the High Life of spiritual immortality, even extending "life in the body."

Ω

155.

A

The physical world is riddled with opposites: predators and prey, male and female, night and day, summer and winter, etc. What is that state of being that has no opposites? One who loves does not know to hate. It is a state of being beyond opposites, even beyond the limits of physical form. The Void, or Nothingness, has no opposites. No judgments, no opinion, no desire. Who am I to be of the Void? A state of absolute Peace, because the conflict of opposites no longer exists. My meaningless thought begins to fade away, and a new certainty emerges, one that is not attached. I can observe my thought and see that it is motivated by fear. Renunciation of thought is necessary. It is the turning away from fear to be who I am as Love created me. God is Love. That's all. And this kind of Love embraces all living things: the criminal and the saint, the good and the evil, the high life and the low life. Sri Ramakrishna said, "until one sees a ditch of dirty water and the holy Ganges River as the same, he will never be enlightened." In the end, all that one "knows" must be dissolved. To be as a little child, not knowing, is closer to one's original state. That emptiness of mind is holy because it contains all things equally, not condemning a thing, embracing the evil as well as the good, loving even one's enemies of memory. I am grateful to have the opportunity to be free of the known of opposites, if only for a few seconds.

Ω

156.

A

The day is given. Morning light comes, and the earth and all living things awaken. To what do I give my day? To the corporation? To a routine? To something I did many times on many yesterdays? There must be more to life than the repetition of the same mechanical or mental task. I can give my day to my Self. That would be different. I could be at peace with the Unknown. There are commitments which I have taken on which I can complete, so both I and the one with whom the commitment was made can be satisfied and set free. Still, how I begin my day is important. To what do I give my first attention? One could say "to God" but that would be a fallacy. Giving attention to breath is essential. Most people don't even think about it. The wise would breathe a certain way and watch their breath come in and out, holding each inhale and exhale for a certain number of counts. Grateful for the most essential element, the day is now set on firm footing, cleansed of motives. As one breathes, the work of the day is made clear, but not in a pressured way. Certain things need attention. Water is also essential. Drinking warm water in the morning is wise. So, the day begins with something very basic and elemental: air; water; then some food, which is of the earth; heat, which is fire; and then space which is the forum in which the work of the day unfolds. The day is given and now I am in right relationship with it.

Ω

157.

A

There is pleasure of the senses, and this leads to joy. There is also pain, and this leads to sorrow. There is a third place in which both pain and pleasure are transcended—a state beyond the physical form in which Being is not identified with opposites. Physicality contains life and death, pain and pleasure. The Spirit is not opposed to either. Acceptance of what is, as it is, is the Spirit's way. But humans are accustomed to seeking pleasure and avoiding pain. Or making a sacrifice, that is accepting pain as the price of a greater so-called good. "The age of sacrifice is over," Morrnah Simeona said. As well, hedonism, or the main function of life being the pursuit of sensual pleasure, is not it either. Sacrifice and hedonism deny the reality of the Spirit now; the present is overlooked for some more ideal state to be attained. Pursuit of happiness is a denial of present happiness. Pursuit of anything is a denial of perfection of the Now. We want things; we want situations to be different; we want to be happy. Life and liberty are both present states of being—God-given, not made-made. Therefore, happiness is God-given as well, not bestowed from outside. Freedom is freedom of the Self to be. Just that. No more, but no less. The Self contains all the various states of physical experience but is not confined to experience. All is contained by the Self who is in an unbroken state of joy and peace and love.

Ω

158.

A

Having knowledge of the truth and living the truth are two different things. That is why it has been said "truth, unapplied, turns to poison." (Tara Singh) Also, it follows that the deeper truths of life's mysteries come with great responsibility. The Mind of man, consistent with the Mind of God, is the Christ, a state of being in Divine harmony. This is the Self, my Self, your Self. How few know who they are as God created them. The personal self is limited to thought. The God-created Self is not. Few make this transition. Death of the body does not necessarily put one in contact with the Self. An active attention in this life is necessary. Intellectualism cannot make it either. Knowledge and application are not the same. So few live by a truth. We are preoccupied with the activities of survival—of the body. When the day is done, we entertain ourselves with TV and movies. Who gives attention to the Self? "Know thyself" is the ancient directive from the wise. This is twofold: 1) knowing the self of separation in all its impurities—fear, greed, anger, hate, insecurity, pride, attachment, etc. 2) knowing the Self of Identity in its connection to Higher laws of Love, Honesty, Charity, Peace and Joy. And once a person is aware of his or her Higher Self, what would he or she extend to the Sonship—to all other human beings in whose Self we share?

Ω

159.

Α

A person can be inspired when the mind is still and empty. But the possibility of projecting a memory and confusing this with inspiration is strong. It becomes difficult to distinguish memory from inspiration, especially when a particular result is sought. To not seek any result is an attribute of emptiness. Who knows the Good in a whole way? We are divided beings in this dualistic state of separation in which memory is the primary guide to daily life. The possibility of problems is imbued in the very mind we use to make choices and decisions. No one distinguishes between thought (memory stored in the brain as consciousness) and insight (inspiration in the present not of the brain). The first is the mind of all past thought, the second is the Mind of Creation always present. To see this distinction is the beginning of real vision. The body is no longer the focus of attention; the Unknown is now the focus. Space and quiet; into these internal states of being the Creator can communicate because the medium is the same. What is this medium? Love. Love is a state of being free of problems, free of the past thought, free of judgment(thought), free totally and unconditionally. The empty mind can receive from the mystery of Life. This is the Path of Reason, not science. The cause and effects of thought are done. Now real Life can be extended and experienced.

Ω

160.

Memory is the culprit of problems and therefore the cause of sorrow. The mind has fallen into physicality in the sense it has forgotten its spiritual Source. Spirit is not physical—it is a Force, a mystery of Life which creates. It is the Cause Supreme. So, memory is mind separated from the Reality of the Unknown; it is the accumulation of thought gained through the perceptions of experience, which are the contacts of the senses with their physical surroundings, happenings, and events. Interpretations of these events and surroundings form memory as well, giving the mind opinions, beliefs, motives, etc. This "consciousness" of the known is limited; therefore, it is important to "see" beyond our memory, our thought, our conscious mind. Memory is illusion because it is so limited. Yet there is a memory of Self—who I am as God created me. It is possible to remember the Self when memory is undone or transmuted to nothingness. But who has taken their mind to Zero? We are students, at best, of the Mystery School of the Self. Though not outside of each person, the Self is difficult to know because the doorway to It is one of constant vigilance and undoing. Fear is a block and the human psyche contains it; it must be undone for Love to rise in our awareness. When fear is overcome, the mind is free. Freedom brings peace, and peace is of God, of Self.

Ω

161.

A

I am not my memory. I am not my body mostly caused by memory. So, who am I? *I am Spirit. **ACIM, Lesson #97*** Three words which state a fact. What does that statement mean to me in actuality? To say, "I am Nothingness" or "I am of the Void" are close corollaries. Yet, I am Spirit implies a more total Identity of Self. When I really look at the word Spirit, it is related to breath: *In-spire, ex-spire.* Yet even more rarified than elemental air, Spirit is something non-physical. Life Force is more akin to its meaning, or simply "I AM." I AM is Identity in the Original State. Any word put after it is a limitation, a fence around Being, which has no partial definition. Even an attribute commonly recognized as admirable and good could be turned into a limitation and therefore a bondage. Freedom is not subject to limitation; if it was, it would not be freedom. "I AM" is a statement of Freedom. Who can be with the emptiness without yearning to fill it with something? Almost impossible. The human brain craves labels, partial identities, self-imposed definitions. What Peace beyond understanding is available to one who sees understanding as a block to real Freedom? My understanding is an erroneous interpretation of what is. To go beyond understanding is to embrace the Unknown, the Void, as the Source of all Life—as the Spirit that I am.

Ω

162.

Relationships are the main reason for life. These are various, but all based on love (Self) or fear (ego). Man/God relationship is primary; teacher/student and mother/father/child are important; man/woman relationship is elemental; and then there is friendship. Friendship may be the highest form of relationship in which two unrelated by blood, cease to see any separation between themselves. This is rare. Friendship has no motive. It is a bond of Love, not a bondage of fear. Love sets free; fear binds with conditions. Yet the first friend one must make is with himself. "Love thyself" is akin to "know thyself." It is not the small self of fear that loves, but rather the larger Self that one shares with all of Creation—every seed, every grain of sand, every droplet of water, every breath of air, and every brother and sister are contained by this Self. So, to *love thyself* is to love everything, even the most abject and despised human being. There is nothing the Self does not embrace and encompass. The prostitute and the Madonna are the same. Who can judge one better than the other? Each has a function. In a world of duality, the only freedom is a state of neutrality, free of judgment or attack. *I can escape the world I see by giving up my attack thoughts. ACIM, Lesson #23* When that has been mastered, then I can be a friend of another.

Ω

163.

A

Few can say they "betrayed the faith" because few ever had a real faith to betray. First, to know thought rules our life stored as memory and it is the source of all problems, all sorrow, all impurities, is a profound step toward faith. What we were taught to rely upon is not reliable to produce happiness. Memory replays as problems. To step out of thought is the easiest thing and the hardest thing because outside of thought there is nothing, and we are afraid of nothing. But this "nothing" is the Source of all things, all life, all death; death in the true sense of "ending." But we are afraid of "ending," therefore thought goes on projecting "problems" and also "solutions," which in turn make more problems. The cycle never ceases, because we do not live by faith—we live by thought. Faith is in Nothing. That is why we don't have it. We are taught to have faith in what we can see and hear, taste and smell, touch with the body's senses. These are the workmen of thought and its opinions and conclusions. Faith operates outside the realm of thought. When one can say, "my thought means nothing," then faith begins. To not betray the faith means to remember the importance of *not knowing*. I do not know. Then the wholeness of all Creation is mine—realms beyond the stars, beyond physicality itself. Then I can say, ***The light has come. I have forgiven the world [of thought].*** *ACIM, Lesson #75.*

Ω

164.

A

The poet observes Nature in a direct way with no desire to weigh it down with his own interpretations. Therefore Nature, vast and infinite, yet specific and particular, will speak to him who can be still. Out of the stillness, which is true observation, the poet is given insight. Insight is not a thought as much as it is a harmonizing chord. The notes comprising this chord are present in Nature and in the very core of the poet himself; therefore, the poet discovers what is already there. He cannot, will not, take credit for creativity. The Creative is a Force in him, but not of him. He can be with It, and the more he is, the more insight will bestow upon him, but he cannot make something from nothing. Though His expressions may appear to come out of the Void, these forms are already determined, already present as aspects of the Divine. Because insight does not rely on the body's senses, it appears to manifest "out of thin air." But the physical matter in front of the poet is arranged and related so he can "see" beyond the senses, beyond the restraints of *this time* or *this place*. Time and space are meaningless. Only Love is meaningful as seen in the scene of this present moment. What is strewn about, apparently at random, is not by chance. Each item has a place in the Heaven of right now, in the Life Force that remains intact, even for generations hence, through the words of the poet and the recycling of Nature Herself.

Ω

165.

A

Characters have traits particular to mental makeup and memory. What a character thinks determines his fate until he steps completely out of thought. Then all there is "to do" is to forgive—to let go of all that is not Love. In a world mostly void of Love, where illusions substitute for reality, the only sanity is forgiveness. The character traits I have accumulated are not my real Self. But I embrace them. How could I not; they are the tendencies I need to look at and let go of—in short, the part of me in need of forgiveness. Without first owning and embracing my self-destructive tendencies how could I possibly be free of them? These would continually remain submerged in the computer memory bank of my soul and repeat again and again throughout the ages of my life on earth. Tradition, though to some may seem a security, is to another a bondage of expectation and fear of the unknown. Tradition is an accumulation of past thought; the inherent nature of my day-to-day mental state. Who is free of repetition and routine? Few. Even the people who have interesting work can fall into the pit of redundancy. To remain new, one must live "out of character," which is to say, step out of all self-images and be who the Divine Creator created—empty, free, manifested and whole, at harmony with what is, what has been, and what shall be. In other words, a timeless character.

Ω

166.

A

"I am." Probably the shortest sentence and the most profound. To know "I am" is to be free in one's being, dependent on nothing. "I am" is a divine statement of truth, needing no proof. However, acceptance of the truth, living of the truth, are required to realize the profound nature of I am. "I" is a vertical letter, a shaft of light, a pillar of peace, a column of the Void, like the origins of Lord Shiva—a shaft of light with no beginning and no end. "I am." The tendency of thought is to place an element of limitation after this whole declaration. Anything after "I am" is either a small part of the whole or an unrealized assumption. I could say something identifying me with a religion or ideal—I am *Catholic*, or I am an *environmentalist*. Both may be partially true. But to question the meaning of any conclusion placed after "I am" is to reject anything that would limit my being. In the mind of my Creator, my being cannot be confined or limited. Who is whole? "I am," without a cause other than Love, the Creator of All. "I am" everything. All is me. This identifies me as "containing universes" as Whitman said, and enveloping the evil as well as the good. Good, a force out of which "I am" comes, has no opposite, therefore is a state of being at total peace. I am. Do I need to know anything more than this?

Ω

167.

A

A sound is sacred when the one listening is also aware of his sacredness. A work is sacred when the worker is imbued with an attitude of gratefulness and reverence. Reverence has acute powers of attention. The eyes of reverence observe everything wholly. Nothing is "outside." What is seen is lit from "within." There is no "focal point" of observation. Life places the observer where he becomes the thing observed. That state of being is sacred because it has no judgment in it. True observation does not divide this from that, tree from earth, black man from white man, Republican from Democrat. Even the false and superfluous have a place in observation; they are seen but not judged, forming a forgiven world. Reaction, wanting things to be different, are no more. Acceptance of "what is" has begun. This acceptance is the key to forgiveness, which is the key to happiness. "I am" as "I am." No regrets, no apologizing for "faults of the ego," because one sees these faults are not reality. A shift from thought to stillness and silence is the action of enlightenment. It requires no effort, only a tremendous amount of letting go which begins with acceptance. Accepting my part in "God's plan for salvation" is to accept myself as is—so-called faults and all—so that whatever is not myself can be released, cleansed and totally transmuted to what is of God.

Ω

168.

A

There is a revolution in life. Never static, the forms of existence are constantly in motion. The planets move around the sun and the sun, with all its worlds, plummets through the universe. The galaxies are but specks in the Mind of God. Who knows what is beyond them, numerous as the stars. Evolution, devolution, revolution—the cycles of creation, sustenance, and death are known to continue ad infinitum. We are beings within this motion, yet totally devoid of it as well. The Stillness and Nothingness, out of which All creation comes, is ours as well. We are timeless in an illusion of time, spacious in a field of individuated space. I AM without beginning, without end, immortal. Before the spark of manifestation shaped matter for the first time, eons had gone by—no need to sense and experience. What was "forever" sufficed to satisfy God and His Sonship. The purity of the Word was enough to sustain Beauty. "I AM" needed nothing to define its particular attributes because it encompassed everything. Revolution—that which encircles around itself—could only be a good thing in which change was constantly cradled like a new-born babe in the manger of nurturing forms. Destruction, if it ever came to that, would be the shedding of outgrown skin, inevitably gone, to make way for the new grace of a cosmic covering of communion.

Ω

169.

A

The future is unknown; the past is gone. The instant that holds these words in the time it takes to read them will never come again. What is of time is fleeting—change amidst a sea of change. Man seeks security in the insecure, stability in the unstable, and certainty in the uncertain. The present is the only time that has meaning, but even it is shrouded in the veil of perception, tainted by past thought and future projections. The mind is a powerful determiner of this perception. Seldom is it empty and still, in total admission of its limits. When I begin to see the futility of my own thought, the unreliable nature of memory to produce happiness, I can admit my helplessness to determine things in a way I sought before this realization. Writing now, in the present, with no direction or motive, is to venture into unmapped territory of the mind and its relationship to the Now. Who is fully present with all their faculties in tune with "what is, as it is"? Acceptance of all polarities disintegrates the notion of opposites. Night and day are cycles; light and shadow are elemental states of nature. When compared, they are strikingly different, yet without one, there is not the other. Wholeness envelops both. Wholeness knows no opposites. Accepting of darkness as well as illumination, the Self rises above all judgments and comparisons.

Ω

170.

A

We are spiritual beings fallen into physical existences. The mind, or consciousness, can turn its focus to our lower or higher nature. The spirit is unlimited; the body is an illusion of limits. To discover and lead a spiritual life, the mind seems to do battle between these two "natures"—the limits of the body pitted against the unlimited spirit. Few are conscious of the spirit in actuality. Thought itself, which comprises consciousness, is limited—the source of all conflict. To rise above it to an awareness not of thought involves an arduous process of letting go; arduous because a vigilance is required and the human consciousness is assertive by nature, not self-questioning. The undoing of thought is a stepping out of the stream of consciousness—a kind of a "death." And wired within that consciousness is "fear of death," so it does not want the very thing it seeks—freedom. Spirit is freedom. The body is memory of a bondage to physicality. Being wishes to participate in Creation; therefore, taking a body seems fitting, yet once engrossed, the mind is overwhelmed with survival, fear, tendencies, and in short, separation. These mental "problems" must be erased, dissolved, forgiven, and transmuted to nothing. "I am not a body. I am free, for I am still as God created me." The Son was created in the image of his Father, Spirit, which is to say he is the Void along with God.

Ω

171.

Α

Each day is ever new when there is real space to be with it. What is real space? How one begins the day is important. The pressures of survival, so-called "earning a living," must be transmuted to having the capacity to receive and give. Pressure is a result of fear. Entering into long-term commitments such as getting a "job" with the corporation, can nearly eliminate the space. When routine gets the better of a human being, pressure comes and robs the space. The poet said, "make yourself a mule and someone will ride you." Who has never made themselves a mule for the sake of survival? So few. The financial pressures are so great, the human being is compelled to be the purveyor of some skill in the marketplace. Work has become synonymous with "sacrifice." But productivity is something totally different. Coming not from the fear of self-survival, it begins with a different premise—one of space and freedom. Man, created free, has an intrinsic responsibility to remain so. Never to take advantage of another or to be taken advantage of, is to be with the true space of independence. Such a one is Self-reliant. Yet this is the God-created Self shared with all, noble and impersonal. This Self can face every day with a new energy, a new light, and allow the work of the day to reveal itself.

Ω

172.

A

"Productivity" involves relationships that are honest. Meeting life, I must be true to myself, never acting from "sacrifice," "obligation," or "duty." These are memories of karmic debt. Love is productive in the sense that it only gives and is totally free. Being a child of God, "what would I give to fulfill my function here on earth?" This should be the question of every human. Instead we are more likely to ask, "how do I get what I want?" Wanting is the pitfall of life we tumble into. A life, which is totally given, we manage to turn into an anxiety-ridden torment of insecurity. Who is really content with himself? The world leaves us short because we leave ourselves short and accept the compromises of personal and bodily survival. Freedom is not something bestowed from ideologies of church, state, or education. Freedom is a reality, unaffected by the known. Freedom, like other life mysteries, is so vast it can barely be grasped by human minds. It is a reality beyond our thought, beyond our knowing. To meet a free man is to be turned upside down, as it seems, because we are walking dead in the bondage of our beliefs. The free man will flip one around, so what had appeared normal is now seen as a contradiction to truth. Truth is my Self; honesty is to see clearly my falseness. When I own my falseness, I am no longer false. The humble will always admit to the possibility of self-deception.

Ω

173.

A

I am not the victim of the world I see. ACIM, Lesson #31
The human being is conditioned by memory. His mind, like a computer, stores all the experience of the past and all his judgments of these experiences. Inherent in thought is fear. Its roots run deeply within memory. Frustration and grievances are projected then "blamed" upon a source "outside" one's own mind. This activity of blaming or assigning a false cause is what the lesson calls being a victim. A victim is not Self-reliant, rather he is dependent on something or someone to fulfill his happiness. When that does not occur, happiness eludes him, and the victim consciousness is engaged. All this is in the psyche of man. Therefore, to be free, one must declare independence from external "causes" that have been erroneously assigned to bring happiness. Happiness is a state of mind within. There is only one Source and that is the Divine Creator. D.C. is synonymous with perfect happiness. All of man's real "work" is to ask himself why he projects an opposite. He does. I do. Why? Why am I unhappy, which is some form of victimhood? The lesson liberates any who can accept it as true. "I am not a victim of the world I see" because that world is only my projection. I *can* stop projecting pain and sorrow when I take 100% responsibility for these projections.

Ω

174.

All relationship is sharing and giving, a kind of natural exchange. The tree is related to the sky. Its leaves produce oxygen which replenishes the atmosphere so animals can breathe. The sky carries minuscule droplets of water it distributes as rain. All in the cycle of this exchange are inseparably related. A man is related to a woman. His seed is implanted in her womb; joining with her egg, this union produces a child—co-created with God. The sacredness of a life begins with a loving relationship. Anything not happy would be a violation of real relationship. Grievances do not relate two individuals; they divide them in a real world which knows no division. Why? Separation is strong. Unwillingness to accept wholeness, to accept relationship, to give and receive, is to be a victim of thought. Thought is sorrow. Underlying all thought is sorrow, not happiness. God's Thought is only love and joy, peace and light. To accept my part in restoring mankind to his reality in the Mind of God, which is love, is my only function. This begins and ends with me. I am the one in need of salvation. When I accept it I can give it. When I give it through forgiveness, I know in my heart I have accepted salvation as my own. When I can say to my Self with conviction, "The light has come," then I have forgiven the world. The light and forgiveness are the same.

Ω

175.

A

I am God's Son, complete and healed and whole, shining in the reflection of His Love. ACIM, Preamble to Lessons 351-360 Is this my truth? It is given to me. Can I accept it? My thought cannot because within it is unwillingness—a contradiction to the truth. Only the Self in me can accept my Identity as God's Son. First, I must silence thought. Again, thought cannot do this; it takes a power, an energy beyond my thought to come to real quiet. What is that energy? God's Love, not an idea of it, but the actual Thing, is energy. I have it because it created me. Love created me before the multitudes of galaxies comprising the cosmos. I am "out of the Void." Nothing was before me, and nothing after me can alter my being in any way. Separation from this reality is thought which is not real. What we call "reality," that which can be seen, heard, tasted, smelled or touched by my five senses, is the great deception. It does not admit what is sensed. A physical phenomena is temporal, destined to fade and decay by the erosions of time. Self-Identity is beyond experience and the body. It alone is real. It alone has my Creator's complete support. Spirit am I, a holy Son of God. I am free to forgive, free to save the world. I am free to be my immortal Self. And applied to these physical planes, I can even alter matter and time/space existence. I can create a Heaven on Earth of Pure Joy.

Ω

176.

Within thought is the tendency to manufacture problems, even in situations where they do not exist. The best approach to a problem is to disengage from it. First, I own it, and then I disengage through forgiveness from it. Sounds easy, but the ego will throw up all kinds of roadblocks. Thought thrives on problems—upset and conflict. The whole complex of thought has no answer within it. That is the one problem. Thought is separated from the one Source of the Answer. Thought will seldom, perhaps never, admit it does "not know." In fact, thought is knowledge. Knowledge is a "problem." We are taught knowledge will free up the human being, "improve" him, give him a better life. But what we call knowledge is only partial; I "know" only part of everything. Therefore, I am inadequate toward the part I don't know. I see it. But "total knowledge" is impossible in the realm of thought. Knowledge that is partial is meaningless. Total knowledge, or the Absolute, begins to enter my mind when I see clearly "my thought does not mean anything." Or in other words, I don't know. Then when I witness a "problem" I can see I made it up and I can "unmake" it. I do not know, but the Christ, the Self in me, knows to dissolve all problems. I need but invoke the forgiving power of my Self to step totally out of a life of problems.

Ω

177.

A

Standard religion promotes an ideal, usually embodied in a memory of a past saint or being who was pure in heart and true to his words, who had mastered the art of living, which is to say the art of Loving. Christmas is a day commemorating the birth of Jesus, the Christ, a man who lived 2,000 years ago, who according to the written accounts of a few, merited our utmost respect and reverence. His main action was forgiveness. When those who resented him condemned him to death and he hung on the cross, he said, "Father forgive them, for they know not what they do." He had no attack thoughts toward his killers and tormentors. Why? He did not defend himself. Because they could not "kill" his reality, which had nothing to do with his body. They could "kill" his body, do it harm, bring it to cessation, but they could not kill him, a nonphysical Entity of pure Love—the Holy Void. Many believe, on the account of the apostles, that he brought his body back to life. He arose from the tomb of death and walked again among the living. After three days he arose, thus cementing the faith of his students, the apostles, and providing mankind with an unprecedented example of Life's triumph over death; good's ascendance over evil. On Christmas we accept or reject Christ's being in us. We choose Life or Death, happiness that is total or imperfect sorrow. Thought cannot choose, but the Christ in us can.

Ω

178.

Learning is touted as a necessity to self-improvement. People who are illiterate are thought of as dumb and uneducated. Learning is the pillar of education whose highest degrees are aspired toward amidst the ivory towers of academic circles and institutions. Yet, in fact, learning is the storing of memory. In the present moment the new is vital, yet once the new is learned, it becomes the secondhand memory of tomorrow. Reality cannot be learned—it just is. It can be recognized, owned as part of myself, but it is not to be sought and attained, because it is already there in me. To seek would be to deny my own reality. Recognition, however, requires a good deal of undoing of quietude, of trust in the words and deeds of the wise. The wise have already been touched by the light of true love, the reality of Identity. "I come forth from the Void into Light." This Light is in them but not of them; therefore, they are the channel through which Light is brought from the Void. The Light is present in every atom and particle of the Cosmos. Learning is an activity of indulging in ideas, but never living by the absolute application of a truth—in a "whole way." We have learned to be greedy, angry, depressed, ungrateful. When these are truly observed and forgiven, the content of my mind is closer to my Reality. Then the Light has come. Learning was not required.

Ω

179.

A

Family patterns of relationships are perpetuated by memory. The negative, self-destructive patterns go on because they are within the minds of the family members. Without looking within the mind, one cannot see that he is the perpetuator of a negative pattern. Someone in the family must take 100% responsibility. Through repentance, forgiveness, and Divine transmutation a negative pattern can be ended in myself. That is where it begins and ends. The great life work of emptying my mind of memory—the perpetuator of "problems"—will take complete attention. Who has that attention? So few. Do I? What other work is there to do but to liberate my mind from thought, the jailer of problems? An empty mind, a still mind, is neutral; the body is neutral as well, neither good or bad, neither destructive or creative. It is the mind that contains memory—thought—which is at war with good vs. evil. Families are governed by thought. That is why so many problems are repeated. None have stepped out of thought; therefore, destructive tendencies are handed down from generation to generation. This is what is meant by "the sins of the fathers are visited upon the son." That is, what is not undone by the process of Atonement goes on as memory, reprocessing dismal results of pain and sorrow. When I step out of memory, I break the pattern that was so destructive.

Ω

180.

A

The wise take birth to liberate mankind from his lower nature. In the life of the wise, liberation—freedom— is the highest value. Freedom is given and freedom is received. He awakens others to this freedom as he discovers it in himself; giving and receiving, teaching and learning become the same. Thought is the domain of man's lower nature. Within it is fear and the defenses fear has made up. Thought is sorrow. To be free the wise bring thought to an end, but to do this, the wise must take birth and go into the world of thought. Understanding thought's deceptive nature is necessary; therefore, the wise appear to have been caught in these pitfalls for a time, just as everyone is. Through greater insight, some other determination to step out of the conflicted world of thought, the wise begin to question thought's hold on them. The process of questioning, of undoing, liberates them. Then the wise can say, "If I can free myself from thought, so can you." Usually this is done by pointing out exactly how self-destructive the tendencies of thought are. The wise observes these tendencies in himself and speaks directly from having been through the difficulties of undoing. The other name for undoing is forgiveness. It is a "tedious, patient process" to observe what is inside the mind (memory) and to let go of pain and sorrow thoughts, all the complex of problems. Yet the wise take birth to do this process. They are masters of it.

Ω

181.

Α

What is a true action of the heart? So many substitutes for this; I am fooled. Attachment is not love; obligation is not real giving. Yet goodness will guide and in every action of giving there is increase—to the giver and to the receiver. Fearless, the giver gives what is in his heart to share—the Source of his conviction. Because what is in the heart he did not place there. It was long-established by his Creator. God, in the heart of man, is the Source of All Giving. From that Source comes a true action—not from thought. To contact that Source, a person must go through the veil of fear that seems to shroud the Source. My thought will doubt it is there and attempt to act from its own view, which is always partial and therefore always limited. But the Source is never limited. It is whole, containing everything. Who wants to end this doubt? That would require trust in a Force beyond thought, beyond the senses, beyond right vs. wrong. That state of mind which gives from the heart is one in which fear of consequences is done, no loss is possible, and only increase in peace is the result. It is devoid of attachment, having fully let go of "results." It gives from what is natural, step by step by step. The apple tree, in order to bear fruit, must go through stages of growth: sapling, young tree, first blossoming, and then the patient summer months for formation until finally it gives from the very heart of Creation—its apples! Every step in the way was part of this giving, even the stage before its manifestation as an apple tree.

Ω

182.

A

To challenge my own status quo is required to transcend thought, and to really care for another. Does the ego ever really care for anyone, even myself? God-Realization lies solely in how I treat my Self and my brother. Giving is an action. I must come to it happily and with conviction. This involves putting my own energy into it. I must say to myself, "The lack I witness is my own. I put myself into this situation to remove the lack." It only involves me, not the other. So then, I am 100% responsible for what I say and do, and even for what I "witness." To witness a need and not respond is indifference, yet to respond from the "thought" of good intentions is not much better. To whom lies the priority of my responsibility? Self comes first; Life Teacher secondly; Family, relatives and ancestors thirdly; then everyone else. The witness must be very careful to give from a space within, uncontaminated by a motive to "do good." Who is the doer? should be a question. How do I treat my parents? My teacher? My brother and sister? Life brings to my doorstep those with whom my karmic connections are most strong. With them I am given great opportunity to release, and to be released. Forgiveness, in the midst of all complexities and problems, is the only real caring needed—starting with forgiving ourselves. This is the essence of Self Care.

Ω

183.

Α

My Mind holds only what I think with God. *ACIM, Workbook, Review IV* This statement surely distinguishes between the Mind, which is holy and true, and memory of the ego, which is dualistic and full of conflict, confusion, and contradiction. I always have a choice between these two: to be One with Mind or separated in my ego thought of the brain. Wholeness only integrates. The beginning of this awakening within gives the boon of stillness. What is whole is One, though composed of many aspects and parts, yet all held together in harmonic relationships. The body has arms, legs, organs, senses, yet all work together in a living unit. Similarly, humans all have memory, each individual inexperience, yet all have a Mind that binds them together. Mind and Love are synonymous. Neither can be defined in verbal terms, yet each are able to be felt and experienced; transcendent of particular events—yet made manifest through these events. What I think with God is accessible through my attention. Vigilance requires that I let go of my thought and come to silence. Mind begins to dawn in a state of no thought. Practice is only the quality of my attention. To deny my thoughts of fear and affirm that Love pervades all things and events, no matter how they may appear, is to come to the emptiness of my Mind.

Ω

184.

Α

ove holds no grievances. ACIM, Lesson #68 What are mine? Who can say he holds no grievances? Thought's very nature compares and dislikes this for the sake of that—all "meaningless thought." Who can say he has forgiven the world when he holds grievances from memory? Memory is the culprit of non-love. As long as I hold grievances, how can I say I love totally? And forgiveness is made a sham because it is not perceived properly. To say, "I forgive" by letting you "off the hook" of past dastardly deeds is to secretly hold the grievance that keeps me a victim, judge, and jury of you and those ill deeds. I have judged them ill, not seeing the part I played in attracting the conflict in the first place What a mess human thought is in. Who or what can get me out of it? Some kind of surrender is necessary. What do I surrender? Blame. The instant I stop blaming another, or myself, for results in life I don't like, or which are accompanied by much pain, then I can begin to heal and take 100% responsibility for *everything* in my life. It is this very stance—one of no blame, no "victimhood"—which opens the door for Love to enter. This is merely to be my Self, created in the likeness of my Creator—Love. I don't "know" Love, but when I step an instant out of the syndrome of blame, I am in the ever-present peace of Now, not to be contaminated by my thought and opinions, "my grievances." Here I am closer to Love.

Ω

185.

A stillness is the gift of God. When I am still, Creation's beauty comes to me. I am not separated from the plant, the light, the air, the water that sustains Life. It is a state of being bestowed on me through the wise, from above and beyond my own thinking. The wise person, having awakened that state of stillness in himself, can extend it to others. I am forever grateful to that one, for without him I would be totally caught in the conditioning of my thought. He points the way to Self-inquiry and helps me undo my motives, fears, and internal impurities. When these are let go and cleansed, I can be who I am as God created me. Back to a state of stillness and quiet, true vision returns and I can forgive myself and others. Without forgiveness I am lost in my own thought, memory, and judgments. It is a process of repentance involving only myself, because all problems are only in myself. Repentance is merely admitting my mind has been in error. Needing no other to mediate between myself and my Divinity, I can invoke the help of my Creator to make those internal corrections needed. Then all problems are surmountable, because God's Will and mine are joined in only happiness. Real religion is the undoing of negative and destructive thought patterns. When I am willing to do this in my Self, the help I need is provided to be at Peace. My real Self is only at Peace, in total communion with my Creator. Om Namah Shivaya.

Ω.

186.

A

The good and the pleasurable are experiences of different natures. The good relates man to the mind and the spirit; the pleasurable to the body. The wise distinguish between the two and outgrow their attachment to the latter. This does not mean that pleasure is never again experienced, but it does mean it is not sought. Desire for pleasure has come to an end. Now the real work of life begins—to discover and to extend the Good. It begins with Self-inquiry—Who am I? coupled with the relinquishment of "problems" manufactured by thought (memory). Forgiveness is relinquishment of my grievances. Pain and sorrow are results of wrong thinking. "Thinking" itself is not the domain of the Good. The Good dawns in me when my thinking is made empty. This is an invocation of sorts. The involuntary nature of thought, its unwillingness to admit its secondary nature, requires another Force to bring it into harmony with the Mind. This other Force, manifested as forgiveness, repentance and transmutation (miracles) is the only means to be free from the pleasure/pain syndrome. Otherwise I am caught in past thought. Invocation of Higher Forces becomes my daily prayer; that is my primary work in life. The good can now manifest because I have put my whole being into it. Identity of Self is only this: identification and alignment with the Good. Who am I? This question is now answered.

Ω

187.

A

The day is given, and each is a new beginning unlike all the rest. What is to manifest is not solely up to me. There are Higher Forces governing my Life, but I must undo my ego thought before contact can be made with them. The teacher is in touch with these Forces. He helps the student undo so the student may have divine direction in his Life. What other purpose would the teacher have? "Removing the blocks to the awareness of Love's presence" is the concern of the teacher. First, he has dealt with these issues in himself and accepted himself; this makes him able to deal with them in "others" because he sees the "other" is also himself. Empathy is this kind of compassion. The teacher shares in the suffering and sorrow he witnesses in the "student" in order to remove them in both. It is a balance; not to "identify" with problems, yet to be close to the one stuck in them and open to another way. We all must witness our bodies get old and lose the freshness of youth, yet when we are young we don't think much about this. There is no process in Life not subject to thought, either the ego's or that of the Holy Self. The decision to be with that of the Self puts me in touch with universal laws and principles. These do not change with the passing of the days or in the face of the body's end. These are the day's guide and virtue. What impact even on the body's processes may be affected positively through this total immersion in the Self of the Spirit?

Ω

188.

A

The truth needs to be rediscovered by every generation in the language and manner befitting of the times. The truth does not change, but the language and manner by which one discovers it may. The old ways are worn out. Each age demands a new program, a new process of questioning the values of importance. The process may be totally different from that of our grandfathers and great grandfathers. Plane travel has made the world smaller and brought people together. A global view is possible. Computers link minds and raw information is immediately accessible through an internet link. The important questions posed by the wise are basically the same: "Who am I?" "What is the meaning of my Life?" "What is a problem?" "Is there a benevolent Creator guiding my life?" "What is the Will of God and my will in relationship to it?" How I approach these questions may be unique to my age. A person needs a teacher to shake him to the bare bones of what is essential to living a virtuous Life. Then the challenge begins, a principle is only real when it is applied. Love is not an idea; it is an action which involves my own input and conviction. *A Course in Miracles* is unique. The first scripture written as a step-by-step course, it is the unique means by which the modern man may step out of thought and be with his Identity as God created him. It is the current means of this age to rediscover a Divine Truth.

Ω

189.

Α

Art and music, at their highest level, communicate something of the Spirit. Elements harmonize and come to stillness and silence. Even sound can be part of the silence when it is harmonic. There are no formulas for creating Art of this high nature. Constant attention to the medium and the expression renders something indicative of the artist's inner state. Whatever the medium or the craft, this inner state of stillness is absolutely essential to creating a work that communicates something beyond our thought. And Spirit is most definitely beyond our thought. Yet, it is our essence of Life. Without communion with our Essence we would be ignorant and dead. To be inspired, the artist must empty himself; and from this state of emptiness, he has the capacity to receive. This capacity is the basis for inspiration. It is effortless—a matter of just being present: right now, with no motives or projections. Thought is "turned off," so to speak. And now what comes into the mind is innocent and new; never before thought. It does not come from the reservoir of memory, but rather from the Spirit, the Void, the Great Unknown. Reverence for this Source is supreme, because it is the root of my Self-Identity. Yet contact with it can barely be described with words. In its Presence all external expressions are done, rendered secondary to Silence.

Ω

190.

Attachment to the body and to the things of the body has produced unwillingness in man to know the Spirit. This unwillingness separates him from his Source, his Creator, his fellow man. He has manufactured a thought system in which personal desire is the primary motivation for action. This manifests as "I want," usually focused on a particular thing or result. Yet the wise see this and begin to question the power of unwillingness over them. To have no "wants" is to accept the present as it is. The current situation does not instill a desire for things to be different. The internal issues involving contact with the Spirit—direction of the Good beyond thought—are the primary concern. Overcoming the world of unwillingness is the work of the wise. Greater and greater acceptance of the transient nature of physicality energizes the deeper question of "Who am I?" Identity is something originating outside the brackets of birth and death. A man incarnates to discover his essence, which is non-incarnate. This question is one of immortality. My being is beyond the body, but there is doubt inherent to thought that cannot accept a Spiritual reality as ascendant over a physical one. There is a belief that all physical things are born, live a spell, then die. Man has questioned this process and sought a "life after death" for millennia. What about "Life Now?" One can only be present, and accept what is, to know the Spirit. Then that has its positive effects on the body and all physical Life. That awareness can be realized now.

Ω

191.

Α

What is health? Sanity? We think of medicine as the catalyst for restoring health. Does it? What is a cure? Perception is sick and we want to address it with chemicals. Do these restore health? Or do they merely "manage disease"? Why did we perceive sickness in the first place? A repetition of a memory, the body will "print out" what is held in the mind, involuntarily. As memory of sickness comes to the surface, forgiveness is still the only sane response—repentance, forgiveness, and transmutation. Divinity has the power to heal. Love, yet to be fully realized in the minds of human beings, is the only real medicine. Does it manifest in physical medications? Who knows? We are obsessed with extending the life of the body. For what end? "I am spirit," clarifies my Identity. Does the length of time one spends in a body have any effect on that fact? Freedom from thought and memory is also freedom from the body. Death, or what we call the end of the physical organism, may have no meaning whatsoever. In fact, what many call "life" may not be the whole of reality. Without the "death" of the illusion that equates identity with the body, no one is really free, therefore never fully alive.

Ω

192.

A

Spirit am I, a holy Son of God, free of all limits, safe and healed and whole, free to forgive and free to save the world. **ACIM, Lesson #97** Application of this truth in life takes guts. Survival of the ego will impose all kinds of limits and "solutions" to be free of them. This is why forgiveness is absolutely essential in the process of realizing who I am as God created me. Why do I imprison myself in commitments and obligations that do not set me free? The body has needs, but what are the essential needs? Food, clothing, and shelter. What are the bare minimums? Is ownership wise or necessary to be free, or does it bind me with more obligations? In this highly commercialized society, it is often more economical to own a house rather than to rent one. But with ownership comes attachment. Can I "own" and not be attached? Heavenly Forces provide for my needs. Can I really trust in those Forces and give in a similar fashion? A state of trust is one in which my uncertainty is given no meaning. Divinity is beyond the conventional thought. An idea is not real, a mere reflection of something nameless, without form, not a body. That "quality without a name" is nowhere and everywhere at once. Imbued in all things, yet not limited to anything. Spirit is a boundless state, realized through the undoing of thought. Forgiveness is the other name for undoing, the dissolution of my illusions.

Ω

193.

A

Making contact with the Absolute—the peace beyond human memory and understanding—is the transcendental purpose of this book—*Alpha Omega*. The first thought can sometimes be tainted by memory, but as I write it down, there is a space to really question, "Is that so?" By questioning, there is more space, more emptiness, more stillness and silence. Then some kind of yearning to give enters in; to be productive in the true sense, to extend the Will of God as I receive the certainty of that Will. The conventions of memory fall away. I do not wish to imitate anyone, nor to parrot something I have learned from another. Rather, Self-discovery is the source of energy required to observe the new, and to share it through the words. The purer essence of this Self is always emptiness. The wise would call this the still mind, the empty bowl, the Void out of which all creation comes. My meaningless thought is just that—meaningless. Yet, out of a mind that is certain of this fact, the opportunity for Inspiration is a possibility—even a probability. Alpha is Emptiness, total serenity with no needs. Then comes a yearning to share a joy of this peaceful state. Then an expression, new and spontaneous comes forth. Omega is the last step in the fulfillment of this Action. "I am as God created me," created in His Image of Boundlessness and Absolute Joy.

Ω

194.

A

Practicality is a paradox. What is practical? One would say earning a good living is practical, paying bills on time, not spending more than the income one earns. In matters of health, eating well, drinking enough water, breathing properly, are practical matters. In the case of the old, giving them care is practical. And the last thing in life—death—the transition from a physical state of being to a non-physical state, that is very practical. All death is a choice, conscious or unconscious. To exit the body is a choice one makes with God. Most make it unconsciously. The very rare person completes all the relationships in his life and then lays the body down in total fulfillment. Suicide is not this because it is based on reaction to life. The transition of completion is not suicide, it is an ending of all unfinished business. When that is done, forgiveness is complete and the Son returns to the Father, absorbed into the Void. There is no need to be a separate entity. Why come back? The only reason would be to help others make this final escape. So, I would come to these physical plans to undo thought (memory) then to be helpful through non-attachment. Undoing is most people's work to do. Being free of social and family conditioning will take most of the energy I have. But for a few who go "empty" sooner, they truly have *something to give*.

Ω

195.

Α

Once a man has reached a fearless state, the state of being the Self, is it ever possible to revert to a state of fear and anxiety? Frustration is a reaction to what is, not seeing the perfection of the present. Can the Self ever be frustrated? A man is "chosen" to be the vehicle for expressing something Divine. Once that revelation is expressed, does he remain just a man? Who has reverence for that man, because usually the Divine expression is in contrast to the status quo? Something so new that it cannot be understood with the old thinking. A fearless man has outgrown the body and the personality. He becomes, as if anonymous, needing no one or nothing to validate himself. A man who is himself has no needs, no reactions, no desires. Yet he may see needs to meet, or actions to be taken that fulfill his destiny. Who thinks of this? Fulfilling one's destiny is hardly a subject in schools and colleges. Who asks himself, "Why am I here; what is my God-given function; how will that function manifest?" These are not questions posed by conventional thought which is preoccupied with survival of the personality. In fact, thought cannot ever answer these questions, and barely cooperates to formulate them. To be my Self is my purpose and that takes a lot of erasing of the *false self I made*.

Ω

196.

A

I do not know what I am looking at, even in my own life, let alone another's. The meaning of a situation is beyond my understanding. The whole movement of Creation, of which I am a part, is governed by an Intelligence infinitely greater than my own. Yet when I see this limitation of thought, I can touch upon this great Intelligence within myself. Who is wise? Men of science have produced the nuclear bomb. Is that intelligent? Are weapons of mass destruction ever intelligent? One could say it took very intelligent people to produce the bomb; they possessed much knowledge. But is knowledge of the workings of the physical universe, without knowing the ethical and virtuous workings of the human heart, intelligent? My individual life is not more virtuous just because it has not produced a bomb. What about anger in me or insecurity and frustration? Are these not bombs that destroy the integrity of my Self? The real work to do is inside oneself, not outside. When this course of action is taken, I am responsible for all I say or do, even for the vast majority of my mind of which I am not aware. It is almost impossible to go through this world and not harm someone or something. We are brutal in our unawareness, yet seeing this brutality within, I am always able to desist and invoke forgiveness.

Ω

197.

A

One must reach a point where he sees the futility of his thinking. Atonement requires this confession. The past is gone—an illusion of an illusion, but memory keeps it alive and ever repeating itself. Invocation of Holy Help is to end these illusions of thought. In the ending, one goes beyond thought, beyond the futility, beyond the past (or future), and rests totally in the present. What is the present? Who can be totally present without regretting the past or projecting the future? His mind returns to Zero. "Nothing" is very alive, with the ability to be fulfilled. As an empty receptacle, my mind is free from the preoccupations of survival. As I live, memory will produce results I do not like, perhaps these are even painful. A great proportion of my thought is not conscious—yet, still causing adverse experiences. "Problems" are replaying memories of conscious or unconscious thoughts. What else is there in the brain? Renunciation of thought itself, conscious or subconscious, is to rely on a Power, a truth, which is unaffected by human thinking. This Power could be called God, the Great Spirit, the Merciful Unknown which created everything and nothing (the Void). "I come forth from the Void into light." (Ho'oponopono); "I will there be light."(ACIM, Lesson #73); "Light and peace and joy abide in me."(ACIM, Lesson #93). Always, the unwillingness to accept these statements as absolute facts is the internal issue to forgive and undo.

Ω

198.

A

Let me behold the savior in this one You have appointed as the one for me to ask to lead me to the holy light in which he stands, that I may join with him. *ACIM, Lesson #78* This is an invocation to let all grievances go with one whom I have separated by my grievances. All grievances are an attack upon the Self. Yet the Self, above and beyond conflict of any kind, waits silently for my awareness of its Presence. All my grievances block my awareness; miracles, which replace grievances, occur when I can let go. Thought is an illusion. What matters is Reality, irrespective of thought. An awareness of this, given by Grace, begins with the suspension of thinking. How I perceive my brother is the determinant of how I perceive my Self. Can I release him from my grievances? This is the test. I am apt to react, to project, to "want correction" my way. These are thought's way to make sure real correction, the ending of grievances, does not occur. Grievances are "attack thoughts." How can I be "saved" when I am the one perpetuating "war" through holding grievances? Not possible. A major function of salvation is to dissolve my grievances. Joining my brother through forgiveness puts me in the holy light along with him. In that light of truth, of peace, of Being One, are we joined. Something beyond words. Life gives me a particular person by which I may come to know my Self.

Ω

199.

Α

I am saved when I realize I am—and stop seeking it. Seeking salvation prevents it. Salvation does not take time because it already is. Like saying, "I better go earn money to pay my debt," when the debt has already been paid. What a relief to be free of strife and struggle. Absolution of thought frees me from the consequences of thought. **Nothing I see means anything, Lesson #1 of ACIM,** absolves me from thought and judgment by dissolving them. They don't mean anything—they are *not true*. There is a Power in my mind that points out my errors. This Power is that of the Holy Spirit leading me to Truth. That is the Holy Spirit's function—to align the encounters in my life which bring about the ultimate correction of my thinking, mostly through letting all thinking go and bringing me closer to silence, stillness, peace. **Light and joy and peace abide in me, Lesson #93 of ACIM,** because that is the true nature of my Identity. Grievances are symptoms of my separation from light and peace and joy. Yet because these attributes never leave their source, I am secure in them, whether I am aware or not. This life is given to awaken my awareness of who I am as God created me. Awareness arises from attention given to my Self. It is not "easy" to be aware because one must go through facing one's demons, one's lower self (ego) thoughts before he can recognize he is someone far greater than the conflicted self he knew. In truth he is a Son of Goodness—totally free of all conflict.

Ω

200.

A

To speak of principles is to speak impersonally. Yet, the speaker, for his words to be true, must live by the principles of which he speaks. He must "walk his talk." Otherwise, words are merely ideas and ideas are plagued with the dualism of opposites—this today and that tomorrow. Let us say that the principle, when lived, leads one to a happy and virtuous life, free of consequences. For instance, "speak no lies," a principle of the word, will take all one has to apply, especially in situations when the pressure of self-survival is at hand. We have candy-coated this principle by justifying the white lie, an instance when we tell a fib for the sake of what we feel is "the good." I must weed out these instances of temptation because of their ill effects. What are these ill effects? To speak an untruth dissipates energy, making my true words suspect. Now I am sunken into the mass of the collective consciousness that lives in contradictions. Better to say "I don't know" than to assert a positive word that has uncertainty behind it. Lies in me accumulate, and if I don't clean them out with some process of attention and atonement, my mind becomes muddled and ineffective to direct my life toward the good. The good could be defined as a life free of lies, free of internal contradictions. Freedom from untruth, illusions of thinking, is the greatest freedom, for in that freedom there is great peace.

Ω

201.

Α

There must be space in the day for stillness in which thought is laid aside. Nature is still and surrounding man with incredible beauty. But in order to be one with nature, man needs stillness within himself to meet that of nature, for oneness is still. Light and color are natural. Even in the so-called man-made world of things, the raw materials which compose those things begin as nature. The wood in the furniture grows as a tree. The thread of the fabric grows as cotton in the field. The yarn of the sweater comes off the backs of the sheep. The pigments that form colors are natural dyes and chemical compounds. Light that comes from the electrified bulb is from natural elements and forces of energy. A man who is still is aware of his surroundings and is grateful to be a part of them. Every breath of air is appreciated because each comes from a Source beyond himself. Man did not make oxygen, nor the circulation in his body that can utilize the life-giving properties of air. When he is still, this appreciation dawns in his mind and he is happy to be alive, just as he is in the moment with no striving. Gratefulness does not need an activity. It is a state of stillness. Light gives me the miracle of sight. The physical eyes enable the perception of color and form; the spiritual "eyes" enable one to perceive forgiveness and wholeness. The Light these eyes see is Love. It accepts all things exactly as they are.

Ω

202.

Having something to give begins with stillness. I discover the silence of "I don't know." Then the space into which my being flows is new and pristine, like the surface of newly-fallen snow, not tread upon, uncontaminated by the memory of prior footsteps. Stillness has no direction or agenda. When I am still all that is around me becomes a part of me. What I observe is what I am. The movement of creation, the cycles of day and night, the inflow and outflow of breath, the actions of those around me are integrated into stillness. Then my action of quiet observation is added to this scene, as if footsteps that do not touch the surface of the snow, leaving no trace of having been a disturbance. Observation is a gift. It is an intensity of being in in the present with no motive but to be as I am. Activity does not add anything to the scene, if not born out of stillness. Who am I to think my small gestures would add anything to the vastness of creation, were they not connected to the Source of Creation? I need add nothing; already perfect, already whole, creation merely waits for me to acknowledge my position in this wholeness. When I am in that state of awareness, my problems drop away, and action becomes natural. Out of an appreciation for what is, my actions move to experience this gratefulness. Freedom is in the absolute knowledge of I am not a body. I am free for I am still as God created me. In this awareness even the body becomes part this deep benediction of gratitude.

Ω

203.

Α

What dies? Physical form eventually disintegrates, and we call that death. We have come to believe the end of our life as a body is death—and there is great doubt about the life of our soul after this "transition" out of the body. *ACIM* came to restore man's awareness of his Identity as Spirit. "I am Spirit." Identity is only that. "I am not a body." This is denial of physical limitation. Who knows these truths completely? Who is so certain of these facts that he lives by them? Intellectual "knowing" is a block to application. My unwillingness to accept my Identity is almost involuntary. This is why determination is necessary. "I am determined to see things differently" What is different? I see myself as God created me instead of what I made of myself. Freedom is an attribute of God, therefore of His Son. It is my responsibility to accept this freedom by undoing all that is in my life which imprisons me. The body is just a vehicle. It can be used in the service of Spirit, of Love, of extension—or in some sort of personal striving based on lack and fear. Do I lack anything? Answering with anything but "no" is a sign that undoing is still necessary, and I have not yet accepted my Identity. To "die" is to end; to end my preoccupation with lack is the only real "death," which I need to make while I am alive. The real death is a stepping out of the self I made into the Self God created.

Ω

204.

A teacher comes to teach. A Life teacher comes to teach Life, which is relationships. He is the master of relationships. Having outgrown personal ties, he teaches the impersonal or holy relationship. First, he starts by showing us the state of our lives right now—one of motives, fears, insecurities, calculations, pretenses—all problems self-projected. Second, he begins the process of Atonement, the removal of self-destructive tendencies. Third, he introduces us to our own God-given Identity through this undoing process. Without the real teacher, what we "think" continuously replays as problems. He can bring the brain to silence. In the space of that silence there is great peace. A few moments of that peace beyond understanding are worth one's whole life. To meet such a being is a great blessing, an encounter with the vertical man of the Absolute. The absolute is something true in all time, in all space. Having the capacity to receive this truth requires an open-mindedness and yearning to know Reality. It usually begins with a willingness to admit some falseness inside of me, and an invocation for help to let it go. I let go of the falseness as it is pointed out to me by the teacher. Gradually the process of undoing takes hold and I am transformed inside—getting close to silence and peace. Then the dawning of gratefulness begins in the mind as I see the glory of all Life provides.

Ω

205.

Α

Every instant is new. Each sentence uttered a great responsibility to be true and to be lived. The human tendency is toward an ideal but not toward the actual. An ideal is easy to talk about, less easy to apply. Forgiveness, or "love thy enemies" are ideals seldom applied. Who is the enemy? Is not the human brain all the same—concerned with self-survival, motive-ridden, reactionary, calculating for the best advantage? These thought patterns are the real enemies. Everyone has them, and everyone's challenge is to outgrow these common patterns, to rise above thought and have something of the spirit, something of Love to give. The patterns are so common we have grown to accept them. This is why it takes a teacher, one who has overcome these patterns in himself, to shock us out of our complacency and deal with them. Who leads a motiveless life, one of not taking advantage of another? The one who gives is such a being. He gives the light of undoing, of inner correction, of Self-honesty. Such a being is the true teacher, the Voice connected with Forces of Universal proportion. He is the one whose utterances are ever new, possessing the responsibility of a truth. His knowledge is of the absolute, not the dualism of the relative. He is one-minded, unattached, motiveless, and free. He has accepted himself as God created him, extending this acceptance to others. He is a liberated man.

Ω

206.

An independence bestowed on one by a government is less all-encompassing than one bestowed by God. The Authority of my Creator over me is founded upon the Law of Absolute Freedom. It requires no standing army to uphold, no legislature to enact rules and regulations that ensure this freedom. It is based on the principle of giving and receiving, whereby I am the point of transfer. What I receive I give; what I give I have received already. Free from wants, the Nature of my Freedom defines my Self, Impersonal, and ever complete and whole. The inconsistencies I experience within the thoughts of problems and doubts are but memories in need of renunciation, entanglements to be undone. This renunciation is my responsibility. Separation from my Self is the only problem in Life. Realization, total and complete, of the Self is my only real work. The Self is not a personality, a body, or an entity which is born then dies. The Self is my Identity in God, in the Great Source of All things. The Self is my link to the Absolute, the Immortality of Love. The Self is my refuge and security, my freedom from fear of any kind. More clarity of the Self comes to me in proportion that I disengage from worldly affairs that distract my attentions. To reduce my physical needs to a minimum is to free my thought from all concerns but this Self. I am Free when I stop entangling myself in the unessential.

Ω

207.

A

There is great suffering in the world. Many humans live in a struggle to survive. Tribal mentality promotes division, vested interest, prejudice, and violence. These are more or less all over, even in the industrialized nations; corporations seek success and power in the marketplace. Individuals working for corporations are used and discarded according to the rules of competition and productivity. Jobs have become the lifeline for survival. Man has become a part in a large machine of corporate interests. Where is Love in this equation? Tribal man had enemies and modern corporate men have enemies as well. What has changed? The enemy has been sanitized, that's all. Internally, fear, motives, reactions still dominate the human psyche. Our minds need housecleaning, yet education is focused so totally on external skills that the light of Self-examination is rarely the curriculum. Modern psychology has not solved the problem. Analysis of the problem of fear does not dissolve it. Therapy does not necessarily turn on the light for someone who is perpetually afraid of the dark. Analysis of the fear of darkness does not dispel it. Only the one who can turn on the light shows that the darkness was an illusion, thus eliminating totally the "source of fear." Who teaches to undo our illusions? So few. One in a hundred thousand teachers is a real one. He simply turns on the light.

Ω

208.

A brother with whom I have ended my sense of separation is my savior. His trials are my own. His disease is mine just as his healing is my greatest interest. "Disease management" is not healing. Healing is from a greater Cause than the science of medicine. Medicine transfers the problem from one form to another. The Cause for real healing is perfect Love. The rules of medicine are substituted; hence, disease is only managed, not overcome. The body has its own dynamics, it seems, as we have accepted disease as a natural outcome of aging and hereditary patterns. But the problem of disease is not solvable in the physical areas where the symptoms manifest. The problem is in the mind and must be dealt with in the mind. Who is the patient? Who is the healer? What is the disease? Disease is a thought of non-love. Within the mind of the patient is a memory (thought) of fear, of non-love, and this thought manifests in the body as disease. Is the brother's disease different from my own? As he is ill am I not as well? Healing is mutual, or not at all. What is in me that I am a witness of disease? What will be my response to it? Will I "fight it" with the expectation that physical agents can heal? Will I take 100% responsibility and invoke Christ's Power of true forgiveness? Does the former expectation shroud my faith in the latter's efficacy? I am repentant. Illness is my illusion. When will I be free of it?

Ω

209.

A

The tools of any trade help define that trade. A carpenter does not build a house with pots and pans, nor does a chef cook a meal with hammer and nails. The tools are specific to the task. The philosopher, one who loves wisdom, possesses tools that expose the false through serious questioning. The question is his tool of Self-inquiry through a process of undoing. Another tool of the philosopher is to withhold conclusions that would prematurely abate the Self-inquiry. Most often the premise of any real question is "I don't know." Inquiry holds the space open for new discovery—the revelation of something previously unknown. There are basic questions concerning Identity. Who am I? What am I here for? What is my destiny? What is my work to do? Why do I fear? Are there Higher Forces moving my life? Thought cannot answer these, yet the questions themselves have tremendous vitality. The truly wise face the Unknown without despair because they are certain that Joy and Love are the ultimate laws that govern the universe. Even in the face of great human suffering, the wise see this as a veil of the ephemeral, a passing mirage mankind just goes through in order to see the real peace and joy beyond. The tools of the trade which arrive at a truth replace appearances with the reality of facts beyond these appearances. Love prevails, no matter what external sufferings would suggest otherwise.

Ω

210.

A

To simplify life, one needs to be with the essential. Many of our possessions are superfluous, cluttering our space, our minds, and our lives. Beauty is in the simple, composed of quality elements. A quality of elements is classic, evoking a sense of the eternal and long lasting. Each possession becomes essential when its absence would detract from this sense of the eternal. The objects of style which close in a space and make it heavy with unnecessary goods, can and should be eliminated. But we are creatures of attachment, enthralled by the complexities of over accumulation. What have we to gain by such extravagance? Our lives are clogged, stuffed to the point of immobility. "You can't take it with you," the saying goes, but that does not make us question the reasons we take so many things along for the ride. Thoreau said, "Man is rich in proportion to what he can do without." It is obvious then, we have become impoverished by over-abundance, becoming a culture of waste. The salesman can manufacture needs, then sell us the accoutrements to fulfill those needs, no matter how artificial and unnecessary. Simplicity is possible, yet it requires a discipline of renunciation, so unpopular in a land where anything and everything is available. Getting more has become the means of *being more*, though at the expense of being just fine as is. As is, that would be too simple; then I need nothing.

Ω

211.

A

What can there be in us that needs forgiveness when Yours is perfect. ACIM, Chapter 16, Section VII We are caught in the illusion of time, memory, and thought. Divinity knows we are caught in these illusions, but we do not; therefore, enlightenment is a slow process of waking up, disenthralling ourselves from the unreal. What would the awareness of perfect forgiveness do to us? What joy and freedom would ensue from this awareness? Awareness differs from belief, in that it is actual, something more definitely lived. One begins to observe the unwillingness to forgive, the tendency to blame, or to feel guilt. Awareness of these is the beginning of letting them go. We have made mistakes; forgiveness erases their effects because in the real world these mistakes have no meaning. The meaningless world of fear-based thought has a dreamlike quality; when I awaken from the dream, the fear effects are gone with the dream as well. Such is perfect forgiveness—cause and effects are dissolved together. Thought is transmuted to Zero—out of which comes the Peace of God. It is given to me through grace, although my attention and energy is required. Forgiveness is a sustained vigilance to repent from fear, motives, advantages, and self-survival in order to have something to give. Without having to give, life is empty. Having something to give is an action of co-creation. One who gives is honorable.

Ω

212.

A

Thoreau said most men lead lives of "quiet desperation." No longer tied to the tail of the farm as in Thoreau's time, man is connected to the cogs of the corporation. His energy is given to jobs and they are subject to hierarchies of management and labor. Few have their own work. Skills are acquired to serve massive corporate interests and to earn wages. Does a man have time or energy left to devote to his inner life—the evolution of himself into higher levels of being? More often his energy is spent and the interest to question himself is not there. Even seeing the dilemma of pouring his life energy into a system that may not be life-enhancing, he may feel the trap of survival pressing him to stay—put within the predictable security of the status quo. Who will challenge himself to be true to himself first and foremost? Few have this tenacity because more often than not it means standing alone, without the support of people. Not isolated, the person with his own convictions is related to Higher Forces. These provide for his needs, not the endeavors to acquire. Relationships are based on sharing, not on the motives of getting. Man asks, "who am I" and "what is my relationship with my Creator?" These are basic questions which need the space of leisure to pose and ponder. One is no longer "desperate" when he asks these questions. He is part of Divine Action which created the planets and all the universe. What greater Power is there?

Ω

213.

Α

Salvation is my only function here. ACIM, Lesson #99
One would naturally ask, salvation from what? And what is meant by "here"? In this life we accept a variety of so-called roles: husband, wife, employee, employer, carpenter, lawyer—a vast variety of ego definitions. "Here" is my life now. Where else could "here" be? Here is where I am now. Period. So being here, now, the lesson says I have only one function. This is *salvation*; to be saved or spared the consequences of my life now. What is my life now? I live with a sense of lack, a sense of uncertainty, a sense that my life is somewhat incomplete, a sense that my thought is ever unsatisfied with the status quo. To be saved from this complex of shortcomings is my *only function*, as the lesson states. To be absolutely liberated from the fears of these uncertainties and shortcomings is the mandate of this lesson. It goes on to state "salvation and forgiveness are the same." We are deceived as to what forgiveness actually is. We have no idea what salvation is either. Caught in the repeating patterns of memory, our problems are replayed in the mind, producing demonstrable effects. Memory must be cleansed. Salvation is my function here; forgiveness is the means. The past and future are unreal. Is time my jail keeper? Salvation is the end of time. Only my present innocence is real when I repent from the patterns of past errors. The Mind, emptied of memory, if but for a moment, is *saved*.

Ω

214.

A

What is shared with a brother? What do I give to another? That is a major concern of life. To give to blood relatives is good and often expected, yet to give to one who is not related by blood is a higher form of giving. What do I have to give? Apart from the needs of the body all I can give is my own peace, my own stillness and clarity. Am I there, empty of my thought? Do I have a motive, a wanting a desire to get something? These must come to an end before real giving takes place. What is real in me is already given, just waiting for me to awaken in it. The process of Atonement, or undoing, is one of letting go of all that is not supremely happy. Conflict of any kind is self-projected, therefore 100% my responsibility to undo. This begins when I own the conflict and admit "I was wrong." Now the light of correction can come into my life. Only real correction brings peace, because it helps me to let go of separation, the only problem. Separation from my Source is impossible, and in seeing this "impossibility," it is undone instantly. I have gratefulness to bless my days. All that I have received, all that I have let go, all that I am yet to extend, these are integral to the inner peace of gratefulness. Life provided the teacher, now it is time to stand on my own feet. What do I have to give humanity? Will I rise to my greatest potential? What I give to each brother or sister is the real indicator.

Ω

215.

Α

Most encounters in life are given as opportunities for forgiveness. It may seem the reasons are friendship, business, or otherwise, but the main reason is to release and to be released. A life has a function beyond the obvious, beyond the personal actions; a purpose which is God-given serves the whole, as well as uses the strengths and talents of the individual. An individual's function is to realize the Self. ***I am spirit. ACIM, Lesson #97*** Who has fully realized this? He would have outgrown many lesser levels of being in the process of Self-realization. In the end, there is no body, no thought, no movement. A few seconds of this state of being are worth one's whole life. Having this encounter of complete forgiveness, nothing else would come close to the peace, the bliss, the total fulfillment of these holy moments. They are given, not achieved. They occur when the brain is still, and one has dropped thoughts of self-survival in whatever form. There is nothing to do in this state. Only Being is still and peaceful, unattached, yet permeating everything. Only Being can satisfy my Mind because it has let go of all problems, striving, seeking, all needs for anything to be different from what it is. How does one meet those encounters? Is being my Self my first concern? Can I arrive empty? Each day is an opportunity to live by grace, to extend the will of Absolute Serenity.

Ω

216.

A

Gratefulness must face the nagging doubt of ingratitude. Goodness must face the dark forces in man which drag him down into depravity and murder. There must be more to health than taking a pill. Medicine does not necessarily heal. What is an error, a problem, a disease? Gratefulness must face all of these, in the end, to dissolve them. **Only salvation can be said to cure. ACIM, Lesson # 140** Salvation is the end of guilt—a deep sense of wrongdoing, a regret of past mistakes. The end of self-attack is salvation, for all attack is of myself. Sickness only arises where some form of guilt was invited it. With the end of guilt, no sickness can enter. For every pain I would experience, I may ask myself the underlying guilt that is the perpetrator of that pain. That is the part of mind where God is now invited in, instead of guilt. The cure is the transmutation of guilt into light and love by Divinity, based on my holy invitation; a recognition that my mistake can be corrected when I confess to it. There is no place where God is not. Even where guilt seemed to be, it was not, because guilt and God cannot co-exist. This is the thought that cures. I will rejoice and be glad in it. A truth must be fully accepted in order to be my truth. I have been so conditioned to accept the false as true, it takes the gentle reminder of the Holy Spirit working in my life to accept the truth as true. Only forgiveness, complete and total can cure.

Ω

217.

A Lord, may my mistakes be brought to light and may the smallest inkling of guilt be rooted out of me by Your forgiveness. May I accept the Atonement for myself and be as You created me. I do not know my mistakes, that is why the Holy Spirit is needed to mediate between truth and illusion, between the Mind of God and my mind. At some point I must side with truth, the part of my mind which is God's Mind as well. In that is the realization of my Self, the Son of God. **The Son of God is my Identity. ACIM, Lesson #252** My thought cannot "know" it. Yet the part of my Mind which is God's Mind can know my true Identity. My thought need not "know;" it can't because it is limited. It is like asking a first grader to solve a calculus problem. Or like the calculus professor accepting the reality of the Unknown. To be as a little child in the presence of Divinity's Truth is the only honest approach; not with doubt but with the certainty of our Creator's love and care. In the face of all our memory there must be forgiveness. Otherwise the sorrow would never cease. Separation from Self is a lie of desperation, and we often do not even realize we are suffering from separation's "effects." The past, looming like a testament to our mistake, is but a mirage, a projection kept alive by repetition. I may not realize my Self, but I can realize my past is not real, mistakes are past. Atonement is mine to accept.

Ω

218.

A

The mystic, if he would write, would be very clear. Mystery, or the Unknown, is the domain of the mystic because he is clear that the known world of thought is loveless and deceptive. Love operates in the Unknown realm, yet in very concrete demonstrations. A person does something kind to another; what causes this action is something great and pure, a Force originating beyond motives of thought. To give, just out of joy, is the action of the mystic. He has no motive other than to be free of self-centered motives. What he sees, he sees. Joy is in what he sees, as well as the Source of his sharing. What he shares is increased by the "giving away," because he gives something of the Spirit, something strengthened by sharing. Give a man a fish, he will have a meal; teach a man to fish, he will catch his own meal for all time. The mystic is one who is certain that the Mind is not thought; it is something beyond the intellect, memory, thought—all functions of the brain. Beyond the organs of capability the body possesses, the Mind stands apart in stillness, in silence, not relying on the brain at all. Undoing is the main function of thought, through the guidance of the Holy Spirit. Without the help of something beyond my thinking, I would deceive myself, seeking some Nirvana, artificially projecting some image of peace when real peace lies at the end of all projections.

Ω

219.

A

"Life, liberty, and the pursuit of happiness"—words of the founding fathers put at the head of the rights of mankind; therefore, the responsibility of any government of the people to safeguard liberty, or freedom, is at the core of these Self-evident rights. Without freedom, life and happiness would be conditioned and dependent. Independence is a new concept at the governmental level. When had man not been under the chief, the king, the pope, or some authority? Now he ponders freedom in the New World. What is the pursuit of happiness? What is meant by pursuit? To pursue is to seek, to strive for, to endeavor toward. Is there not an element of the opposite in seeking something? What I seek I do not have, so why do I pretend to already have what I seek? Seeking or pursuing excludes having. What do I have while in the pursuit of happiness? Non-happiness, called sorrow. To question what is meant by life and liberty may yield similar contradictions. What is the Source of life? Something Great and Unknown. Man can play around in the test tube with it, manipulate it, but he cannot create it. Can a government be the protector of something so sacred? Who bestows freedom? Not a set of documents or group of people upholding the rules of those ideas within the documents. Freedom is God-given from the Great Unknown, the bestower of life and liberty, and even happiness.

Ω

220.

A

Within the human brain is the memory of brutality. Victim and perpetrator memories are both present. To rise above these thoughts remains one of the most important steps in man's evolution to realize the Self. Ordinarily, people have jobs; they exercise a skill necessary for the system to work, and they are rewarded for this productivity, usually with money. Do jobs introduce people to their highest potential? Employees are directed in the system by employers; often executives of the corporations are paid excessively at the expense of those who work at lower levels for lower compensation. There is a pecking order. Within ordinary life, there are still predators and prey, those with the upper hand and those who are victims of the upper hand. When viewed in this light, what is common practice is still a form of brutality. But people need jobs. Slaves are directed by masters. People live at the level of survival. No blame, just fact. Humans become mechanical and the systems that need these workers will exploit their "survival instinct," and get them to perform. The poet said, "make yourself a mule and someone will ride you." I am responsible for my thought, words, deeds, and actions. Do I make myself a mule? What I have to give will determine the level of my freedom. To the extend I am self-centered and mechanical, I am dead already. To the extent I am creative, what I have to give will lift me out of my bondage.

Ω

221.

A

What is a body but a few pounds of matter in a universe of billions and trillions of pounds of matter? So much attention is given to the body, no wonder man has forgotten the truth of "I am spirit." Living in this physical world the body's senses are supreme. Man has sought pleasure of the senses and attempted to eliminate pain. But pain and sorrow seem to follow him. Like a shadow, the joys are tainted by the looming possibility of sadness. Within this pleasure/pain syndrome there seems to be no hope of escape except the acquisition of more pleasure. Man has sought solace in religions which have told him to bear the pain in this life and to do good for rewards in some "heaven" after death. He has sought cures through chemistry and science for bodily ills, yet one cure becomes the cause for the side effects of different disorders. He has analyzed thought and memory and sought psychological solutions in the unearthing of past thought which produce their effects in the present. Attempts to be free have not liberated him from the strife and struggle of daily existence. Preoccupied with the body and the personality, man remains in the rat race of achievement and self-improvement. *ACIM* makes clear a way out. "I am not a body. I am free." And, "My thoughts do not mean anything." These quantum shifts are where the solution exists—outside all past associations.

Ω

222.

A

"A peace beyond understanding" does not involve thought. Thought, though subtle, is still a material thing, and peace, immaterial by nature, is a state of being unaffected by the changes of time, space, matter, decay, or movement of any kind. The wise speak of *stillness*, and this is synonymous to a peace beyond understanding. A state of being does not oppose anything. It is a matter of degrees. Physicality is part of a continuum called wholeness, or Reality. At the lower level of this continuum is matter, and of matter there are various degrees as well; earth is more gross than water, water more gross than air, air more gross than fire, fire more gross than space or spirit. Yet all are imbued of the highest element of Love. The closer one gets to this Reality, all pervasive in its nature, the closer one gets to peace beyond understanding. It is a narrow path up the disciplined spiral toward Reality because it involves outgrowing the lower levels in such a way that all reaction is done. Opposition will cease the progress toward the Spirit. Ingratitude for any event in one's life, no matter how difficult or painful, will sink the ship of forgiveness, and place the aspirant on a lower level of identification. To be free of the "body identification" is a rare state of Mind. This freedom lies in stepping through the doorway to the Still Mind where thought has no meaning apart from the God-given.

Ω

223.

A

We base our trust on the ephemeral, the things in life which are subject to change. Virtually anything material—money, car, house, job, the body itself—are often subject to the erosion of time, decay and an end, depending on our programmed "thinking." Trust is placed in the untrustworthy because at the core of our *trust* is the uncertainty that what I am trusting will change. Only the eternal merits our trust because trust must first be in our Self, which is beyond time, change, limits, and decay of any kind. Value is determined by this simple question: "Is what I value ephemeral or eternal?" This discrimination will determine what is trustworthy as well, because only the trustworthy is valuable. Now we are faced with the fact that: I value what essentially has no value, I have chosen to trust the ephemeral over the eternal. For instance, I may trust the power of my bank account over the power of love and because I have very little knowledge of love's power. Not being aligned with love's power, I may earn my money by means which exploit or take advantage of others. This may increase my bank account, but can this truly be productive? Forgiveness is the only sanity in an insane world of my thinking. I have a body, a house, a car, a skill, and a bank account, but my reality is in Spirit. Let these lower levels of the ephemeral serve the Eternal of who I AM.

Ω

224.

A

Conventionally a book is a stream of thought which has a beginning, a middle, and an end. The poetics of drama pose characters in a situation, a conflict, a "good guy" and a "bad buy," and the resolution of this conflict or catharsis. Life has similarities. One is dealt a hand which have cards of character, environment, family patterns, personal aspirations then meets life in the struggle to realize these aspirations—and one realizes them or not. And then one passes away, all so tidy. What about another way? I am writing differently in the sense that what I start I finish in one page. I begin, which I call Alpha, and I end, which I call Omega, in the space it takes to write down thirty or so lines which go down into some thought of subject, examine the good guys and bad guys of my thinking, and arrive at some resolution. One need not read the whole book from start to finish to get the content. Either one page contains the whole or it does not. What I write down is either meaningful or not. True or false. So then, because of the brevity of each page, I am more determined to get to the point beyond thinking. How quickly can I dissolve the problem of conflict and arrive by the end of the page in the little green garden of peace? This is the challenge, and intention of this work. I was not aware of my Self, but now I AM.

Ω

A

To simplify my life, I must pare it down to the absolute essentials. What are they? Thoreau established the facts in this area. For the body: food, clothing, shelter and heat. For the mind: lofty words that are true. For the spirit: a healthy relationship with Nature. His two years spent at Walden Pond would have an impact on the thinking of America. Open now to a Voice that draws religion from the very breath of air which life abundantly offers, the new American is a melding of the intellectual heritage of Western thought and the nature reverence and relationship with environment embodied in the cultures of the native people. Thoreau incarnated in the period prior to, and on the edge of, the industrial revolution. He died before the black man was freed from the institution of slavery. He wrote no comments, as did Whitman, pertaining to the carnage of war. His voice preceded, though anticipated, the demoralizing impact that work without virtue would have on a population dependent on jobs. Simplicity to him amounted to living life with the absolute bare necessities materially so that space could be devoted to contemplative and spiritual concerns. The inner man, and intimate knowledge of that inner man, is the core of Self-Identity, and is the primary relationship in life. Without knowing Thyself, life becomes drudgery. Simplicity therefore lies in Know Thyself.

Ω

226.

A

Truth is something beyond our thinking. We may intend to be honest, but as long as we have a motive, our thought will lie in the face of threat to achieve our goal. Then we will say the ends, which we perceived as good, justified the means, which were latent with contradictions and manipulations designed to achieve our ends. To some degree, thought will always lie; its nature is self-survival in a world it perceives as dangerous and threatening. Lying is justified in order to achieve our desired effects, which we say are for the good. We say as a nation, "In God we Trust," and believe in Christianity, then we go halfway around the world to kill our enemy, whom we believe deserves to be killed. Do we ever see the contradiction? Christ said, "forgive your enemies," Either we kill and admit we are not Christian or desist from killing and endeavor to forgive. We cannot have both, for this would mean we are hypocrites—knowingly. As an individual, my thought is no different from the collective. I can say I am above those forces which justify killing, but the instant I separate myself into a bubble of self-righteousness I become a hypocrite. I have murdered in my mind; therefore, my thought is just as deceptive as the rest. Forgiveness is the only way out. Repentance is the only sane stance in a world based on the duality of relative thought. There is only One real thought, Love, which silences my own.

Ω

227.

A

Basically, the mass of mankind is uneducated, even those who have been to college. Education, in the highest sense, is the familiarity with the highest and wisest thoughts of mankind from all time. A call to wisdom is no less than to be disenthralled from our self-deceptions and self-imposed limitations, and to be interested in truth, however unpopular by standard conventions. We approach the wise as if befuddled by our own lack of insight, but somehow alert to a superior intelligence. And it is this we hear by contrast to unexamined elements in our own life. Sometimes this contrast is too much to bear and our own lethargy a shame. But as it is, the wise are now in our radar and their incoming objects of moral clarity fly to the center of our awareness. They are on our screen, no doubt, to dissolve our ignorance. That is, if we admit to it. So often we don't, in some bastion of unwillingness to see how much we do not see. Vision is a light from the sun of the wise. They cannot help but shine. And likened to them are those they study, as wisdom is passed from age to age by certain torchbearers and the words from centuries passed—touched, wick to wick, to the minds of those with current aspirations. So few can see, so few can hear. But only one is necessary; one who puts his ignorance before the altar of truth to be dissolved.

Ω

228.

Silence, a state of being with no words, is an incredible blessing needing no particular place or time or circumstance. What is needed is attention that observes thought, for an instant it's not engaged in thinking. This instant is Silence. I read the other day in *Walden* the dynamics of Thoreau's morning. He would get up early, bathe in the pond, then sit in the doorway of his cottage in a quiet contemplation, totally aware of the natural surrounds. Often this span of being still and quiet would go on well past noon. Now some would call this laziness, a shying away from productive labor. But is man a beast of burden? Mr. Thoreau made contact with Silence, a state of being beyond thought. And all of Nature was at his disposal—not to exploit, but to commune with and be a part of its transcendental blessing. This is the reason he went to the woods, to discover a reality not subject to the conventions, expectations, and bondages of society. Independence, not bestowed by government, is the birthright of a truly religious man who has outgrown the conditioning of church, state, and corporation. Education that imparts no freedom is no education at all. The "pursuit of happiness" equated with the pursuit of material wealth was a danger and a sham in Thoreau's eyes. The real wealth worthy of man's pursuit of happiness would be wisdom, the kind that undoes thought, freeing us to be Silent.

Ω

229.

A

To read the words of great men and women I must rise to the level of what they are saying. Otherwise learning is a sham, a preoccupation of thought, and not the impetus for a new action. All academia is based on learning ideas, skills, systems which make the human being a "marketable item" in the world of jobs. Those who bypass academia for a more entrepreneurial lifestyle often exploit the skills and energy of others toward their ends. People of conscience go into social services, yet the intention of "doing good" can fall into the same corruptions of practice. A wise person stands alone. To depend on others is deception. He works with his own energies—for better or worse—and leaves others alone. I have enough sties in my eyes to not be concerned with those in others. Fortunately, the wise have left a trail of crumbs of true words and deeds behind that I might follow through the woods of myself. Similarly, my challenges now were theirs then, though in slightly different form; one of these being Self-discipline. What is Self-discipline? It is not conformity, nor is it some imposed habit of ritual. The act of questioning itself is a discipline. Who am I questioning but myself? The wise would ask questions that thought cannot answer: what is the meaning of my life? What is love and happiness? What are my blocks to joy? In being honest there is an atmosphere of receptivity which is disciplined.

Ω

230.

A productive day begins with gratefulness. I am on the planet one more day. How will I use the time and space of that day? Will I isolate myself or will I extend something of love? This question begins an internal action; to strive toward a particular external result can be deceptive, even if that result is perceived as "good" and in the best interest of myself and others. The extension of Love begins with the awareness that Love created me in Its own image. As a creation of Love, I am something beyond the body and the thoughts of the body. I cannot recall my Identity with memory of thought, which is of the past. Yet, there is a "memory" of the *present*, in which my thought is silenced. In this state I am with whatever it is I am with. It sounds redundant and over simple. But to be in the present, memory must be silenced, if but for a few instants. Then what is in front of me, beside me, surrounding me is freed from my associations. All things are free when I am not naming, judging, comparing, calculating, etc. This is a state of mind I rise to when memory is silenced— even for an instant or a few seconds or minutes. Great Freedom abides in the statement "I don't know." But memory is persistent. I don't just shed it like a snake does its skin. It is a long, tedious process of repentance, forgiveness, and transmutation which form the Atonement in my Life. And only Atonement is productive.

Ω

231.

Α

When true words touch the planet, mankind is never the same. One Jefferson to utter, "All men are created equal," transformed the thought of Western Man. One Lincoln to say, "As I would not be a slave, I would not be a master," formed the basis for eliminating the slavery. One Jesus said, "Forgive your enemies," established the basis for mankind to atone for its errors. True words are to be lived, and the ones who utter them are usually the ones who bear the burden of proof and stand stalwart in the face of prevailing opposition. Every age has its prophet whose words speak to the particular need of that age. "Affluence without wisdom is self-destructive." This truth, spoken by Tara Singh, is yet to be realized, though its current effects are apparent. And now the planet is blessed with *A Course in Miracles*. **My thoughts do not mean anything. ACIM, Lesson #10** Thought, the basis for mankind's strife and sorrow, must be set aside. How long the effects of memory go on; now they come to an end. **There is no peace except the peace of God. ACIM, Lesson #200** This is not the God of organized religion which pits one group against another as the standard of the true form of worship. This is the God beyond all thought, all duality, all conflict or opposing interests. The "Peace beyond all understanding" comes from a Source unfathomable but nevertheless *actual* in bestowing this Peace.

Ω

232.

A

I am responsible for my unhappiness. The causes are within me and I can say I am not the "victim" of external circumstances beyond my control. I have actively pursued an unhappy life, knowingly or unknowingly—a repeated memory. All the experiences I have had I asked for; none came to me without my consent. The problem is a thought, a judgement I have had before, which I continue to have. This "thought" produces a result of fear and pain. Fear and pain isolate me, maintaining a self-imposed separation. Seeing this, I would repent by taking 100% responsibility for my memory replaying as fear and pain. Then I ask Divinity to release me from these thoughts. "Forgiveness is the key to happiness," when I see myself as the maker of unhappiness. To be my real Self, who is pure light and peace and joy, I must let go, through forgiveness, of my made-up self. I am responsible for letting go. This is a process of petitioning Divinity to dissolve the falseness manifesting as depression, ingratitude, and general melancholy. I cannot fully direct the results of this invocation, but I can be responsible for petitioning. Vigilance is required to question my thought—what I am aware of and not aware of. **Father, let my forgiveness be complete, and let the memory of You return to me. ACIM Lesson #291** Once I have taken the step to forgive, my life is in God's hands.

Ω

233.

A man takes delight in the world of the five senses of the body, sight especially. The visual world of light and color is incredibly beautiful. When the mind is still, nothing has a name and objects flow into a scene of melding colors, shapes, intensities, shadows, lines. What the body's eyes see has no judgment. One is grateful for moments of stillness. Each item is like a jewel, its colors brilliant and pristine. Without the space in which there is no pressure and no particular focus or motive, vision is partial. To be whole, vision must rid itself of judgment or "thoughts of." I am happy to admit I don't know. In this admission there is the space to receive, in this case the visual beauty of what my eyes perceive. *ACIM* states, "The body's eyes do not perceive the light," in reference to seeing a "forgiven world." Non-judgment and forgiveness are the same; in them is freedom. Freedom is needed to *see*. To see a forgiven world is a vision of freedom. Then what the body's eyes see is different. Colors, shape, and lines of things are seen exactly as they are, not tainted by the association of memory. Every object is new, divorced from the past. Its presence can be appreciated, no matter how humble. Even "junk" takes on a new glow. The peace within me extends to touch everything I see. I am blessed and what I see is blessed. Beyond the world of judgment, fear, and pain is one of great beauty, peace, joy.

Ω

234.

At the end of the day before bed, can one give thanks for the life that was given? Productive or not, so many breaths were taken, so many billions of gallons of water fell as rain or flowed to the sea, so much sunlight emblazoned the earth for so many hours, the earth stood frozen at its two polarities, thousands of people were born and thousands of people died, a breakfast was eaten at the local diner, and the teacher who opened our eyes sat alone and somewhat forgotten in an outpost for the aged in some foreign Iowa city. Care is given, but not directly from you. Paying homage from afar is too easy. Others manage his care; you play no active role in that. But who has joined with his heart? Have you? He would say of Jesus—the people came to hear his true words; they ate the fish and the bread, and never came back. Who would walk out of their life of mortality, conditioning, strife, and struggle to enter the immortal life of the Self? Would our egos let us? We ate the fish and bread and were uplifted. But were we transformed by the truth of his words? Now he is "managed," but not by us directly. The professionals have taken over. Some say there was no other way. We who beseeched and offered were turned down. Let the "friends be the friends" and the "professional caregivers be the caregivers." This was the Life Action. So say those in charge. Now I am still with the question: is there a better way, or am I compelled to accept all things *as is?* This is a nagging question.

Ω

235.

A

Light and Joy and Peace abide in me. My sinlessness is guaranteed by God. *ACIM, Lesson #93* There is a distinction made in this lesson between my God-created Self and my ego-based personality self, which I made. To discover Self-Identity is a renunciation, or forgiveness, not a judgment of good or bad, of my made-up self. Beyond thought is who I AM. **You are what God created or what you made. One Self is true, the other is not there.** *ACIM, Lesson #93* What is "made" is of thought; the accumulation of memory, conscious and unconscious, of experiences, forms the personal self. This needs to be "let go" in order to encounter my One Self. Light and joy and peace abide only in this One Self. Few have ever found it because so few have really let go of the man-made personality self. Yet, I am responsible 100% for my own salvation. No one else is; therefore, the state of the world is not a concern because "the world" is *in me*. I am the world I see. I see either the self of duality and conflict, or I see this Self of Light and Joy and Peace. I waste my time trying to "improve" upon the self I made. It is not really "improvement" that will liberate me. In fact, it is the play of the go to "improve." When I "give up" improvement I am closer to the Light and Joy and Peace which assures me of my One Self, sinless in God.

Ω

236.

A

My friend is one who can see my Self-deceptions and gently point them out to me. A deception is anything that makes me "unhappy." I must see the ego for what it is, a memory bank of past problems, pains, struggles, and desires. The friend helps me to observe my memory and to make amends for past mistakes without pressure or judgment. The past is gone, actions and courses taken cannot be "untaken." Future actions and courses are unknown. In this present moment, which is the only real time, I need only to be my Self. Then what happens is incidental to being my Self. *All things are lessons God would have me learn. ACIM Lesson #193* Even my mistakes are gifts from God because I can see them and invoke forgiveness. *Salvation is my only function here. Salvation and forgiveness are the same. ACIM Lesson #99* Life becomes an invocation for forgiveness, Atonement, in which I am healed of the past through "letting go." My friend, also included in this process, can help me forgive myself. And I can help the friend do the same. We all seem to have an "Achilles heel" or a blind spot of weakness we don't readily see. The friend helps me to see the blind spot and to correct it. It is the Grace of God that delivers me to the inner state of Light and Joy and Peace. My thought cannot do it, but my Self can. And the friend is a major part of my Self and part of that God-given grace which helps me to reach inside to Light and Joy and Peace.

Ω

237.

A

Depression results from the thought, "I am trapped in a situation I would like to be different." Feeling helpless to affect a change, I have judged the situation and cannot accept the way it is. There is a thought that "I am a victim of circumstances beyond my control." These are thoughts the ego uses to maintain melancholy. Unless they are faced and dissolved, light and joy and peace will never be reached within me. External situations are neither good nor bad, because they are not the source of reality. The externals are acted upon but have no ability to change in and of themselves. Depression results from a world I have disordered in such a way as to make me depressed. I have done this to myself. It is a form of self-destruction. The ego would say, "I'm a victim," which is to say, "I'm not responsible for my depression." The Holy Spirit undoes this self-deception by taking 100% responsibility for all that goes on inside myself. I can work with what is in me. I have absolute dominion over that, therefore, that is where change must occur. Depression is a decision to be depressed based on the external "evidence." Thought always precedes form. *I am determined to see things differently. ACIM, Lesson #21* puts me in touch with another way of seeing, one of responsibility. I have the power to decide to be happy. It is in my hands along with my Creator. *Heaven is the decision I must make. ACIM Lesson #138.*

Ω

238.

A

Within the day are the physical tasks that can be as delightful to the mind as any meditation. The snow falls and blankets the earth, over the rich and poor alike. Shoveling snow is beautiful, especially when it has immobilized a whole city. There is a muffled atmosphere; sound is softened, people are like hermits coming out of their remote shelters in the woods. It is a blessing to live on a street which is not a main thoroughfare. There is time and space to say hello to the neighbor a few houses down. The conversation is more than a quick hello. What starts as casual goes deeper. One's work and its principles, never to take advantage of another through business. What are the means? The tendency is to justify the means with the ends. Desirable ends can well justify the means, but what are the consequences? It seems reversed. One can control his means and keep them impeccable. This is the real virtue. One can have an end which may be noble, but it is brought down by means which are not pure. One could state the means simply: "I will not lie." This will test you. Every situation will be thrown at you to test your means. Is the purity of your means more important than your ends? Would you let go of your ends to keep your means pure? Who will face down the possibility of utter defeat to remain impeccable? These are the questions the snows brought along with a conversation with a neighbor.

Ω

239.

A prayer of prayers which undoes my thought: *Steady our feet, our Father. Let our doubts be quiet and our holy minds be still and speak to us. We have no words to give to You. We would but listen to Your Word and make it ours. Lead our practicing as does a father lead a little child along a way he does not understand. Yet does he follow, sure that he is safe because his father leads the way. So do we bring our practicing to you. And if we stumble You will raise us up. If we forget the way, we count upon Your sure remembering. We wander off but You will not forget to call us back. Quicken our footsteps now that we may walk more certainly and quickly unto You. And we accept the Word You offer us to unify our practicing as we receive the thoughts You have given us.* **ACIM, Workbook, Review V** Without the guidance of my Creator I am but lost. Without my Creator's love, I am without love myself, as all love is originated from the Creator. Let one remember Him and say firmly, *God is but Love, and therefore so am I. This Self alone knows love. This Self alone is perfectly consistent in Its thoughts, knows Its Creator, understands Itself, is perfect in Its knowledge and Its love, and never changes from Its constant life of union with Its Father and Itself.* **ACIM, Workbook, Review V** This is the Self we share, in Love. It is the Christ.

Ω

240.

A certainty is not of thought. The changing nature of thought cannot know that which is unchangeable. *Let our doubts be quiet and our holy minds be still and speak to us. ACIM, Workbook, Review V* Thought is "doubt." Let thought be quiet. The prayer invokes the state of stillness—the capacity to receive. Invocation is usually just a ritual. Without the quiet and stillness, it is like calling for help falsely, and when help arrives not listening to it. Do not invoke without the quiet to listen. Having the ears to hear is the most important responsibility. *We have no words to give to You.* Who is that still? Am I? Do I still think my words mean anything? Having let go of my own directions, there must be another way of being guided. *We would but listen to Your Word and make it ours.* And these are powerful words. The lessons of the Course *are the directions.* Just live by them. Again, stillness and quiet are necessary. Application is not in "doing" but in "accepting." Who can be guided like a little child? Giving up my long-held ego plan of separation is something that requires determination. That is never to give up aspiring to be my Self. *God is but Love, and therefore so am I.* The personality does not know love. It substitutes advantages, attachments, kinship, philanthropy, for Love. Love is something beyond explanation, yet as concrete as building foundations. My true Self is that. Know Thyself, say the philosophers, and be happy.

Ω

241.

A

The power of decision is my own. *ACIM, Lesson #152* What is that power and what will I decide with it? Power is energy. The two are synonymous. Without energy there is no power. The lesson refers to the "power of decision." There is an energy associated with decision. To decide to take a job with a corporation will inevitably give that corporation my energy. I will give them my energy of work in exchange for their energy of structure, purpose and finance. The question is always one of value. Is my work (in energy) worth their compensation (in money)? This has been the perennial question of man—that of value, self-worth, due compensation for work, etc. But this power of decision reconsiders my energy and to what I give it. There is only one decision to make: to be my Self or not to be my Self, to be who I am as God created me or to be my self-made ego, and essentially to be or not to be—Love. The power resulting from this decision is totally my own. To decide in my own "strength" is to limit my energy to my thought, my body, my separated world. To decide for this strength of God in me is to connect myself to a force so vast I can literally do anything. These are the two powers between which I must choose: God's or mine. God's is given me when I see I can do nothing by myself. It is a matter of God's energy working through me. Then I have the energy to undo all that is not my Self. I am accepting of this force to undo.

Ω

242.

A

The call to God has been heard faintly or strongly by men and women throughout history. Those of the so-called more primitive cultures may have had the greater ears to hear this call. Because we are more advanced technologically does not mean we are closer to Divine Will; perhaps progress puts us even further from the truth—that of the absolute and unchangeable—as we may think we are more advanced than we actually are. Administrations and governments come and go but the voice of a wise man sets a vibration on the planet for all time. Buddha said the nature of physical existence is suffering; attachment, and unfulfilled desire lead to sorrow; all things in this world are transient and passing. Impermanence added upon impermanence. These are observable results of thought, like it or not, describing the status quo of our conditioning. Man thinks in terms of a finite body identity, not in terms of an Infinite Spirit Identity. This body identification will always end in disappointment. Seeing the futility of identifying with the physical senses, sensitive and wise men have asked of a reality beyond the senses, beyond the known world of thinking and memory. This question provides the fuel for the call to God. A man who has let go of the world and forgiven himself for past errors of memory and thought, can invoke his Creator for guidance. "What would You have me do, Father, to be consistent with Your True Will, which is also mine?"

Ω

243.

A new day begins with a prayer. "Divine Creator, Father, Mother, Child as One, thank you for this day. Help me keep it holy. Let me do your will which is also mine. And that is all. Forgiveness will show me the truth, and truth will correct all falseness in me. I need not condemn myself for past errors, but only recognize I have been wrong. And now I do not know, but You do, and that is all that is required. I do not know what this day will bring. Steady my work to do what needs to be done and no more, that I have space to give my mind to stillness and to peace. What You give is far beyond what I receive. Give me Your blessing, that I may give as well in Your likeness, from the Love I AM and all my brothers are. May I be consistent in Your will and overcome any doubts and self-destructive tendencies. Help me see unwillingness for what it is—an impossible dream of separation. I am Yours to guide. I cannot be apart from You in everything I do. You are my blessing and my strength. Without You I am nothing but with You I am all. I will rejoice in knowing You are closer than my breath, closer than my own thought. I cannot think apart from You. What You have given is mine forever. Help me to accept who I am exactly as You created me to be. There is no Love but Yours for me and mine for You and all my brothers. Let me see You in them, for in them I witness to my Self. Amen."

Ω

244.

A

Great artists, painters in particular, are often solitary men and women. Solitude is the atmosphere of the creative spirit, conducive to the unpressured space of action. Out of stillness and silence comes an action; not from the conventions of academia, but from a deep place inside. One cannot be fully aware of that place, but through years and years of practicing an art such as painting, the demonstrations of insight, not necessarily even sought, prove the place is certainly there. The results occur after the fact in the paintings themselves, perhaps even in a state of unawareness at the time of their making. There is a difference between "thought" and "awareness." The lion is aware of the zebra, its movements, its speed, its location, the wind, the scent, etc. But he may not be thinking about it. The same with making a painting. Acutely aware of the process, the color, the mixing, the application, the additions and subtractions, the range of doubt to certainty, the mystery and the revelation—all these aspects are in the forefront of making the thing, but the painter isn't "thinking" about it. There is a point where the conscious mind must let go and trust the subconscious mind will receive the proper guidance from "above," from the transcendental "mind" of God. Solitude is the most conducive environment for this awareness to be full and productive. Awareness needs no people. It is a communion with the Spirit.

Ω

245.

A

When I use the word God, I do not mean it in the conventional sense. It is a word used to describe the *indescribable*. In no way does the word fathom the unfathomable. I want to be certain that God is more equitable with the Unknown Force that created and permeates all life and all things—universally whole—into infinity. Our human brains are so incapable of even conceiving what God is, I feign to use the word. But a word we must use to communicate, so I use the word God as a point of entry into that area that is far, far beyond understanding. It is a word on the edge of silence, a word to end all words, and take our minds to the furthermost outpost of words of thought, before leaving us at the gate through which all words end. Into that realm we cannot go alone. It is there, at the gate, we stand united, brother in hand, waiting for the final step to be taken by our Creator. It is where all words end and only silence reigns. We wait expectantly for a promise to be fulfilled, that we have done our part to forgive and forget all things except Your Love, the Love which created all things and us as well. Here we would stand forgetting all the hurt and sorrow we inflicted on ourselves. The age of sacrifice is over. Now would our minds be one with God, which means our thought can safely cease to be.

Ω

246.

A

There are people with whom I have grievances. They represent the unresolved part of my mind. A grievance is an "attack thought." These are showing me what I need to let go. These people give me an opportunity to look inside myself because the grievance is inside. It is a thought of separation. It is the part of myself I "hate." We are conditioned to have grievances about ourselves and others. Likes and dislikes rule our life. Now is the time to let go of grievances. They are self-destructive. I must admit to my Creator I was wrong, and then the correction of grievances comes—replaced with the miracle of forgiveness. **Let miracles replace all grievances.** *ACIM, Lesson #78* My responsibility to be attentive to my thought is for letting go of grievances. There are ones I am aware of, and ones buried in my subconscious. This is why a sustained attention to setting right (Ho'oponopono) is most needed. I hold the people I "don't like" in my mind where I must let them go. The one with whom I hold grievances is my savior because he shows me what I need to forgive. What is in him is in me; forgiveness releases us together. When we are released from grievances and attack thoughts, we are both free. Release is freedom. Divine Creator gives release when I repent. The work of the day is repentance, not because I am a "sinner," but because I deceive myself with grievances. I miss the fact that my Self and others' Self are One, totally free of all blame.

Ω

247.

A

Gratefulness to life for all my past experience lays aside my grievances. Difficulty and painful memories can be cleansed and set free by gratefulness. Even these memories can be forgiven, thus being transformed from a grievance to a miracle. That I have made mistakes is obvious, yet the power of decision to accept my God-created Self is also mine; the Self who knows no error. This is my one Self. All memory not of this Self is a passing dream. It goes the way of water down the stream. Out of the torrent, the Self steps out of the passing events of time to be certain in the present. All the adjunct memories are done, forgiven, and gone. *"I" am the "I."* is from Ho'oponopono. It is similar to, ***I am the holy Son of God himself. ACIM, Lesson #191*** This "memory" of my Self is the only memory that need occupy my mind. It is given me by God Himself. Would I not accept it? To reject my true Identity is foolishness. Why would I continue in the false self I made that was born to die when I can claim my Identity as my Self which cannot die? Death or everlasting life are the only options. Forgiveness of the physical and certainty of the mind that looks toward Spirit are my only functions here. My happiness is dependent on my acceptance of my function. I can accept it. Will I? For me to be among those who have taken this step I must also take this step. Gratefulness for Life to have brought me actually to this crossroads overcomes doubt and unwillingness.

Ω

248.

A

Today our theme is our defenselessness. We clothe ourselves in it as we prepare to meet the day. We rise up strong in Christ (Self) and let our weakness disappear, as we remember that His strength abides in us. *ACIM, Lesson #153* I will not attack today, especially myself for what I have not done or failed in doing. Self-blame is a defense that keeps awareness of God's strength away from me. Defenselessness is strength because it would acknowledge nothing real can be harmed in any way. The body is a neutral thing to be protected with care and wisdom, fed and clothed and housed and used to communicate defenselessness. Remembering the Christ in me is my strength who does not condemn, nor does he see this passing world as real. What is my condemnation but attachment to the forms of material things I want to possess? Defenses witness to fear. Defenselessness witnesses to Love. I am safe in a world in which I am not attached to physical forms. The body was made in separation from my Source, but as nothing is separate from that Source, it can be transmuted to a tool in the hands of that Source, a harbinger of Christ's Love. He needs my body to communicate with other brothers who have forgotten their Identity in God. Let me not be a "priest" of ideas, but rather minister to the work of freedom for myself and all.

Ω

249.

A

I cannot be my Self by an act of effort. The Grace God gives is centered in my Self and there I must be satisfied. It is not my effort which gets me to my Self; in fact, when effort stops, will wisdom shows the way. The Self I am already is. So my concern is not to be, but to remove what never was, yet appears to block my own awareness of the Self I am. Forgiveness is the only means to God in our dualistic world. The split between the good and bad does not exist in Self. The Self is only One. This is what holiness is—all in One. Any thought of division is to be undone. A grievance, a sadness, a dissatisfaction, a hurt, all stand in the way of knowing who I am in my Self. I need help. The help is there in the form of dissolution. Dissolution is of thought; dissolving the block where the block was made is the only real solution Thoughts of separation from the One are forgiven: **And God Himself shall wipe away all tears. ACIM, Lesson #301** Transmutation is from God; miracles are from God; God is Undefinable, a Force that permeates and enlivens all things, the Force which dissolves illusions and the blocks that keep me from awareness, direct and simple, of my Self. My thought can be silenced. To know thy Self, it must be quiet. Inside of me my thought needs to be still; for only then will awareness return to me and my blazing Self be revealed.

Ω

250.

A

Miracles "remove the blocks to the awareness of love's presence." In stillness and silence, I am closer to that awareness. ***My thoughts do not mean anything. ACIM, Lesson #10*** This is a necessary lesson in order to be still inside. Thought is a block. The miracle of the lesson removes it. Who would need to say anything in light of the miracle? It is so. I accept it or not. Nothing I say about it means anything. Am I grateful for the space of stillness? In stillness, "I am not a body; I am free." Escape from the world of thought is possible. I need but accept the truth of the lessons with gladness. To be free of thought is a blessing. The ego's way is thought and activity which it perpetuates. It wants to seek liberation but not find it. To end seeking takes the miracle. Thousands of people have sought enlightenment in numerous religious practices all born of thought. Thought does "this to get that." Already the premise is off. Love, or Being, cannot be "sought" and then "found." It is already in me. Stillness, the removal of blocks, is my only need. The first and the last action of healing my mind is this undoing: Repentance, Forgiveness, Transmutation (Ho'oponopono). The emptier my mind becomes the closer I am to Love's awareness. I am happy to know this one fact. Undoing is forgiveness. Forgiveness is my function on earth. It transmutes hell into heaven. It is the first and the last fulfillment—Alpha and Omega.

Ω

251.

A

There is quiet and there is light. With no particular activity there is space to observe these. I do not want to do anything but observe the quiet and the light because their beauty is so intense it makes me happy. The light envelops everything I see, bringing color to my eyes like rainbows. A dog barks off in the distance, an automobile drives by, in the next room a person turns the pages of a magazine, the sound of my own breath is heard. And the silence between the sounds is louder than the sounds themselves. The wind rushes between the two buildings, whooshing against the windowpanes. The radiators make a clank; all these sounds compose the silence because the silence itself is within me. And the light, the light—how beautiful the light. What a gift of God, the greatest painter of all. The glowing green of the translucent leaves lighting up the plant as if from within, the rainbows of colored light on the walls refracted from the glass prism perched on the window sash, the orange to red colors of the Indian blanket draped over the end of the bed, the gray-brown shadows on the wall and in the hallway and the overall glow of a well-lit room in the midday winter sun. I am still, as is the earth, as is the whole of creation. What need is there for anything? The gentleness of quietude is mine.

Ω

252.

A conversation I have with myself is recorded. The inner life is that—a conversation with myself. It is between my conscious mind and my subconscious mind; between my mother and child. It is between the two together, invoking the mind beyond—the super conscious mind, or spirit—the father. Mother and child holding hands, asking the father for clarity and guidance. Mostly it is between the mother and the child first. I have a problem in the body, the child. Pain is a problem that manifests, an imbalance, a disorder. "What is it my child. What is bothering you?" then I listen and don't project "solutions." I take responsibility and ask forgiveness. Also, I have to accept that the condition may be around for a while. Forgiveness usually is not the quick fix of the problem. Divinity knows how fast I may be free of problems. Trusting the process of forgiveness requires faith, because desired results may not occur. Can I let go of disappointment without getting disillusioned with the process? The problem is always something *in me*. I invoke the Lord's help to clear judgment, reaction, depression, and self-destructive tendencies. There is another way to live in which a vigilance for Higher Forces proceeds the thought of the brain. This vigilance is an internal application. Vigilance means there are uncertainties, but my power of attention can dissolve them.

Ω

253.

Α

I must forgive myself and accept the Atonement. What would my life be then? The same old patterns of behavior and self-destructive tendencies would not apply. Discipline is necessary. Consistency with what is given, not because I impose it on myself but because it is the only right course of action. The road to the Self involves a lot of letting go, a lot of inner correction. Life shows me my mistakes. They are gifts—signposts to inner correction. Why would I condemn myself? Why would I be dejected when my Creator promises me a "happy outcome" in the end. "No one can fail who seeks to reach the truth"– about himself. Will I follow my own inner guidance? That is the question. Unwillingness and laziness are powerful forces in me. What would undo them? Alone I cannot overcome them. I would need the help of the Christ, which is also in me. Each moment is always a decision between the help of my Self and the self-destruction of my ego. Self is Father, Mother, Child as ONE. Consistency in all levels of my being—spiritual, mental, and physical. I can receive what is given; I can digest it, and I can extend the new Man. This newness is an awareness of my God-created Self. It is my responsibility to undo (correct) all that is not that in me. I am as God created me. Can I be only that, a being with no conflict? This is my challenge and my legacy.

Ω

254.

A

We must be clear on what is meant by the Christ. The Christ is not just Jesus. The Christ is a state of being human. It is a state of inner awakening in which one's Identity in God, the Universal Force of Life and Creation, is made manifest and known. Every human being, no matter from what belief system, religion, or no religion, has the Christ within himself. The awareness of it is potential, not actual, so it needs to be awakened. Like a candle is lit by another candle, a brother more aware of the Christ inside can awaken another brother to the Christ in him. It is a sharing in which the separation between individuals normally perceived is suspended. This suspension is the *miracle*. Only the Christ can work miracles. There have been very few humans who have reached this high pinnacle of being—Jesus, Buddha, Mohammed, Hermes, Moses, Krishna, Krishnamurti, Sri Bhagavan, Dr. Schucman, Morrnah Simeona. They all faced the depths of the human challenge—to undo within themselves the lower nature of the human ego for the extension of the high nature of the human Self. They reached the top of the mountain of Self-Identity and provide the candlelight which can touch the light in each human being, regardless of past belief or past experience or memory. The Christ is the only real part of us, our only real Self. All else is our memory of hell which only the Christ can dissolve and undo.

Ω

255.

A

Stillness is a state in which thought slows down and silence reigns. Forgiveness is the only real thought because it ends my conflict and undoes thought. It is the means toward stillness and silence. Once my world is forgiven, what would I have to say of any meaning? What would the Christ in me say? Something like "love ye one another." What would love do? Bringing order to my life first is the priority, and that would require clearing out the unessential. This is everyone's task on the road to fulfilling their God-given function. The Self is empty and unattached. Because it is free. It can respond to situations that are not free. To be my Self takes vigilance and practice in removing the blocks. The work of forgiveness seems long and tedious only because thought is so conditioned and entrenched. Just knowing that thought must be undone is half the battle won. But the real day-to-day, moment-to-moment undoing takes energy and determination. ***My thoughts do not mean anything. ACIM Lesson #10,*** but the thoughts I think with God mean everything. Aligning my mind with His is the work of the day. One can be easily fooled in thinking he is doing this. The light the body's eyes see is nature's great beauty; but the light of the mind of God, which is also my mind, is far greater. That light is within me. I look toward it now.

Ω

256.

A

Reverence for the teacher is the most sacred thing in life, especially when that teacher is the real one. How would I know? The real teacher has nothing to teach. He points out thought and learning are false. Identity of who I am as God created me is the only lesson. All that is not that—my own self-deceptions—the real teacher works to remove. When this one is found, all lesser teachers drop away. I have found the real amidst a sea of unreal. Who is he, this man who knows my Self better than I know it? The teacher has transcended his own thought and gone through the many levels of spiritual awakening that lead toward liberation. It is not possible to seek and find such a person in the conventional way of finding a teacher As destiny would have it, the teacher comes into my life when I am ready to undo my memory, thought, toxic personal issues, and awaken to my Self. This Self is the source of what I have to give in this lifetime. My function, my Self, my service, become one when I am led by the real teacher. I must overcome my unwillingness to be led. When "I think I know," I am lost. To stay attentive without projecting a direction is the challenge. To live each day fully with no regrets or plan, to be guided what to do, that is the real test of reverence for the teacher. The snares of self-deception and self-sabotage are all around. It is reverence for the teacher that gets me past them.

Ω

257.

A

I desire to speak somewhere without bounds like a man in a waking moment, to men in their waking moments; for I am convinced I cannot exaggerate enough even to lay the foundation of a true expression. Henry David Thoreau uttered this statement in the conclusion of Walden. A man would give everything he had to make a true expression. A whole life would need to be put into it. Who speaks "somewhere without bounds"? Aren't we saying things to achieve very particular and narrow results? And because of this preconceived motive of speech, our language is limited to what we have learned, confined to the predictable utterance of memory. Something wild, something new, something so natural and awake it cannot be denied as a statement of fact— that would be the spray of the crashing waves against the steadfast rock of our being. The cool droplets of mist that gently strike us in the face are the facts that wake us out of our morning stupor. Who can hear such a thing? Most of us have only the ears for "news," and not the least interest in a statement that will stick to our bones like a healthy breakfast. Who speaks in a state awakened? Most of the time is spent half asleep in a routine of rote. To speak "without bounds" would mean we have to live without bounds. And who could do that? Most of the time our lives are confined to convention.

Ω

258.

A

There is a space in life where belonging to anything artificial is a travesty upon the Self. I can be part of life, which is whole, but to join any other cause or organization or to gain survival by succumbing to working for another, is to separate myself by fear and limitation. We are tied in a knot to do this to ourselves. The boundlessness of our nature is violated. Everyone will say I'm crazy to be this unilaterally focused on freedom from man-made dependencies and organizations. "How do you earn a living," they ask. There is day labor, but that labor does not begin and end with some mechanical task, physical or mental, in which the routines of a system are perpetuated. Work is to be aware of my Self. That job transcends all others. To be employed by Higher Forces is to be guided along in a fashion totally unknown. "That is just lazy and stupid," the detractors might say. But who is truly free? And isn't it the tendency for the bound to ensnare others in their bindings? To be practical and support the body one must work and be productive. That work must be for something absolutely essential. Man/God relationship is essential. To be aware of that is essential work. The artist is one who makes contact with Divine Forces and expresses his love of God through his life of giving love to his fellow humans. Mother Teresa in our time is one of the greatest artists. Probably greater an artist than Picasso.

Ω

259.

A problem is persistent, lingering, recurring with frequency. Memory is the perpetuator. The process of forgiveness is the means of release from the problem. Ho'oponopono is a threefold process: repentance, petition for forgiveness, and transmutation. My mind is the container of my Self, pure in its original form, created by Love. All that is not Love, which I have introduced into my mind out of separation, is my sole responsibility to mend, to clean up, to release. I can invoke my Self for help in the cleaning. The process is clear and given. *ACIM* gives lessons, or thoughts of God—one a day for a year. These are very specific in changing my mind from one of memory, problems, toxic thinking, to one consistent with the Will of God—which is also my Will. This Will is a mind free of problems. I must not get discouraged if the symptoms of problems persist. To go through the pain, which seems unavoidably brought on by subconscious memories, I need faith in a Power that is helping me release the "thoughts of pain" which are its cause. Faith in final release is my need to keep. **And God Himself will wipe away all tears. *ACIM*, Lesson #301** is another way of saying God, the Great Unknown Force of Life, will take the final step in my process of salvation. My responsibility is to let go of judgment and accept all happenings and situations exactly as they are, as manifestations of God's Will. In this acceptance they are cleansed.

Ω

260.

A

To accept my world as it is, exactly as it is, without judgment (because acceptance is freedom from judgment) is to see forgiveness in the correct light. Any "problem" is a judgment I make of non-acceptance, a rejection of forgiveness. This perpetuates the problem which leads to death. Any problem I have now I always have had. It is coming up to show me I have not yet accepted Atonement. This lifetime is first an opportunity to accept Atonement for myself. And then it is up to God to send me my work, whatever that may be. My first work is to accept Atonement—not to judge anything. When will I accept Atonement? What is preventing me from stepping through its glorious and open door? Why would I fear? Do I think I must give up anything? Is sacrifice still part of my thinking, therefore a "fear" I impose between myself and acceptance? Is attachment the issue? I confuse Love with attachment, then use this false love to justify not moving forward to accept my function. It is all very wily of the ego to seek but not find. I can find nothing by myself in isolation. Only when what I "seek" is for all my brothers as well, am I on the path of true correction. Wholeness is just that—all inclusive. *Everyone* is God's Son. There are no enemies in truth. My pains and suffering are curable by my acceptance of salvation. To let forgiveness rest on *everything* is my work to do.

Ω

261.

A

A person can excel in an art form, be it music, dance, sport, painting, science, etc. Discipline and practice are the most important ingredients to excellence. Giving yourself totally to your art will produce excellence, but will that intense focus along particular lines make the individual one dimensional? Or is the art just a metaphor for the whole of my life? What is the purpose of art? First, to introduce me to discipline and practice that leads to transcendence—a meeting with my Self. The wise point out the only real art is the art of living. What would that be? Painting and drawing are fine, but what will I paint? Mastering the art of living seems essential because the painting is only a mirror to how I live. It is the metaphor of my thinking. Conflict and doubt in myself would automatically surface in the painting. Peace and joy would surface as well. Which do I choose? Wouldn't the art of living be the most important source of creative energy for the art of painting? Beauty, joy, happiness are the perfections of any art. We aspire to those states of being. I am responsible to *live those states of being*. There are specific obstacles to overcome in my internal state. Guilt, regret, inaction, procrastination, laziness, unwillingness; these are the dragon's teeth of my inner impurities which are to be undone. When these are dissolved through forgiveness, I can excel in being my Self.

Ω

262.

Α

Student: "Does life take care?" Teacher: "Yes, when you completely let go." Who has completely let go? One in a billion? Have I completely let go? What does that mean? Let go of what? We think we have a plan to improve ourselves, to achieve happiness, to go for the gusto, even to aspire to our highest good. Can I let go of all that? Not to seek anything would require great wisdom. That would be "letting go" completely. I have certain responsibilities: wife, elderly parents, elderly teacher, sister, etc. These relationships must be honored and seen through completely to their loving end. End, in the sense that they exist in total freedom, not in obligation or attachment of fear. Higher laws establish key relationships. These are the opportunities for my own evolution toward total liberation. Liberation is from all sorrow, pain, illusions of any kind. To ask if life takes care is everyone's question because everyone is concerned with their own life and what actions or what source take care of them. It also implies a larger field of care. Life, in this question, is something Whole and Universal—something beyond our thinking, our limited field of knowledge. Call it God, Allah, the Void, Jehovah, whatever. The Great Unknown. Is it safe to "not know" who or what "takes care"? This is implied in the question as well. And when the question is my question, then comes the answer: "Yes, when you completely let go."

Ω

263.

A

A meal was shared. I was struck by the fact no formal grace was given. We have fallen into taking providence for granted. What comes to us was acquired through our efforts, so no one really is grateful to Life, to God, for providing what we need. We think we "get it," therefore, why thank forces beyond ourselves? I can see why. We are fed up with false platitudes and rituals. "God" and religion have ben overworked and used as the basis for justifying conflict, factions of good pitted against those of evil. And as a result of this falseness, many stay totally clear of this question of Divine Forces and the providence from those forces. It is no wonder people are fed up with saying grace before a meal. They are burned out with all that *God business*. But the fact remains: the elements the body needs to be healthy do not come from us. Air, water, food, heat and fire, space, or all that sustains Life, were not created by man. These are God-given elements. One might say vegetables were farmed by man's efforts. Yes, but man did not invent an apple tree. The chicken that was slaughtered and cooked and put on the dinner table was not man-made. It was God-created, and it gave its life to sustain ours. Without forgiveness and grace in this picture we are stuck with the unspoken arrogance that our life is only what we can get and accomplish. In reality, other Forces play a great role. Who can truly give thanks to them? That would be a *real grace*.

Ω

264.

A

Who *is most dead, a hero by whose monument you stand or his descendants of whom you have never heard?* **Henry David Thoreau, Walden, p 206.** We remember the one who stands tall in the face of great odds and adversity. One who is disciplined and good at what he does, one who overcomes impossible odds at the risk of annihilation; this one we call a hero. Thoreau will be remembered as a great American writer. In his own time, he was not recognized except by very few. Now he is in the pantheon of great American minds whose written legacy forms a pillar in the building of literary greatness. His "monument" is his writing. He had a way of communicating the sublime through an attentive discussion of the common and ordinary. By seeing into the depths of things—nature, society, commerce, history—his commentary transcended those things to give light to a constant and higher principle. His insight lives on into the future, being as clear in its vision today as it was when he wrote it down. He didn't marry and had no heirs to this legacy, but he didn't need any. His words spoke a truth *that he lived.* In the face of much detraction he did live his life according to principles of virtue. This consistency to be true to himself came through all he wrote. This truth is what we remember through his work. His immortality is assured because his words speak to the aspirations of all generations.

Ω

ALPHA OMEGA

265.

A

What is valued in the world may have no value when it comes to the eternal. Man is an idea in the mind of God. When he realizes this, he may have little need for his own ideas. They are of use in the world living in a body. But ideas at the body level are split into a duality of opposites. Opposites inevitably generate friction, and friction results in decay or conflict. The mind of God is not dual. It is One. OM is the universal vibration of Oneness. In OM are all things brought to a close—not in the sense of "death," but in the sense of the everlasting. The idea of Love in the Mind of God is constant. This idea never deviates from its Source. The Source and the Idea are One. Most people do not rise to the level of wholeness and Peace, a level that is within them. Rising, or resurrection, is attained by first going deep within. First, going down into the depths of the subconscious brings up the memories of separation and conflict. All the Pandora's Box of thought forms of a self's destructive nature are within the mind, waiting to be transmuted to pure light by the energy of forgiveness. The instant the Pandora's Box let loose its pestilence on Man was the instant forgiveness was given as the perfect antidote to human suffering. Suffering is a reaction of pain; everyone feels pain, but not everyone reacts to it by suffering. Pain is a sign that my mind is identifying with my body. When that ceases, so does suffering.

Ω

266.

A

"Know thyself," the wise say. Which one? The first step to know the God-created Self is to be familiar with the ego self I made; to know its deceptions, fears, doubts, errors, etc., and to release it from the mind. Release is the goal to know Thyself. To let go of all past hurt and sorrow is a cleaning of memory. To come to an empty state of mind that embraces the Unknown is a state deep as well as high. Undoing would simplify life. When I don't want things, I find I don't need things. The basics of food, clothing and shelter are essential. Beyond these are desires with motives and consequences. Simplifying life does not mean doing without, it means being aware "that which I thought I needed and wanted, I do not need or want." The price is too high to pay in energy. One desire can consume my life. Why? To give my life to God means to keep my mind free from unnecessary desires. Even things I need must be kept in moderation—enough food, enough heat, clothes which are neat and classic and hold up to long wear but are not extravagant. Simplicity is an inner state of stillness in which peace and quiet are valued above all else. To know thyself is to outgrow the lower stages of desire. I may desire art and music in their ability to lift me into a lofty state—but at some point, art and music may be a hindrance, needing to be left behind as well. The closer I get to the Self, the more I will relinquish as simply unnecessary.

Ω

267.

A

The times I have heard wisdom and not heeded it are numerous. Thought seems to have its own momentum and unwillingness. It is inherent to every person. But the superior man overcomes this resistance. At times I have this resistance, therefore, I have the symptoms of conflict, pain, and suffering. Thank God there is the Atonement. When will I accept it for myself? These writings may appear to be in the form of a confession, or an admission of shortcomings, but I think they are Self-honest statements of my status quo in relationship with the external status quo. They aren't much different. Every day is new and every day is an opportunity for me to forgive myself. Whitman, in "Crossing Brooklyn Ferry," discovered his relationship with not only the good in the world but also the evil. Both are in the mind and I must own them because this is true—then there is something in forgiveness, Ho'oponopono, inner Peace, or the Self. Regardless of the content of the mind which holds these "opposites," there is a place of acceptance which is not in conflict about it. No matter how many times I have fallen into doubt and unwillingness, this place in me is always accessible; a decision I make to forgive myself. That's all. And it is a constant vigilance to remind my Self that forgiveness is my function moment to moment. This is my work to do, and I will do it.

Ω

268.

A

With every inspiration there is an expiration; with every birth there is a death; with every inhale comes an exhale. I have died a thousand deaths and lived a thousand births. The cycles of physicality appear to change, but I do not change. With every end there is a new beginning, but I have no beginning and no end. I am my Self. I am aware of who I AM as God created me. "I am that emptiness, that hollowness beyond all consciousness." (Ho'oponopono) What I experience is only a memory; beyond memory there is no need for experience. Life is the great dance of memory, and Life is the Great Void out of which the dance came. I am the beginning and the end, the Alpha and the Omega. All bird songs are mine, all mountains are mine, all oceans and stars are mine. There is nothing that is not mine. All the good and all the evil as well are mine. There is nothing I do not contain, and when there is nothing, I contain that as well. Understanding of me is not possible because it cannot know all of me. Awareness is possible because it can open greater to witness who I AM. Be still and simply know I AM. That is all you need to know. "Nothing real can be threatened. Nothing unreal exists." Herein lies your Peace; "not the world's peace but only my peace, the Peace of I." What would you give to have the truth written on this page also written in your heart? I am you and you are me. Truth must be shared. There is no separation. So be glad in your life, you cannot die.

Ω

269.

A

Is my life being guided by God or am I just repeating life from memory? My thought which I use even in writing this sentence is never sure. That is why forgiveness is absolutely essential. Forgiveness can admit, "I don't know." Forgiveness cleanses the mind of memory. It is important for the mind to be empty. This is not often the case because it is filled with thoughts of doubt, uncertainty, unwillingness, fear, etc. Forgiveness is a process of emptying the mind from memory. The door to the Absolute of my identity is open, but memory prevents me from going through that door. Forgiveness helps me go through the door. Peace is when there is no thought. "No thought" is when I have no judgments about my perception. The body's senses are in contact with what is, but my sense of Self does not judge or interfere with what I perceive. **The body is a wholly neutral thing. ACIM, Lesson #294** What God created is not corruptible nor is the body "sick." It is the mind, not the body, which needs healing. The body can be used to communicate forgiveness—forgiveness of what? Forgiveness that I confused my body for my Self. When I think the things I have done will define me, I rely on memory. God is. Self is. I AM. We are in an age when Self-Identity is the most urgent thing for us to know, of which to be aware.

Ω

270.

A

Mysticism begins with the admission "I don't know." It is acceptance that *My thoughts do not mean anything. ACIM, Lesson #10* A person who has risen to this state has come to an inner silence. Without a teacher to confirm this state, it would be mistaken for something else. For most it would appear as "insane" because they do not see their conditioned behavior and beliefs are more insane. The mystic is vulnerable because he does not defend himself nor attack the status quo. He values silence and the action of stillness. The status quo of beliefs is something the mystic deals with inside of himself, because it is his "memory" to overcome. He is no different than the ordinary man, except he sees the problem is memory itself; thought is the prison house of everyone. The non-mystic is caught in what he knows; the mystic has freed himself from the known. He is comfortable in the Unknown. One could ask what does the mystic do? Nothing. His principle action is to undo. Then Life works through him, but he cannot take the credit. Emptiness is his first concern. He cannot say he is "good" nor can he deny the "bad." But neither are the domain of the Self. The Self is everything. There are no "villains" and no "saints." The one who reaches the peak of this *mountain of being* is enlightened. He is the mystic who has overcome the world of thought, which is the only thing to overcome.

Ω

271.

A

The Chinese sages refer to the way of life by the name of Tao. Lao Tsu, one of the greatest sages, wrote of the Tao, which in these modern times is widely translated in a book called the Tao Te Ching. He said, "Tao abides in non-action." "Nothing is left undone." This non-action is movement free of thought such as the river whose water moves to the sea without thinking. Nature is an action of non-action, thus it is never lazy; it completes all things. He speaks of the "simplicity of formless substance." The tree is conceived in the seed, grows tall then dies and returns to "formless substance" – an idea. "Without form there is no desire, without desire there is tranquility. And in this way all things would be at peace." Physical form is a replayed memory, an artifact, a printout of an idea. All "wanting" is some desire for form; this requires "work" to make something other than what is. To accept the formless as my reality puts me in a state of no desire. Then, without desire, I am at peace. In the modern world of acquiring things, it is almost impossible to be without desire. That is why the voice of the Great Rays of wisdom is so necessary. That voice can clarify the actuality of this status quo and the liberation from it. "Without desire there is tranquility." Who values that peace? The first obstacle is the desire to get rid of peace. Yet, when I value peace above all else, I will have it.

Ω

272.

A

We know God through our fellow humans. The person next door is our savior when seen in the light of the Self. He and I are one. In this binding am I also one with God because I have not separated any part of His creation from my Self. In this view what a person does or has done in a body has little meaning. All have certain tendencies to overcome but so swiftly does forgiveness wash them away. Memory, thought, conditioning are all words that describe the ego which keeps me separated from wholeness. Within memory there is fear, and fear holds Love away from its awareness. Within a more ancient memory there is Love, a remembrance of who I am as God created me, along with all my brothers, in the image of my Creator. I need but accept who I am. I need but call his Name, which is my own, and His presence will be felt. The breakthrough occurs when I see my brother's interest as my own, his pain is my pain, his need is my need, and his joy is my joy. **God's will for me is perfect happiness. ACIM Lesson # 101** This is not a state of being which is here today and gone tomorrow. The Source of this happiness is unchangeable. And because it cannot change, *perfect happiness* is not of that which can change. The physical is not its source. The Source of *perfect happiness* is liberation from the thought of death. Immortal Life is happy and only awareness of that life can be perfectly so.

Ω

273.

A

My salvation comes from me. *ACIM, Lesson #70* It is the attention I give to life, to love, which determines my salvation. I am the master of my mind. I choose to love or not to love, to be or not to be. The great sages of old knew that salvation was something pursued and achieved. The attainment of peace, therefore, became an internal issue. Weapons of mass destruction are not the harbingers of peace. "Peace through war" is a contradiction that can never be reconciled. The real wise men knew this and so few of them exist. Intelligence is equated with status and power and the ironclad arguments of a cause. Sophisticated people can make the true seem false and the false seem true by the mere eloquence of their language. But the truth is true regardless of what I say about it. The world is round, not flat, no matter how much I purport its roundness is a fallacy. The most I can know is that I don't know. The sages of old admitted their human frailty and bowed to the holiness of the Great Unknown. To be humble in the face of the Unknown is wise. Because nevertheless, needs are fulfilled, food is provided, what I am ready to learn is taught, even the lessons you can't learn from books, but only from life itself. The teacher/student relationship has been provided so that I can discover I am my own teacher and student. The teacher is inside of me. The One Self is in me. From Him comes my salvation.

Ω

274.

A

The undoing of what is in me, not my Self, is the tedious work of the day; there is much to undo. Not a day goes by in which my memory does not attempt to sabotage my peace of mind as it would replay some ingratitude, some hurt or some put-down of myself. The energy to put these thoughts aside is needed. It would take all I have to face it. When my mind was so preoccupied with the activity of survival, I did not notice that my ego was in charge. Now that I am not so "busy," I have a lot of time to look my self-destructive tendencies in the face, and it is all I can do to remember I am not that, and not to dash myself upon the rocks so to speak. Somehow, I am grateful I can face myself, and in the end, not condemn myself for all the mistakes I have made. At the time I made them, I did not know they were mistakes. Now that I do recognized mistakes were made, I need the release that forgiveness offers. There is no other way out of the birth-death or high-low cycle. The reality of my Self, beyond the opposites of good or bad, stands waiting for me to let go of my little memory of my conditioned self—for the whole remembrance of who I am as God created me. The intellect alone cannot accept this. But the intellect with the memory of the body, can invoke the Spirit of the Father to help. In this reception of forgiveness am I safe and healed and whole.

Ω

275.

A

Man, to perceive his world in terms of good and evil, is missing the point of wholeness. Therefore, he disconnects himself from a larger reality, for a limited point of view that divides "what is" into two opposing factions. There is an inhale and an exhale in life; a night and a day, but there is also the One Life which encompasses both apparent opposites, accepting both as active parts of wholeness. All is as it should be. There are predators and prey at the physical level, yet at the spiritual level there is no conflict about this. Man is meant to rise above it all. He is "in a body," but his Identity is not limited to a body. He is whole in a detachment from physicality. This wholeness can then return, incarnate, to bless that which seems to be "caught" in physical terms. Divine terms are real because they do not change. All things which move and change in life are just the dance of forms—forms which only reflect higher laws of wholeness. I am an artifact of my Self, as is every human, every entity, every atom in creation. What seems to be so small and separate in a body is like a passing leaf on the tree of life. They come in the spring from who knows where, up and out of the sap, the rain, the earth, and the sun. They fill the tree full of verdant life, and then fall in the winter and die into the dust of earth. Always to come again.

Ω

276.

Ω

Having the energy to face myself requires I not waste it on nonessentials. What is meant by "facing myself"? Psychology, the study of the mind, comes close to this. But it is more than the methodical study of thought, personality, the cause and effects of experiences, analysis of the past, etc. which can reveal the Self. I must distinguish between my personal self, the ego, and my impersonal Self that is my God-created Identity. The ego is particular to me, though conditioned along lines that most people possess—self-interest, motives, attachments, desires. My Identity is shared "all for one and one for all." I still experience my Self with the body's senses and mind, but something beyond the body and thought enters my awareness. I may not have language to talk "about it." The "known" cannot define the Unknown. The finite cannot describe the infinite. Self-Identity is revealed to me when I let go of memory, thought, ego, experience; all that is of my past. Then I am in the clear moment of an uncontaminated Now. "Facing myself" can mean a couple things, i.e., facing my condition, my fear, my selfishness in order to *undo it*. Or, facing, once this undoing is complete, my God-created Self—whole, peaceful, connected to all. Energy is needed to face illusions. Facing the Self gives energy to undo what is not my Self. This is my function—to face myself. In that, is my real salvation.

Ω

277.

A

Having a body, I find myself doing things. Life is productive in its movements. The tree converts massive amounts of carbon dioxide into oxygen which animals need to breathe. The atmosphere of the earth is thus an exchange. Most of being productive is a kind of exchange—I give what I have for what I need. What I have is another's need. The exchange is a movement, an extension of being. Insight into the reality of things is something the wise have. They give it through words and deeds to those whose insight is asleep, thus waking up a tired humanity. They may not do things in terms of building houses, or roads, or countries, or governments, but what they do "build" is a bridge to the spirit, a clarity of mind that can be taken by the one who hears their words, to the clarity of mind in himself. Fear and sorrow are undone by the wise. They point out one's being is far beyond the body, or memory, or thought itself. Clarity of mind is an enlightenment in which prior behaviors and beliefs are virtually erased, leaving a vitality of emptiness, stillness, and peace. One could ask what value is emptiness? It is like a great bowl into which all the problems of man are poured to be dissolved. What greater productivity could there be than this?

Ω

278.

A

We have become a society of robots. We justify anything which is profitable. The body has become the most important aspect of our Self. Hardly is the life of spirit sought, let alone found. We are preoccupied with everything physical—bodies, cars, houses, clothes, food, jobs. Pursuit of happiness is equated with affluence and success. Who lives a spiritual life? What would that kind of life look like? Is simplicity something which people want? Simplicity could not need so many things—only the essentials. But this simplicity is not a sacrifice or a denial. Virtue is not in the guilt of denial or the self-righteousness of sacrifice. It is in outgrowing the appetites having first fully satisfied them. Morality is not some strait-laced denial of the flesh; morality is in being myself, not harming others, being true to my convictions. Who is true to themselves? The person who hears and follows his own voice, even in the face of unpopular opinion is the one who will prevail in the end. In the end, I mean, who will not die with regrets. I would rather follow my guide into the demise of a thousand defeats than follow the crowd into a superficial triumph. Consciousness is just being true to myself. I will sink or swim on my own. Sinking, I am my Self; swimming, I am that as well. The opposites of loss or gain are transcended in the light of complete forgiveness, which is also the fact of my Identity in Spirit.

Ω

279.

Α

What can one say regarding silence? He listens to his thoughts from a place disengaged. This place is silence. If something needs to be done, he does it. No problem. Silence is a neutrality of thought—not judging, therefore neither "good" nor "evil." The "good" of thought judges the enemy "evil." The good of silence has no enemies. Men will do what men will do, killing one another in senseless conflicts as they have done for thousands of years. Fear runs the human psyche. Underlying the affluence of the status quo is a fear of losing a position of dominance, of security, of safety. Is fear ever safe? What would a fearless life look like? Just because a man is willing to kill an "enemy" for the so-called protection of his country does not make him fearless. There is no denial that destructive forces of hatred exist in the world, but hatred is not overcome by more hatred, and the willingness to kill another is always based on hatred. Hatred is overcome by Love only; and forgiveness in this world is the truest mechanism of Love. Jesus could say, "Love your enemies," because he had none. Even of those who crucified him he said, "forgive them for they know not what they do." This is not a statement of hatred. It is one of unconditional Love, the only reality of the true man, the fearless man, the man who has realized in himself the Christ.

Ω

280.

A

What am I giving to life? Am I using the talents given me to their highest potential or am I wasting the Given in some inaction, some form of fear or ingratitude? I question myself; there is no other person to consider. To continue along the same lines as the past is to stay at the survival level of "doing things" that produce money. Money is necessary, but what else do I have to give other than certain skills for sale? I could say all the pictures—paintings, drawings, and photographs of the past 30 years. This is so. Their value is yet to be assessed in terms of art. My life for the past 17 years has been attentive to a teacher, Tara Singh, who is now in the decline of old age. It is time to stand on my own and give something of what I received from him back to people, to humanity, to even my Self. That is it. To give to my Self first is the beginning. What is the greatest gift—forgiveness. He gave moments of Absolute Peace by undoing the conditioned thought which rules our minds. A conditioned mind is fearful. A mind that is free of conditioning, judgments, etc. can Love. Love is peaceful. It is fearless. For my main concern to be survival of the body, I miss the point of my life. My purpose is to Love, to extend, to be who I AM as God created me. To do this, I must put away depression, fear, and all the self-destructive habits of my memory. All I can do is to invoke Divinity's help in erasing these from my mind.

Ω

281.

A

Why does the human being fall into depression when life calls him to be happy? What is the discontent and sense of futility he feels that leads to depression? Man-made systems: governments, corporations, religions, even households—are subject to change and decline. Yearning for a sense of the permanent in a world that appears so impermanent is a factor in depression. The body and the personality form a sense of "self," ego, "me." Most often this "self" is seeking something; something better than what is. The discontent from the difference between what is and what should be lends itself to depression. What would free me from this difference? Questioning the status quo begins with a sober acceptance of the mess I'm in. I somehow chose depression over joy in wanting the situation to be different. A change of perception is needed, not a change in the external situation. To see not with the body's eyes, but with the eyes of forgiveness, is the way out of discontent. There is beauty in the world. Am I in tune with the God-created or am I preoccupied with trying to control the man-made? The God-created is not physical; it is meta-physical—manifested in the physical. A person who sees the Grand Canyon, though the experience may pass away, is still touched by the knowledge of that space. The real space is *in me*. In this space is no depression, only Joy.

Ω

282.

A

When I say, "I feel," who feels? Is it memory replaying or is it inspiration from my Holy Self? Feelings are not reliable to indicate truth or reality. They are reactions to stimuli, to situations, to things I perceive. I feel pain What is pain? It is an intense feeling that draws my attention to the body. It usually marks an imbalance or lack of flow; we call it dis-ease because some negative thought of guilt is stuck in the body causing pain. Desire manifests a body; further desire requires energy to be fulfilled; unfulfilled desire creates emotional pain—sorrow. Desire is wanting something I don't have. When what I have is everything I want, desire ends, as does sorrow. Stillness has no desire. Silence wants nothing to be different than it is in the present. Feelings are useful indicators of what I need to undo by letting go of the thoughts that produced them. I tend to cling to the feelings I deem desirable and tend to run away from feelings that are painful. Both sides of the coin of feelings are unpredictable, changing from one to the other. What is a state of being unaffected by feelings? Can I be a witness to my feelings without being blindly sucked into them? I own them as mine, but I see beyond their present tone at their deeper meaning and reason to be. I lead my life from intimations. Feelings may or may not lead me in the right direction.

Ω

283.

A

There is nothing greater in life than the real teacher/student relationship. All light is in it. Without the one awake, the one asleep will remain asleep. So, the one awake agrees to be in a body so long to awaken the students, his students, from the sleep of duality. The lesson is simple, but in order to receive it, the student must be willing to put aside the conventional habits of learning. The real teacher undoes the propensity for intellectual learning so the student may face what is actually in himself—all the impurities that need to be removed—so by looking inside they *can be* undone. By not looking ahead or backward, but directly at the present, the student wakes up to a new freedom, one that sees perfection in what is now. He accepts what is, corrects disharmony, and comes to gratefulness for life. There is nothing to achieve. In fact, the empty aspect of his mind is the most valuable. The preoccupations and labors of thought are brought to question. "What am I doing? Why am I doing it?" would eliminate most of the students' former activities. He begins to see the greatest virtue is in stillness and silence. These are states of being closest to his essence, his Identity as Spirit. To be aware that what he does in a body is secondary to Being Still. Being Silent, the student is awakened by the teacher and forever grateful for the light he imparts.

Ω

284.

A

To be with the emptiness of no thought is energetic. "I don't know" is a vitality which is honest. Each day is given to realize the Peace of God and to accept the perfection of every moment. Nothing needs to be added to "what is." If there is a problem, I am 100% responsible for choosing its hell. Otherwise, heaven is now, not later in some projected place beyond the clouds. The body, though subject to our thought, is our own best tool to experience "as above, so below." Though the film is not the movie, the movie would not be known without the film. The body, though not the Spirit, has a function forgiven to know the Spirit. And thought, not empty, has a function to be empty—that is its highest function. Without thought there would be no *ACIM* whose function is to liberate the mind from thought. I am not adverse to sensuality. It is part of the human experience best accepted for what it is than denied in some puritanical finger pointing. Pleasures of the flesh are still pleasures. Who would live a life devoid of pleasure? This does not mean pleasure and virtue are mutually exclusive. Self-honestly somehow purges away the whole problem of guilt. I vowed to marry one woman, but my nature has fantasized with many in my mind. Would this exclude me from a Spiritual life when the beauty of a female sets my inner fire going? Sex is innocent. And the highest spiritual knowledge is certainty of this all-pervading innocence.

Ω

285.

A

What exactly is "my body" to which *ACIM* states I am not? There is a separation of sorts from who I am as God created me that is the principle malady the *Course* aims to correct. But this body thing is central to the correction, so, therefore, essential to know just exactly what is meant by it. ***The body is a fence the Son of God imagines he has built, to separate parts of his Self from other parts. ACIM, Preamble to Lessons #261- #270*** Inherently the body is not separate. How can it be when without it, I would not even be able to ponder the question or write down a few impressions. The problem is I "imagine" it to be a "fence," a separation device to limit my being, keeping me isolated from my real Self, etc. In fact, it may not be a fence at all, but I imagine it to be one. The problem is not the body, it is always my "thoughts of" the body. My body is a living thing—living, breathing, eating, having sex, defecating thing. It is part and parcel of who I am, not separate or frozen in time but a living, moving thing in this world. Why would I want to flagellate myself by denying it? It is a subtle lesson because we interpret it wrongly. Already hating our body being "mortal and fallible," we use the statement "I am not a body" to beat the thing even more. Really now, I need to stop imagining myself without a body, a pure conjecture. Now I have one, and my whole Self can be glad of it. ***My body is a wholly neutral thing. ACIM, Lesson #294.***

Ω

286.

A

Dreams are fantastic. Incredible things happen in dreams that do not directly happen in waking life. But what part of waking life is a dream? We are under the tyranny of belief systems and authorities. Are we ever free? Could it be said we are in the bondage of thought and belief? Who questions them? Who is free of belief and dreams of authority man has instituted over other men, over himself? Freedom is an aspect of being. "I am free" has meaning only in a world in which mankind has imagined himself in bondage, in a prison of sorrow and discontent. Without a world of bondage there would be no need for freedom. An eagle doesn't think of freedom until it is caged. The waking dream from which we all need to wake is a thought of bondage, of being under another's authority, of being a victim of circumstances, of working for a living doing something absolutely meaningless—the various entrapments in which thought has entwined us. What would break the bonds? The first step is to see I am a prisoner and notice what imprisons me. Then I see what I think is necessary is not. Food, clothing, shelter are necessary. My beliefs are not. Nationalism is not. Suspicion, hate, judgments are not. Gratefulness is necessary, even for my mistakes that can be recognized and not repeated. When I see a mistake that keeps me bound to sorrow, and I can give it up – then I can be free and awaken from the dream. Awake I am free.

Ω

287.

A Self-centeredness of the ego possesses a person and mental masturbation results. Isolated in this ego self, there is a sense of despair and frustration. A meaningless world results. Mental masturbation turns to sexual masturbation and futility and ineffectualness permeates one's thinking. What would it take to break out of this rut of self-centeredness, to be whole and related to life and other fellow humans in the fullest way? Human thought is separated and isolated, almost by its very nature, because the mind has been unfairly wrenched from the body in a kind of puritanical demise. And it *is* a demise. Sex has become naughty in the consciousness of Americans, and even more perverse, associated with the worst kinds of violence. One need but turn on the TV and witness the insanity of it. Murder and the most ghastly of crimes dominate the media and the dramatic versions of criminal shows, and sex is a tease. Commercials use buxom and skinny women to sell products to arouse the human urges to a purpose—to sell something—which is a perversion of the whole purpose of our original intuitional/sexual body and mind. Diversions are good for business. Advertisements play on and perpetuate a pervading unfulfillment. The body is no different from the mind. Innocence begins with the integration of body with the Mind which is whole. What is good is whole, without violence. It is our choice to stop being mesmerized by the violence and diversions.

Ω

288.

A

Mysticism begins when I honestly say "I don't know," which is admitting that seeking and striving to accumulate knowledge has come to an end. It doesn't deny anything which is real—like rocks, trees, my body—but it doesn't accept ideas and opinions, acquired skills, etc. as the measure of wisdom. At the root of my being is emptiness, a void from which my reality flows. I need do nothing to be who I am as my Creator created me. Vigilance is required to catch my memory replaying as sorrow, problems, goals, motives, etc. These "thoughts" need to be released from the mind. Talking doesn't release them. Writing doesn't release them. Only having a good look at myself and questioning what is inside me releases them. What "makes me who I think I am" is a kind of non-judgmental vision and questioning process. This process of questioning will help me release my "educated ignorance." Forgiveness releases, yet even my "understanding" does not comprehend this release. Anything I "know" is questionable. The questioning and the rejection of the known, the conditioned, the patterns of memories, is a process which awakens my awareness of Who I Am. I go closer to emptiness, peace and joy. In order to escape from a prison, first I must know I am in one, then atone for the "cause" which got me there, then be grateful for my release. Without being grateful, I will not recognize my freedom. Without action to undo my thought, I fool myself.

Ω

289.

A real poet, a mystic, is in touch with the outer edges of thought—at the edge where thought itself ceases—and beyond that is a reality not contaminated by the past or by predictable conventions. To the status quo of conventions, a real poet is a revolutionary, a threat to the prevailing order of things; therefore, he represents chaos, or the "destructive" side of the Creative. And because he represents chaos, pundits of conventional "wisdom" reject him in his day because they cannot reach the heights and depths of his new insight that would require real change, a letting go of old and dead thought forms, and a total shaking up of the hierarchies of power and dominance. The poet does not care for man-made rules. His only concern is for the natural laws which govern life itself: the Love in creation that puts the milk in the mother's breast; the rain, sun, and air which sustain the vast vegetation of the earth; the mystery of the stars; and the infinite size of the universe. A poet brings himself and his readers or viewers into crisis. This is the crisis of being, one which shows the falseness of the limited self, so it can die. And die it must because until it dies, I cannot totally embrace my Capital Self who is free, who never dies. Without a "death" of my conditioned self, the original Adam, my new man, cannot emerge. A long and tedious process of emptying myself is the work of a poet. And for that most of society often ignores or rejects him.

Ω

290.

A

Writing about fictional characters, drawn from life with all the descriptions of psychological subtlety, is the work of a novelist who weaves a story from their actions and interactions. Fiction is not really "made up" in the sense that it is derived by the writer from his life experience or an attribute of a distinct and striking character—again from the author's life or observation of life. There is no such thing as fiction; what is drawn is real in the sense of the artist's view. Even the most surreal or mythic setting and action can have some direct metaphysical relationship with the way things are. Even in so called "real life," thought taints our experience; perception often predetermines the quality of action. A story is of life. Life tells a story. The novel, called fiction, is the story-telling format. These are facts. But what is not so obvious is the relationship between the author's cosmology and the story itself—his or her philosophy of the universal Life Force. The characters become spokesmen for the author to get across major aspects of his own world view. And it is false to assume the author works diligently to describe in great detail his characters and spontaneous accounts of their interactions without some intention to communicate some moral issue. Not the moral of "good or bad," but the moral that presents Life as accurately and vividly as the writer can. This true-to-life quality makes fiction a good measure of the artist's insight and Self-honesty pertaining to his own character and Life observations.

Ω

291.

A

"Beauty is only the first touch of terror we can still bear, and it awes us so much because it so coolly disdains to destroy us." From Rilke's "Duino Elegy #1." Beauty does confront our hideous shortcomings and therefore requires we bear that terror to face ourselves. What it "disdains to destroy" in us is non-beauty, of which we are full; therefore, the terror of being exposed, of being seen for the paltry thing we are. But we are in awe of something so powerful that it *can* destroy us—as if we are certain of being burnt so totally that the new phoenix of our Self can newly arise. Why not? That is where human doubt gains all of its horrible momentum, and why the psyche cannot ever allow itself to be fully destroyed. Hence, we can only bear that "first touch" of beauty, that first touch of "terror," that the ego sees as a certainty of its inevitable end. And at some point, we turn away from whatever form beauty presents because the terror becomes unbearable and our death un-faceable. We skirt the real issue, the death of our own mortality, the doorway into our own immortality. "And death, once dead, there's no more dying then," said W. Shakespeare. But we succumb to the terror and bolt, never going through that doorway to the angels. As it would be, life consists of that terror to embrace immortality, to look with ever gazing eyes toward beauty, and not to look away, allowing our illusion of temporality to be destroyed.

Ω

Elegies Between Heaven and Earth

1.

A

Where have you gone? How deeply do you go, you who does the cleansing, my spirit, my love? Is that mystery where you wait under the other side of death your soul sent there in haste to find the keys in that akashic book that unbind my ties to ancient mortal sorrow? I am waiting because I have not chosen to depart, rather to stay unto the end of time when I can say, "Yes, it is finished." Would endurance be the hourglass, sorrow my sand falling, falling down to leave my upper half free and empty. There my sand has fallen still to remain so collected in lower regions of my mortal half, my body yet intact, and memory those crystal bits so uncountable and still. Inverted now you go above, leaving those regions prepared, the new receptacle of silence, transmuted sand rightly so below. You in my top half now, above that tiny channel through which my sorrow flowed. As above, so below, and when birth again would turn endurance over once more, begin that fall of sands through the crescent of your love, again would I fall down gladly through you, gladly to my lower regions where my sorrow turned to gold, my sands of sorrow stilled. My soul is free to rise into my upper half, up again through you, through the tiny funnel to the sky above, free of obscuring sands, empty now into an atmosphere clean. Would you prepare my way, you who domesticate yourself for me, you who are my devotion?

Ω

2.

A

There is a point where my body and mind are lodged between space and time, and the Infinite. Where else could I be, but here and now? The obvious locutions of my thought in language—not sought but given—rest on that pinnacle that places me between two worlds. I am here and now with observances of memory, without which I could hardly feel my body or write my thoughts upon the paper of a long tradition of speaking. Speaking of those things we knew before, those things that live barely in regions available to my reach, dimly defined in the present, enduring—yet, into the persisting worlds of my attentions. A point is where I am each moment; but where I place that point is the question. Between two worlds it is. Now, would I lament or rejoice, given to my solitude or my melding? Am I sanctioned off, as you from me? Is there much of a difference between you and me; between a star and me; between all the galaxies I do not know, and my Self ? Like an invisible universe that can't be seen no matter what my method employed to view—there, at that point between two worlds, I would position myself securely between the known and the Great Unknown, an affiliate of both memory and emptiness. Experience is like an immortal wick, one that never burns out. Then, is my mind/body lit in truth, exactly where I am, as who I am still, now without a time nor place to hem me in? Why wait to leave the body behind while still in it? Go to that point now between the worlds; why wait for hell to run its course? Uncertainty is but the mirage of clinging to a need to know. I do not need that when a universe so much larger than accumulated memory

ALPHA OMEGA

awaits me. The point of my Being is here, between two worlds—amidst the one of finite atoms numbered; the other Immeasurable by any instrument of thought I may apply to enhance my limited understanding. Who needs to understand to be? Could a tree tell you how many leaves it has on any given day? Were you around when the foundations of the universe were being laid? Do not lament; relinquishment of knowledge is the beginning of wisdom. Love need not know all the details of physicality, nor speculations of things beyond. It knows "I AM" and nothing more. Nothing more is needed.

Ω

3.

A

I hover over a query, the one of sustenance so basic as the very food I put into my mouth and the shelter that keeps me from freezing to death in the winter months. Yet now I live in the midst of money, as if I could eat those little pieces of green paper and small metal discs, forgetting all from whence the very air I breathe exchanges its oxygen within me. There are forces of life I do not see; beginnings and endings constantly exchanging their formations and dissolutions. Amidst them, there I am, some small dot on a cosmic plane of infinity. I almost disappear. I go to speak, and I cannot. What have I to say that is not predictable and dead already? Newness comes to me as something not my own, giving life and sustenance in a life otherwise devoid and wasted. Yet, every breath an affirmation I am forgiven; and I become the very air I breathe and the light that makes my vision clear is within me also, otherwise how would I see at all? Matter moves by other forces I do not perceive, but in the movement would I know these forces are the founders of a universe and me a player in the great dance of creation, appearing as a tiny aspect of appreciation. I ponder providence. So long as I have purpose here, will I be held sustained by Hands of God I barely dare to mention, too massive in scope on the scale that holds my daily being balanced.

Ω

4.

A

Inundation of words falling into my consciousness from who knows where; is it from memory or from some other Source, the One Who is Creator of all things speaking through these little hands I place within those larger Ones, the Ones now moving worlds? What could I say that possibly has not been spoken a thousand times before? So much thought and so much sorrow has the human utterance endured. What would it take to be new and clean, something of an inspiration from on high pulsing in my veins and waiting to come out of these fingertips, these Hands of larger Ones? People pass along the road; a convergence that I witness, each going his own way, each absorbed in thought of his own making. What would I be to them as mere observer? Yet as a brother would I be as friend, if only from afar, non-obtrusive in their flow, an ambient witness adding some distant communion if only known by me in silence. Just my very looking gives its notice, adds some vital heat to the surrounding air. I converge for a moment with them, then go elsewhere in my mind, the blessing gone, my attention placed on new observances, none ever quite exactly like the former, those passing movements of a tactile actuality, those passing convergences, those passing people, players in some cosmic dance of outermost communion.

Ω

5.

A

It is night, and I am still, in waiting for your voice. There is silence and the sound of my breath, and outside a world of cacophonous sounds as well. The automobile rumbles, starting from a distance, loudening, then just as quickly fading; the voices of the people walking, laughing, unaware of being heard; a car door slams; then I return to silence, always silence, what greater sound than this, the one sound encompassing all the rest, the one sound contained in all sound, the ringing sound of silence. It is night, and I am still, in waiting for some strong voice that speaks a truth from sounds inside this space in front of me. It is a matrix of envelopment, an air around the bodies of close orbit, some passing, some staying, yet all a part of stillness reigning, even the moving things impress their strokes into the vapor of observances. My body whole moves beyond its bounds; why can it not contain the sounds and the night and shadowy forms, and the light from the lamp, and the black trunks of trees outside my window, and the coffee cup empty, the disparate pens flatly lying on the surface of the desk, papers in thin flakey layers, a lone clip, the keyboard and its sounds of fingers clicking, moving over the letters in search of words? Indeed it does. I listen again to hear a silence, and the enveloping sounds of night so still, so quiet, so myself.

Ω

6.

A

Speak not about things, but what it is to be a thing, uttered, more real than mere words can describe; rather something touchable, palpable to all my senses and not just a verbally formed veneer. If I talked about water you could not drink, what good is your thirst? The weaver I would be of lies. A simple nothing is better. As I fill my lungs so would you, a moment of notice in this ever present Now. I could remark on what I see; would you see the same with sharing eyes? Between us can all sense of separation end? You have your own observance of things. Can I bring yours into mine; would you wish to take an empathetic part and see behind my eyes, the same as I see, what I see, and how I see it? What would I see so silent, so distilled in my field that even words appear superfluous? Ahead of us is space, marvelous open space filled with myriads of matters beseeching to our minds; hold these in our thoughts as we spot them with eyes of blamelessness, so pure, so uncontaminated by our sieve of judgments and veils of interpretations—color like an aqua glacier, the bottle of ice-blue, crystal glass as an elongated cube, sculpted full, with solar water almost to the neck, so still, held contained by a cylinder of cork.

Ω

7.

A

I, on a seat somewhere between heaven and earth upon which I ask of Heaven, "Are you a place with firmament over and ground underneath curving outward in all directions under me? Why could you not be here and now where I sit, inasmuch as I can devoid myself of thought, memory but a mirage of passing, already gone? Why could your compass not circle my own cosmos as I circumambulate into you leaving all imposed barriers behind, like tiny fences made of matchsticks? So much I do not know of you, Heaven, a state of mind 'where conflict is done.' I would not really be anywhere else, unless I choose a hell, a denial of some original Self that could not conceive of opposites. All I have made of unhappiness but a persistence of memory, imagined separation, a station outside the gates in space and time, excommunicated, an exile of my own making, alone and isolated by thoughts of ancient sorrows. The door to joy is in front of me, behind and to the side, above and below me, within my own eyes and ears, my hands and feet, but at the service of a decision. Will I enter this portal by the Liberty of my own Reality? The door is open, and I am but a fool to linger longer in my little world of horrors."

Ω

8.

A

There is a space inside me that has no sound, where my senses do not creep about in search of things to eat, always hungry in their appetites, wanting constantly to bite into some experience. The ones who renounce the senses are tied to them. I do not renounce them; I have a body, so let it be itself, senses and all. The space of no sound is something else. The body comes to rest, along with the mind; nothing to do or feel, and no cause to live or die for, only what already is, as it is. It is a state of Zero. When I get closer to Zero my thought gets a chill. Some remote threat takes me over and I am frightened of complete obliteration—but it does not come. It is a death of no death, the kind where access is open to empty realms while I am still filled up with memory. Memory is persistent; but this is an awakening of a state of being long forgotten, received through the undoing of attacks on myself and attacks on other people. No disparaging thought; can you imagine what that is like, a state of mind totally carefree? No fear of death comes into it. There is no sound but silence.

Ω

9.

A

Isolation's error is just a yearning to meld with everything. Otherwise I am just as I am, not wanting to be a tree or a frog or a mountain. I would rather be myself, an observer of all this stuff we call a universe. When I want anything, I don't have it. Otherwise there is no need to want it; but when I already have what I think I want, and recognize I do, then there is nothing to want. I am still because I have everything. Tara Singh told me, "When you don't want anything, you have everything." It is a rare person who can say that as his truth. Most of us are unfulfilled in some fashion, seeking something we do not have. This puts us in the march of time—in some kind of dissatisfaction. Desire is a powerful force; wanting things takes a lot of energy. Not wanting anything takes little energy. Conservation of energy keeps my inner forces intact. When I contain myself thus, I have more energy to act; action is then something natural, like when the trees get their leaves in the Spring or water falling over a cliff and running downhill. I do not yearn to meld with anything, because my body cannot meld, and my mind is already joined with other minds, otherwise you could not read this. And my spirit, unknowable by thought is in everything already. So, where's the problem here? I think there is none.

Ω

10.

A

A fasting of my whole Self is a thing I must do. Is it possible to keep the senses free of their objects and fast my heart too? My eyes, could you be blind for a moment; my ears, would you be willing not to hear; my hands, refrain from touching things; my mouth and nose, no more taste and smell? The fast of the whole Self is more difficult; it is a meeting with the Great Unknown. All those things I thought I was I am not. Things I pursued to accomplish don't mean much. Learning was a function of some self-imposed restriction; my body itself, but an artifact of some memory pattern; my character tinged by some predestined events. I need to fast from all of this; a complete fast, like a cleansing from the inside out. Jesus went into the wilderness for forty days. Walked right out into the desert with only the clothes on his back. Gone. Didn't ask permission from family members, just headed out without purse or script or even a lunchbox. Imagine that. I don't know if I could do it, but I've pondered it more than once. Can meeting my Maker face to face happen within the confines of a conventional life? I doubt it, but maybe. Most of convention is from a security based on fear. I need to fast; the form it may take is unclear to me, but I see the need. That awareness is like a message, is like a cry into the night of my being, is like an oath to some dynamic solitude.

Ω

11.

A

He passed today, 4/7/2006, if I could call it passing. His body soon to go into the fire he so loved, where it is turned to dust, and scattered to the winds, and out into the four corners of the universe. He used his body well, to teach the world he was not a body, but representing Love, which often looked like the lion's face two inches from my own in some kind of roar. Tara Singh, which means the Star Lion, returned fully to the Spirit world today, far beyond thought, out into the constellations where he may join those other stars, so silent and so still, not speaking, but only sending light from a million miles away. Up there with Orion and Andromeda, up there with the sages of old, the Great Rays, the ones who came and left their light for all the world to see. He is with them now, with the timeless only. Now it is I who must open my eyes to the Self and see the light inside he left with me, the light of Truth which he imparted, beyond my thought, in our life-for-life relationship. He is fully in me now, as much as I can bear, into the dark night where he can be seen to flicker in my firmament, a beacon still and silent, like a guiding star, the lion of my life, the one who holds direction sure, the one whose words live on inside my breast, the one who laid his body down today and went to join the angels in his rightful place. Tara Singh, you are father and mother to me, you are brother and friend as well. I bid you my farewell.

Ω

12.

A

Accountable to my own conscience, there I would face my Maker and say whether I lived up to those talents given me. None but I will assess in the end my life and what I gave, to what I aspired and fulfilled. Can I look myself in the mirror and say OK, you gave it your all, and then go to rest? Until I can there is work still to do below the heavens, and I in body and mind set myself to do it; each day but a microcosm of a whole life, and my thoughts, words and deeds but a trailing set of footprints along some bidden way, longer and larger than I can fathom with each incremental step of daily actions. Where am I going if not to be who I am, at peace with the sunrise within myself? There is no place else to go. All paths lead inward to the depths, past all the raucous memories of things gone awry, events gone asunder, to a place of peaceful vistas of spring mornings cool and bright, lime green leaves sprouting on the ends of twigs. Much in this world is sham, but Nature isn't; Her elements are diverse and still, even in their broad and determined movements. Stillness is the nectar of wisdom, because within its embrace are all things, no problems, and vast space to observe the beauty of what is right in front of me, totally free and forgiven. Peace comes to one who extends peace, as the great oak along the terrace waits patiently through the last of the cold days, catching the new warm light, higher in the sky, ready to burst.

Ω

13.

A

Having my own voice is not that easy, to say something new that hasn't been said before. Mankind goes on in the same kinds of conflicts, mostly over Self-interest—don't mess with my money or my oil or my woman or my, my, my whatever. Here we are in an age when men will die themselves to kill other men who they have decided are evil, or not fit to live, or just plain not in agreement with them, the victims in a drama of *God on my side*. We got this God thing all wrong, like we made up a "Big Guy in the Sky" who listens to us and nobody else and has our best interests in mind, but not really the interests of those who don't believe in our particular Big Guy version. It's all a bunch of baloney. That's not to say there isn't some Great Divine Intelligence that we could call the Great Unknown, which is a Life Force that created and moves all things, me being one of them. But this is in all other humans too, no more or no less than in me. So how could God be on my side and not on the other's side as well, being equally in everything? The human being is still in some kind of a belief sleep—I believe this or that thing which divides me from people who believe something else. No belief is better, the intelligence of not knowing has more honesty than a skill-based education that makes everyone a wage earner to fit into some corporate system of necessity.

Ω

14.

A

Would my muse be but myself? Within me is the universe still, like a seed before the great sycamore grows. There I would be to burst, then *bang* into form, spewed upon the Void and gathering my trunk and limbs together spread toward you, my sun. My sun, great light that ceases not even here in the night of my dark—would I grope for a toggle switch to turn you back on to me. My branches to the outer ends so thin and delicate, nearly shrunk to nothing, here twigs of supple fiber ending almost into air itself. Now would my winter end, my silence cease. Through snows have I stood dead appearing to not be, so frozen was myself within a forgotten world so dim, so cold, so long I went unnoticed. And now does a new spring light come to the outer edges of my reach, would my tips tremble as I come awake. This light would draw my juices up from roots below my ground, firmly would I grab this matrix of massive earth and draw moisture into me, a drink to quench my thirst and send fluids up and out into my furthest most tips, the ones so delicately filled with light. Together these, liquid earth and light would sprout anew a myriad of growing things, thousands upon thousands, none alike, but all never to be found before and never again to be. Now would they come out quietly and slowly as little yellow sprigs of green, springing out in a miracle explosion, composing a whole tree, the sycamore of stalwart being that is me, with leaves so turned in search of light from thee, my sun.

Ω

15.

Α

Flat on the earth am I. We call it round but would I leap and bound on level planes of my vicissitudes so tiny I cannot tell what curvature there is to earth, except from pictures sent on high, from lonely outposts orbiting my home? It is a world on which I walk convex, over hill or dale, beyond the crest imagination goes. "Walk on," it says, "onto some unknown plain or valley low." Flatness would I seek at night to lay my head; rolling off this orb of earth I would not want, into abyss or crags of jagged rock, plummeting off a sloping edge, falling there, into my own oblivion. No. Flatness is a good thing. Galileo was right to recant. For heaven sakes, who ever heard a man could perch on a mountain slope forever, or on the side of an orb plummeting through space? So here I am terraced, a ziggurat of ascending stairs each level flat and sure, each place for good repose. There would I rest on flat terrain, in my bed alone, complete in my solace of solitude. No heaven or hell but just what is accepted here and now, terms divine, no more but no less. I walk upon the planet new, no past or pre-ordained future to tweak untold anxiety, but only this, the flat place where I am, my feet on ground secure. Roundness is a reality untouched. It is a shape of a practical unknown. I am satisfied without a view around the bend. Within me is the world, flat or round would cease to be conflicting roles, I play my part upon the plains of my own abode.

Ω

16.

A

Hands are the portal into the soul. What but they can move the mountains that would make me worthy of God's Son? Even an utterance unheard before alone cannot take form without my hands. How would I say to you into eternity those thoughts upon my heart, down in my breast, into my eruptive regions? Were it not for my hands, my mouth would betray me, uncertain of what I saw until written and pondered for a while. Like a scratch into the growing wood of my impressions, a carving from my hands that shape an instance, a reflection, a nuance in the figurine of language now. What I'm thinking is shaped and molded by my hands, those dutiful servants of my craft. I am grateful for my hands which lead me along and stay in tandem with my innermost parts. My hands that seem to be the guide, the willing workers of my direction taken, the ones who lead the way in present time into the certainty of an unknown future as long as they are working true in time I call the Now, why would my future not be true as well? I am responsible for Now only, and it is my hands which shape my gestures into that. The Now is who I am. Only Now. Now only. Hands are present Now. Where and when could they be? I have never seen future hands nor past hands. So would these be forgiven hands in a posture still, one of general repentance, so what they do is cleansed into the seventh generation.

Ω

17.

A

Who are angels but the dead returned? How would they come but in a shape from a passing time, a long-ago person in the Now who lives? Need they a body having gained such certainty without one? Glad in those regions unbeholden to space and time, they move freely to the very threshold of my desire, waiting only for my invitation to enter. Yet have they already made escape and cut their bonds to earth, released to go into the farthest regions of creation. How much further could they go, these messengers returned from Andromeda or some such galaxy afar? Return they must. How could they leave one brother behind still tied to some corner of the earth in ropes of physicality? How could they not hear cries of agony within the mouths of starving babes, an earth embroiled with suffering? Without ears and eyes and bodies solid, compassion but a memory still held within their mind, they fly to us on wings of return and would embrace us crying and wipe away those tears without delay. Their joy uninterrupted. These are angels who died already; why would death deceive them anymore? So would they come back to us, the living, reminding that our souls will rise to them at last and be released. In grace do they convene within the dome around us; are ever present unaware they do not share our sorrow, and thus would empathy bring them closer to an earth forgiven and we through them our joy returned.

Ω

18.

A

The senses of myself include those of my body. Condemn them not because God does not condemn, but rather gives them use in service to my happiness; the sinless portion of myself who God has said is all there really is of me. Would desire be fulfilled? It must, or in renunciation denial gets the best of me. Only desire fulfilled can be renounced, for then the news is known and all the facts are clearly seen for what they are. Desire unfulfilled would be a block, an unrequited love, a memory of lack in a universe of no lack. Then would my desires be direct and simple, basic to the essential part of me, already in my character and makeup. Something natural in the course of my life to grow into, like the tree grows into itself from the potential seed. Nothing God created is denied. Life is a mystery—mystery is a life. I would follow my own real nature into the very acts which make me whole. My own goodness is the motion within my very cells. Let not my body be a thing of scorn, in revulsion from a higher part of me. As above, so below. Body is spirit and spirit is body. Have I died enough to be alive? Have I suffered finally to be free of all pain? As what is, so am I in this present moment. I would accept myself as is, throughout the pleasure and the pain. I deny no part of myself. My juices flow vital, and I breathe the inspiration of life and expiration of death simultaneously.

Ω

19.

A

What could time be but a chance to replicate myself? Like the cell divides to make itself again, repetition is the law of growth. What I grow into is my Self again, more enhanced and defined in the focus of multiplicity, each facet whole, never lacking a thing in its independence. So would the artist be the portraitist of the Self, not of narcissism but of Him who lives in everyone; call him the universal man in me, the new Adam and Eve, the man and woman both. I am the Father, Mother, and the Child—the seed, the womb, and the newly born—all these at once. At the juncture between heaven and earth am I, on the pinnacle of an Everest would I exist at the beginning of a firmament, and there between the upper and lower regions of my being still reach up and down to both. As above, so below. Would these not be mirrors in my mind? What is one but the other as some Great God would have them be? I, at that juncture, at the point of disappearance, the middle of an X, receive my manna still. Where else could I be? My mind goes empty here, here where all matter is held on the tip of a pin and the ethers converge to be manifest. That is my natural place where I sit on the throne of my domain, at the union of heaven and earth, the tiny portal reduced to almost nothing, through which the whole universe may flow—matter to ether, ether to matter, the constant exchange. Spirit and body come together whole.

Ω

20.

A

Do I want to see what I denied because it is the truth? Truth will correct my errors. Do I want it? There is no vacillation in it. I cannot want the truth then "not want" it. Once I ask to see the truth and it is revealed to me then I am awakened. Once I am awake, it is not possible to be asleep. If I am "not happy," then I have not accepted the truth as true. There is a peace, a stillness, and a happiness. These are the truth. I have denied them in my insane "back and forth" from so-called happiness to sorrow. I have chosen to vacillate because I have denied the truth. Now would I stop attacking myself as incapable of receiving the truth. I have already received it. I need but stop denying it. That's all. When my mind "seeks" for evidence to make it "unhappy," this is a denial of truth. All depression is this denial. I am the one who perpetuates depression. I am the one who has been denying truth all along. Defending my positions, rejecting my own happiness. It is my ego which does this, not my Self. When I finally decide to be my Self this denial will cease, because my mind will now be in the service of my Self, whose only state of being is happiness. I can decide Now. There is no future decision. The present is all there really is of "time." Forgiveness is a total release or not at all. Though I thought I had forgiven myself, I had not. It must be complete and constant to be real forgiveness.

Ω

21.

A

Standing on my own, with whatever powers of observation bestowed upon me, I would pause to question, "what do I see?" Hunting and planting, the two most utilized methods of obtaining food are at the root of man's quest for sustenance. But "man cannot live on bread alone." His body needs bread or meat or what have you, but his mind needs something greater than physical sustenance. Practicalities in a modern world require money. Man hunts for money as a substitute for buffalo or deer. He domesticates business instead of cows and goats. The beasts of burden become other men in complex structures of employers and employees. To have a job becomes almost essential to survival. Yet man is more than a body surviving. What is essential to life becomes very simple when attachments are relinquished. Food, clothing, shelter, heat, exercise—the physical needs of the body—then something of peace, stillness and silence are the most important qualities within the mind. Spirit, so rarefied words cannot describe it, is a transcendental reality accepted on these planes by faith, not perception, and corroborated by awareness, not learning. A movement in life toward happiness, toward Self-honesty, toward the correction of errors and the ending of sorrow—this movement, after the fact, can instill a sense of certainty the Holy Spirit is actually at work in my life.

Ω

22.

Α

Patterns of personality are mostly fixed; everything in life has its own tendencies and conditioning. Experience and a person's response to that experience are according to his various attributes of character. "You can't teach an old dog new tricks." Our habits are well entrenched. What happens when I observe myself and become still? The tendencies that run my life are in full view and I can question them. "Why am I doing that?" Letting go of a tendency is the path of virtue, and it has nothing to do with another or with "good works," or with great accomplishments. It is an emptying out of the personality. I cease to strive; therefore, I cease to project and pursue desires. I move closer to gratefulness for what is already provided. My needs become simpler and the most cherished thing in life is the time and space to be still. To keep this space of stillness open, to sustain the peace which it imparts, is the main work. Call it vigilance. There are many distractions to which I need to say no. It is not a denial of the body, but an establishment of priorities. Stillness is paramount, and when I can say, **The stillness of the peace of God is mine, ACIM Lesson #273**, then the things that surround me in number are absorbed essentially into my Self. The awareness of something whole, a state transcendental of the apparent separations of "individual" things, comes about in this stillness. When I am still, God's peace(wholeness) is mine.

Ω

23.

A

To lift myself out of conditioned thought requires a teacher who has already done this. We went to the priests and the erudite people and found them just as caught in their egos as everyone else. So where would a teacher be found? *A Course in Miracles* represents the teacher, the Thoughts of God to His Son, given from Jesus to Dr. Schucman, given from Dr. Schucman to Tara Singh, and given from Tara Singh to me, with instructions to live by those words, not by learning. The teacher's job is to silence thought. Because he comes from silence, that is what he imparts. Everything he says has silence in it; therefore, it has the power to undo. What does it undo? My conditioned thought which keeps me bound to problems. A relationship with my Creator is one of freedom; a relationship with the teacher is one of undoing all that is not freedom. Like a psychic surgeon, the teacher removes misperception of the mind that blocks awareness of this freedom. Things that bind me are undone. Life becomes a blessing, a benediction when I am grateful. I am vigilant now as a result of having a teacher, having flowed into the reservoir of his living water. This water of forgiveness, the undoing of thought, is the greatest gift anyone can give. It brings me into the present in which memory is not so strong, and creation is whole and gentle in my eyes, the witness to a world of inner peace.

Ω

24.

A

Worship is an adoration of the Unknown. The great mysteries in life converge in everyone, but not all give attention to them. For instance, the role death plays in life, that function of "ending," is a subject avoided in most living rooms until it is foisted upon us through necessity. But we are all quite happy to spend hours watching mindless TV. Worship is attention given to something, in most cases something sacred. Native Americans worshipped Nature and her aspects—the land and the animals. Worship of the Great Spirit as seen through the aspects of nature give form to rites held sacred. An animal that provided the tribe with sustenance may be honored in a dance. To them everything was sacred and worthy of worship. Spiritually adept but not as technologically advanced, these natives were supplanted by the white man who came with guns and greed for land and gold. Our "worship" justified killing the "heathens" because they did not believe as we did. Possession was the rule of European culture. Immigrants aspired to acquire land whether it belonged to them or not. Just take it. The more innocent natives, though crude by sophisticated European standards, had a simple view. One could not "own" the land, which as a living being sustained their life. Possession was not their need, nor was building cities. Living in harmony with their elemental surroundings was most important and was a form of worship.

Ω

25.

A conscious life is attention. To what I give my attention is of what I am conscious. Attention given to exactly what is here and now brings me closer to stillness. Memory tries to intrude into the mind, but attention, when intensified, does not allow memory to take hold. In the awareness of stillness is the power of attention. The senses, not given to any particular thing, are fully relaxed and awake. Stillness does not mean the denial of the senses, but rather an incorporation of them into stillness. Moving objects can be part of stillness because stillness is a state of mind which does not hold on to anything, accepts all things, and tends to the needs of the body. All of life in physical form has a movement. All of life without physical form imparts stillness. The two are connected. Life and death are connected. Attention is not physical but what it observes may be. Attention observes something—it could be a physical form or a mental concept. It could observe itself. Attention observing attention slows the mind. When thought is slowed, more stillness enters. Less movement makes more silence. More silence brings awareness of more peace. Peace is happy; it is free of conflict. Peace accepts what is, as it is. Peace is of God, beyond thought. It embraces the Unknown. I erase my thought. What is left when that work is done is only the reality of what is, free of conflict, free of attachment to physicality. What is left is Stillness and Silence.

Ω

26.

A

Who am I talking to in the end? First, I would say, to myself. I write alone, so naturally I would be the first to hear my own words. I do not use a secretary to take down what I hear to say. Therefore, I talk to myself. But as words are meant to communicate, and communication involves two—one to the other and back again—then I write for a reader as well. This is good news, because then I have another who may benefit from what I say, or may not benefit, in which case who can tell me what I write makes sense or not, describes a truth or not, will be read by others or not. But I am the first one with whom what I write must make sense. It is night and I am not tired. I sit before going to bed and write something. Sometimes I read another person's writings but at some point, I am concerned only with what creative things will "come out of me," so I write to discover that. I try not to preconceive what I will write but poise myself at that juncture between the Unknown and this present moment when I am here to take down what I hear within my head. Since I only have access to that and nothing else, I am the best one to take note. Do these thoughts mean anything? I don't know. Are they just memories of another man's wisdom? I don't know. Perhaps some I acknowledge is from the teacher, but even I must venture into my own unknown to find my own voice.

Ω

27.

A

What used to be called melancholia is now called depression, and we have a drug for it. Lincoln had it. Beethoven had it; Rilke probably had it. But this condition did not hamper their greatness, their expression in life which they came to impart. It may have been a symptom of the depth at which they observed life and its apparent difficulties. How could anyone endure the great suffering and loss of life on a first-hand basis as Lincoln did during the Civil War without the somber mood and resolve of a deep melancholia? For a man who deeply felt the plight of the common working man, or the foot soldier, or the slave, or even the undaunted humanity of the so-called enemy, how could he witness the carnage of war and not be a bit depressed? Anger, attack, and man's inhumanity to man, are as old as the hills. When will men stop causing suffering? The artist, though he may not be participating in conflict, has such a keen sense of empathy with those who suffer, it is as if he is the one suffering himself. That is the true meaning of compassion— one who shares in the suffering of mankind. Beethoven wrote in a time of great strife; the Napoleonic wars swept across Europe. The cruelties of war were apparent. He could delve into the depth of human suffering and come up for air in the form of his incredible music. It was an inner sound he heard, one of great melancholia, one of endless Joy and compassion.

Ω

28.

A

There are missed opportunities in life which do not return, and for these I have a deep sense of repentance. In the instance of leaving home to be with Tara Singh in his final years, I could not. He said to me, "You are needed at the Foundation," and I said, "I am needed at home as well." It was my conviction at the time. Both were true. Little did I know the consequences that would transpire. Tara Singh was hospitalized and put in managed care. Others who had long been associated with him and the Foundation were now in charge and I had very little input. In the next three years I would witness Taraji's physical decline and my own deep sense of uncertainty about my own role in it. He suffered and so did I. Visits to Kansas and Iowa to see parents in K.C. and Melanie Coulter, who eventually took on the major role in his care, have been more frequent, and many trips to Los Angeles when Taraji was there have not made this sense of repentance any less. Perhaps it became stronger. I am responsible for what I see. Have I honored the teacher for being in my life as much as I can? I don't know. Have I punished myself for making a wrong decision? Did I act from fear? I have these nagging questions in myself. Obviously, it was a replayed memory manifesting as a decision to stay in my self-made life. Was it wrong? I don't know. Do I feel a tinge of regret for a road not taken? Yes. This is why repentance and forgiveness are so much needed.

Ω

29.

A person takes on certain things in his life to complete. Relationships with people are the primary concern and where most of the work lies. Relationships are with family, relatives and ancestors, with friends, work companions and acquaintances. An even greater responsibility than the relationship with parents and spouse, is the one with the Teacher who silences my thought. A teacher will question everything I think I know in order to get to the bottom of my Identity—who I am as God created me. He doesn't care how many degrees I have. He is concerned with what is actual in my life. The external situation is not real. What is in need of my attention is the internal aspects of myself which determine my external aspects. The teacher confronts me head on to undo my illusions, my lies, falseness, pretense, sentimentality. Because these illusions are not my Self; they are not my Identity. My Identity knows only truth, God, love. The blocks to this knowing are my opinions, conclusions, etc. A real teacher undoes them, or rather, helps me to undo them in myself. Because he never makes me dependent, it is my responsibility to be my own Teacher, to be vigilant, to undo those misperceptions in me. Forgiveness is the means I am given to do this. It is an active role I take with Divinity to erase all the falseness in myself. I owe the Teacher, and Life which provided him, my deepest gratitude

Ω

30.

Α

Rilke writes of a future happening within us, this very moment. Call it destiny laying its foundation to receive the far-off structures of the events. As if the events are more corroborations of something already happened. He also writes of a sadness which, having gone into the core of a human being, has already changed the blood, brought a new level of awareness, and should not be thought of as something to be "rid of" or put down as debilitating a person's inner evolution. Sadness may be a great teacher in life, like a death or a vision could be. I embrace my melancholy, not because I am morbid but because there may be some key in it that unlocks some hidden chamber in my heart hitherto closed off to me. Why should I not embrace it? If its sources are in me already, why should I not treat them as honored guests, get to know them intimately, and be indebted to their particular reasons and motives? Melancholy induces this need to be alone, yet why not admit the need fully without an apology for it to be socially otherwise. What is this love of solitude? Is it fear? Is it a desire to relate only to myself in some limitation of solipsism? Yet fear, like melancholy, may need to run its course. To fight disease may produce a treatment more deadly than the malaise ever was. Symptoms are treated yet causes go unnoticed. The source of fire is not wood but the rapid transmutation of some enduring energy.

Ω

31.

A

One can corner himself and ask in reference to a thought or an utterance, "Is that so?" For truth must come from the very marrow in his bones and nowhere else can it be verified. If I have not lived through a truth in some form of real-life experience or heart-felt insight into the causes in my life, then that truth is not "true" for me. I would be an armchair philosopher who is only speculating on the nature of things. When I corner myself and question the motives of my actions, 90% of activity would drop away as unnecessary. What remains after the body's needs have been met is the leisure to observe my life and comment upon it. Life is vast, nature so awesome and beautiful, the possibilities for this observance are unending. The observations of the inner life of the mind have a treasure trove of material. Just one issue has the power to clarify a truth given proper attention. For instance, loneliness versus solitude, what is the difference? I find myself alone with my thoughts often or with a medium engaged in solitary action, deriving great satisfaction from this solitude and its freedoms. Secluded from the world, I do not feel a detrimental loneliness. Loneliness is a wanting, a yearning to make contact, but some block seems to isolate me from that contact. Solitude already contains the contact. It communicates without words and extends without bodily encounter. It is pure and uncontaminated by wanting.

Ω

32.

A

I will always have some aspects of my past which loom in memory as a small or large regret, just as those actions of positive and happy growth are cause for great gratitude. The choice is mine which I choose to acknowledge. Most important to realize is that the past is gone and all events the lessons given for my evolution. The present is the only reality; what I do now and how I do it are the only real issues. What I have done cannot be changed except in my mind. I can forgive myself for my memory, thoughts, words, deeds that have caused me regret. At the time of their happening, I was unaware. All there is to do is repent for these misperceptions and actions and be grateful that they are showing what needs to be corrected. Who corrects? My responsibility is to recognize the error and petition Divinity for its correction. Divinity transmutes darkness to light. I need only invoke forgiveness to right the misperceived wrong and be vigilant to continue that invocation. Divinity's will for me is happiness, yet I must erase the memories which continue to replay as regrets. Regrets are judgments in the present about past events which cannot be altered. Forgiveness is necessary to end these judgments. I may be imprisoned as a result of a mistake, but I can forgive myself and come to harmony with my past. It is this harmony, this acceptance, which sets me free.

Ω

33.

A word comes forth out of me. Is it new? Is it from memory? Or is it something of a question from my life? Conventional relationships of blood family are strong. Then comes along a teacher who stands outside of these blood relationships, who offers a different light, a love beyond the conventional. By the conventional view he appears as a threat because he sees the conventional is often based on attachment and fear. I would ask, "Is there a step to take beyond the relationships of blood?" Just because I may think there is does not mean it is so. Most of our memory is with family. In those regions of the mind beyond family bonds, there is a bond to God, my Creator. The teacher stands close to this bond because holy relationship is his only concern. He would say, "To love God you must love and care for your brother." That is the real means toward a spiritual life. Words are meaningless unless backed by action. Who walks their talk? Who has made the conversion from memory (fear) to inspiration (love)? Talking "about it" is a travesty against truth. He who has discovered his light within has something to give the world. Repentance is necessary; not because I am a sinner but because I am like a child unaware of my thoughts and their consequences. When will I cease to rely on my own thought? What am I doing with my life, with the time my Creator has given me?

Ω

34.

A

How can it be that I write anything that is my own and not an echo of another whose greater thought has born upon me in some circumstantial way? I was not educated in writing, and though holding a Masters of Fine Arts degree from Temple University I have come to distrust the academic impetus of any work of art. Life is the impetus, and a life which has its difficulties. I have felt the pangs of isolation and obscurity but only now see the benefits of my solitude, and for better or worse, my lack of formal education when it comes to writing. After all is said and done, writing is speaking what is on my mind in the form of the written word. Seems obvious. Yet it is also something deeper. It is a question one poses to himself and the discipline to withhold conclusions and opinions so as to discover a here-to-fore unknown truth. To the extent I can discover and speak a truth is the extent my writing is Self-honest. Writing then becomes a process of Self-inquiry, or the means for something new to be revealed or something old to be better understood. I am a late bloomer. It has taken fifty-one years for me to feel remotely on the verge of possessing my own voice. I am compelled to write to uncover a truth in me. A solitude of unlimited possibilities is my most valued possession. Yet, being in the world is necessary as well. Solitude within a crowd; that is an art well worth developing.

Ω

35.

A

Once killing, war, and violence are justified, they continue to be justified. A common reason is the investment of lives lost. "These should not have died in vain," we say as a justification to "win" the war. Saving face becomes more important than saving lives. So, the war is prolonged and justified in "defense" of a cause. An act of attack is retaliated with an escalated counter-attack. Hatred, divisions, prejudices are at the root of conflicts; even deeper is the self-hate far submerged in the subconscious that gives rise to these justifications. Fear of loss interprets an attack as a threat and prompts a reaction. Governments and men of power take for granted the lives of the people who support them. The imagery of propaganda which enhances the "evil" nature of the enemy rallies the masses behind a cause worthy of war. People are sucked in by this imagery—rather than witness the "evil" within their own natures—and will project it onto an "enemy" who they can, with "good" reason, be called upon to destroy. Self-defense is a fallacy. It is asserted by a "victim" consciousness. Fundamental to the error is the mistake of attaching Identity to physical bodies and forms. We live now as body-mind-spirit, but eternity is mostly identified as Spirit. Essence precedes existent form. To defend our body, and country (a larger version of body), is to deny the invulnerability of Spirit as Identity. "In God we trust" we say, but continue to go to war on false premises.

Ω

36.

A

Without a doubt, it is obvious to any person of real reason, *A Course in Miracles* is the "second coming" of the Christ Jesus upon the planet. It manifested through Dr. Helen Schucman in New York City, was brought to the public by Tara Singh, and now given to me (anyone) to fully realize in my (his or her) life. The language is direct and simple, but it takes a different power of attention to receive what it has to offer. One must observe his own reactions and lack of application first, move through the inattentive resistance of the ego self, and be willing to invite a Higher Intelligence to aid in realizing its truth. It is not for the conditioned brain not willing to let go of its misperceptions; it is for the working person who sees the detrimental effects of his thinking and wishes to heal it or heal his mind, where all healing begins and ends. **To heal is to make happy. – Healing is a thought by which two minds perceive their oneness and becomes glad. That is why the healer's prayer is 'Let me know this brother as myself.' ACIM, Chapter 5, Introduction** Therefore, there is no one on the planet, even the vilest murderer, with whom I cannot use in this exercise. All possess a Holy Self, whether they are aware of it or not. The one I perceive as deranged is the very one I must ask, "Let me know this brother as myself." This places both of us before the altar of innocence because I can only see in myself what I see in another and vice versa. Joy is my holiest state. It is what God wills for me and all humanity.

Ω

37.

A

God's peace and joy are mine. *ACIM, Lesson #105* Organized religion holds many in the grip of a dichotomy between believers and non-believers. This is the justification for much of the conflict in the world. When there is division, the religion becomes false, a substitute for the state of wholeness which is the reason for religion in the first place. It is a deep-seeded error which misperceives the nature of God as being capable of love and hate simultaneously, or innocence and guilt. Hate is a man-made product of separation from truth. The truth is only Love exists. Man's denial of the truth produces hates, mostly self-hate, projected outward. To the degree that I misperceive God my Creator as a force capable of condemnation, is the degree I will hate myself, thus keeping the miracle away from me. *God is only Love.* All else is my own manufactured nightmare. The greatest gift in the world is God's Love in the form of complete forgiveness. The result of this forgiveness, which I must actively accept by giving, is peace and joy. In order to have love, I must give it away. Love is an Idea, consistent with the Idea of God. Within this Idea are my brother and me, equally. I can say to any brother with whom I may have grievances, *My brother, peace and joy I offer you that I may have God's peace and joy as mine.* This dissolves my conflict and I am free.

Ω

38.

April 7, 2006 at 8:05 p.m. Tara Singh passed from his body. The event was peaceful with Melanie Coulter holding his hand. A new tranquility is present since his passing, and an appreciation for my direct relationship with such a great being. On April 8th a 40-day prayer vigil was begun and my time to sit quiet is 9—10 PM. To know God is only to end my separation between myself and my brother. To have no grievances is to know Love. Knowing my brother as myself is the peace of God. There's no such thing as an enemy and no one is beyond hope. The prison of thought, belief, prejudice is surmountable because these are not true. Truth is in silence, in stillness, in peace—in the space beyond thought. To the extent I have simplified my life, I have the energy within to be who I am as God created me. Words become fewer and silence is valued beyond anything else. Tara Singh was a life teacher who dealt with the entrapments of his own life and freed himself from them. I knew him for 17 years, almost to the day. Now he belongs to the ages, and I am blessed to have his presence within me to call upon when I choose. It is my responsibility to see the Christ in him and in myself. ***Let me behold my savior in this one you have appointed as the one for me to ask to lead me to the holy light in which he stands that I may join with him. ACIM, Lesson #78*** This is my prayer to him who was my teacher, my savior, and my friend.

Ω

39.

A

In the holy light of true words, true being, true relationship, there is only gratitude. Someone remarkable came into my life and undid my illusions to the extent that I can now undo them myself. To not deceive oneself is a great gift. This is what the true teacher imparts. He is the destroyer of illusions by which we live in unawareness. Because he undoes, many are threatened by his revolutionary vision and either dismiss it as insignificant or outwardly attack its validity. Even attacking the teacher has been done. An authentic teacher is a master of relationships; he would say, "Come with me and be a fisher of men." Life for Life relationship is what the real teacher gives and demands in return. He does not teach by adding more to memory; he teaches by means of subtraction. Taking away my misperceptions by pointing them out to me in such a clear way I cannot be deceived anymore. He frees me from my own thought. I get closer to 100% responsibility for all aspects of my life and no longer pretend I am a victim of circumstances. I am responsible for every thought, word, and deed—past, present, and future in my experience. When true words come to liberate me from my thought, I must have the ears to hear by not defending myself against them. It is only my ego that can be "hurt." Part of my waking up process is to see the meaninglessness of my thought and come to accept myself as God created me.

Ω

40.

A

To the extent that I am not happy is also my need for healing. Love is joyous; my unhappiness is a refusal of love. Yet I am given a teacher, *A Course in Miracles*, and the means to realize my Self. What is the cause for this discontent but my refusal to be grateful. To be grateful for all life has given me is all that is required. My unhappiness is a thought and I am assured "my thoughts do not mean anything." The vigilance needed to cleanse constantly begins with determination not to judge or condemn myself or another. Atonement is the gift of Christ's mind, and I have that in my mind as well. Discontent is with my unwillingness; I see it, but what would end it? Who am I to place limits on God's Son? Unwillingness is a refusal to love myself. Why would I condemn who God created whole? I need not do this self-sabotage; it is my lower self of thought which does this. Conscious and subconscious mind need but unite and ask the Higher Mind, beyond perception, for the perfect and right inspiration. Before there was thought of separation there was only wholeness and joy. Separation introduced a thought of sorrow and guilt which before did not exist; therefore, Atonement was not necessary. The Comforter was given by God the instant His Son perceived discomfort. I am at the end of pretending my activities can liberate me; only acceptance of the will of God can save me, and **God's will for me is perfect happiness. ACIM, Lesson #101.**

Ω

41.

A

The purpose of the Holy Spirit, the voice for God, is to return my mind to Joy. It is possible to listen to that Voice without a trace of memory to contaminate it. I need not be an enemy of memory; events have transpired which I cannot change. I can accept them as necessary to my process of awakening. The past is gone, but memory persists. To what aspect of this memory I give my attention is my choice—Love or fear, joy or sorrow. I may choose Love and be joyful in the face of a memory of sorrow. Love is all, in the end, and I am blessed to have had a direct relationship with a great man who had risen to the level of the Self. His body and personality are no more, but his Spirit with which he continually identified, lives into eternity, and into my Self as well. The mind we share is all that matters, and sharing will always lead to the realization of unity, harmony, and peace. Who am I but a child of God within that great Self who he created? We all will eventually know Identity, but my particular urgency is to be with it now. What other time is there? If I do not claim my Identity now when will I ever? Now is the time to be at peace. Actions projected into the future to achieve this "goal" will perennially keep awareness of the Self at arms' length. Time is an illusion, a defense mechanism to hold the miracle away from me. But only Now I can accept who I am as God created me, an integral part of His Love.

Ω

42.

A

We use the word Love and have no idea what it means, like the word God. Perhaps it begins by revealing what it is not. Love is not fear, not hate, not doubt or dissatisfaction. It is not the various other tendencies resulting from some inner deficiency—greed, anger, lust, pride, attachment, etc. Love is one of the great mysteries which defy understanding yet continue to manifest themselves demonstrably in our life. We don't know the source of stars, yet there they are. We have certainty they exist. We know they are unworldly—we won't find a star at the bottom of the ocean. We may not even know what they really are; perhaps the light of great souls of men who have come and gone, risen to greater heights of their own being; pinnacles of the evolutionary process. In order to see a thing, that thing must already be inside of me. I see the light from a distant star, perhaps even long after it has burned out, but what is it in me that "sees"? Some desire to be free of worldly constraints of the body and personality gets me to look at stars and ponder their existence. Had I not some disillusionment with myself, would I even consider the light of stars? The light of the stars must be in me, my essence. When I see my denial of light, joy, love, and practical demonstration of that which truly is, I can repent of this denial and place my mind back in charge of the preconditioned state. I am love.

Ω

43.

A

How do I know a truth? Knowledge is relative or absolute. All the various reasons from the past that repeat a memory happen in my life. Yet my essence is not in these "reasons." For instance, a man might think, "I have difficulty with women because I feel betrayed by my mother." This would be a relative memory that could have continued detrimental results. Was he betrayed? Who was betrayed? Can someone be certain to be betrayed. Are events ever not according to God's plan? An absolute truth would be something unchangeable. "My Self is incapable of being betrayed." This is a different paradigm altogether. The desire to be a certain way and the possibility of a betrayer to prevent that way has no function in truth. As long as I can identify with truth, I have no unfulfilled desire. Therefore, no one can actively prevent anything of my good, as though someone could stand in the way of my being who I am as God created me, beyond the personality, thought patterns, conditioning, beyond even my sense of Self. The holes left behind in my personality are the very guideposts to my essence. Seeing my sense of loss in exact terms, specific terms, sets the stage for working through them toward a remembrance of Perfect Providence. I am whole when I observe my tendencies and question the "loss" which brought them about, and through this observation of a truth inside of me set myself free. It is the work for every human to do.

Ω

44.

A

What is the source of fear? It arises out of separation from my Self, from my Source, from Life. I have a litany of various fears—fear of financial lack, fear of dying, fear of confrontation, even fear of God's judgement upon me which is actually my own judgment upon myself. I am told **There is nothing to fear. ACIM Lesson #48** and **God is the strength in which I trust. ACIM Lesson #49** These two ideas question my own fear. Without illusions I have made, my false thinking, there is nothing to fear. It is an issue involving strength. Strength begins by recognizing my own sense of weakness, ineffectualness, etc. Strength in this world is associated with money, the body, military defenses, social status, affluence, etc. These are all false means of security because they are "threatenable." Without real strength there is reason to fear; but these false strengths do not abate the fear, obviously. Insecurity reigns the human psyche. What is real strength? God is a Creative Force unknowable by thought. I can recognize God's effects—the mountains, the stars, the rivers, the human race, the universe of the infinite of which I am a part. Inside me is this Force, as it is in every atom of creation and again inside the Void of my own inner space. This is my strength, and with it in my awareness there is nothing to fear. Letting go of all my personality traits is the day labor making this strength and trust possible.

Ω

45.

A

The wise say there is a state of being beyond choices. Krishnamurti called it "choiceless awareness." *ACIM* calls it "decision." The state is unalterable—unaffected by the changing moods of choices. I have made wrong choices that brought about unforeseen consequences. My subconscious is producing ill effects. I attempt to erase these unknown thoughts, yet "effects" of illness seem to persist showing me I have not let go. I might think my situation is hopeless. Yet, is there something like the hope of hopelessness? I am not fooled; nothing I do can change my situation. There are no more choices to be made. I may have the persistence of disease, yet I am not looking to "fix it." Rather, I would pray that my Self-projected "causes" could be dissolved. Nothing I do can liberate me; nevertheless, the wise say it is possible. Choices must come to an end. Disillusionment can be a positive force. Negation, or the elimination of the false, is the path to truth. Most of what I "know" is false. The wise speak of Self- knowledge, awareness, attention, transmutation, forgiveness as the keys to liberation. There is the personal self and the God-created Self—or Essence. I made the first, God created the second. Dissolving memory of this self I made is the work to do, yet the fearful side of me does not want *to die*. This is the hopeless part of me. Seeing this, I do not identify with it; underneath is the hope of salvation. And salvation is merely awakening to the Self who I already AM.

Ω

46.

A day is given to be harmonious with "what is," even with my "dark side." Thought contains joy and sorrow. But truth, with no opposites, is only pure joy, unaffected by time, moods, or change of any kind. My thought will try to assert itself. This is why constant vigilance is necessary. By vigilance I mean Ho'oponopono, or forgiveness. Atonement is unceasing forgiveness because I recognize I don't know the effects I am making, unaware. It is necessary in this mental world of thought. Neutralizing memory that repeats "problems" is the real work to do. I may have an issue with "authority" because I have an issue with "authorship." I have grappled with this issue. I did not "author" my Self; God authored me. Once I get that clear I cannot take credit even for my abilities. Nor do I need to defend the personality self I made. It is my "child." Can I not condemn it but rather see what is underneath its numerous deficiencies? Tending to this "wounded self" is the work of the Holy Spirit. It is my work; probably my only work. All being "in the world" is to observe myself and my effects because behind these effects are my memories, my illusions. Behind the illusions which I use as defense mechanisms, is my true Essence, my Self-Identity. A tree is known by its fruit. My effects are my "fruit" defining my tree. I must learn to forgive everything and be clear, which allows my best and highest fruit to come forth.

Ω

47.

A

What is written in the moment is my level of awareness, not necessarily absolute truth. As it becomes undone, it is no longer my truth. Like a childish practice outgrown. Emerson said, "I write after a truth which I find, then lose, but I doubt not." Am I speaking from memory or inspiration? I don't know. That is why constant questioning, vigilance, is necessary. "Ceaseless cleansing" is the way of the man who moves toward spirit. To what depth can my thought be silenced? Why do I write if not for that silence? Is writing a block in itself? Have I ever said anything new and of my own voice? What need have I to draw attention to myself? What insecurity in me needs attention? Do I feel lonely, wanting acknowledgement? I am alone, as is every human being, separated in a body. Yet minds need not be alone. Minds can join. What does it mean to come to one mind? Have I ever been of one mind with anyone? It was difficult to observe Tara Singh's physical decline. Others managed his affairs; they said according to his will. Was it according to God's will? I must accept it was without judgment. The results were not pretty, just as the events around the crucifixion were not pretty. Taraji accepted this suffering for reasons beyond my understanding. Could I have intervened and abated his suffering? I did not have the clarity or even the authority to do so.

Ω

48.

A

Being willing to die for a cause is not courage. It is insanity, the obverse of killing for a cause. Courage is to stand up for a conviction and bear the humiliation that may go along with it. It is an internal issue. I am dealing with own self-destructive tendencies and impurities. What do I fear and how does that fear keep me isolated? Unhappy? What is a real action of giving from my heart in my life? *There is nothing to fear. ACIM Lesson #48* All things I fear I have manufactured. I fear I will not wake up in this lifetime and my life will have been a waste. Yet when I remember my value does not come from me, but from my Creator, this fear dissolves. I fear I will remain unwilling, ungrateful, and isolated. Yet when I observe my life, it has been one of Self-inquiry, undoing, working on the inner man. I fear that my daily activities will stay at the level of survival and never see the light of miracles or real transformation. Yet I give less time to activity and more to stillness and silence, and attention to forgiveness. *Forgiveness is my function as the light of the world. ACIM Lesson #62* This is inner work. Where else can a change of mind occur but in the world of my mind? Being in the world, but not of it, is a willingness to look at my bullshit and invoke Higher Forces to transmute it to light. In the end there is nothing to say. The wise have said it better than I ever could. I am totally dependent on God's mercy.

Ω

49.

A

One is either liberated from thought or not. Understanding of thought is not real understanding. Intellectuality and sentimentality are opposite sides of the same pitfall of thinking. The purpose of writing is to observe thought and to bring it to silence. *Alpha Omega* is to start with thought, which is involuntary to being human, and by questioning it come to dissolution and peace. What is non-peace but some form of thought? The *cleaning* is the very process of dissolution of my thought. There is no such thing as another's thought. If I am hearing another person's thought, it must be in my mind as well. This eliminates the whole concept of an enemy. One may observe grievances and contradictions, but that is the nature of thinking—everyone's thinking. The one liberated is free of grievances and contradictions because he has transcended thought. This does not mean he never uses thought; as long as he occupies a body some thought is necessary. Liberation is transcendence to go beyond, above, or below to the heights and depths of reality, past human understanding which is mortal (death-like) to Divine Understanding which is immortal (life-giving). When I end my belief and practices toward death, then I am still and empty enough to receive something from the Will of God. Receiving is most often just recognizing what is already there in its Divine Glory, and having it is the capacity to receive it.

Ω

50.

A

A religious life must be conducted within the structure of everyday affairs and relationships. To be in the world but not of it means that relationships are honored with values that are transcendent: love and care for all people I come in contact with, not taking advantage of another, Self-honesty, a love for quietude and the gift of repentance when things go awry. These moment-to-moment attentions, when truly honored, amount to a religious life. I am fortunate to have the guidance of a real teacher and to be born in the same age in which *A Course in Miracles* manifested. Application of the *Course's* principles became more focused in my relationship with Tara Singh. He provided what the *Course* calls a *holy relationship*. It has been the boon of my existence for the past seventeen years. In tandem with this principle relationship, I have had other great and authentic teachers: Yogi Bhajan, Sondra Ray, and more recently through the lineage of Ho'oponopono – Ihaleakala and Kamailelauli'I. How could I not be grateful? The body may experience aches and pains, yet I cannot let that prevent me from knowing my Identity, my joy, my function in life. The subconscious may have a terrible dark side, but I am willing to let it surface so I can *let it go*. When I examine the conditions for my fear and see these are my own projections, I am free of them and fear as well.

Ω

51.

There is only the stillness and peace of God in reality, but his Son, who was given free will to mis-create, has made a hell out of this freedom. Separation is the culprit of judgment and interpretations which divide humanity into parts, making some affluent and others impoverished. When someone asked Mother Teresa why God made a world with poverty, she said, "God did not create the poor, man made the poor by his unwillingness to share." She did not preach a cause or assert others were wrong, she simply began to share and serve those people who were in the most-dire need. She brought to the attention of the world the neglected, the cast off, and the poorest of the poor. She who was the servant of God in Christ, would cite the words of Jesus: "What you do to the least of my brothers, *you do it to me.*" In a mission in New York I saw a crude drawing of a hand with the five fingers outstretched. On the tip of each finger was word. Together they read "You do it to me." Each of the poor in her eyes was the Christ in disguise. The Christ is me and you. There is stillness and peace in non-judgment. When I relinquish my judgments, I can return to my natural state. Man's natural state is to be at peace, not war, and though we are divided by various languages and cultures, we must see humanity as one big whole. I must revise my thinking. Only what I contribute to the whole has meaning.

Ω

52.

A

Tableside conversation is usually centered around what we do for a living. The self we made is the subject of conversation. Ambition becomes the accepted motive of activity. To make ourselves into an "image of ourselves" is the main preoccupation of daily life. What if a person found within himself another purpose for being totally unrelated to this fabricated "self" of motives and projections? It is a matter of identity. The world will always promote the personality—achievements, talents, abilities, etc. This identity is man-made. Yet, above and beyond this self is a question, "Who am I," which is one of a broader and deeper Self, one less concerned with individuality as much as with wholeness. I am not my skills and good works, nor am I a working animal in a career I made up. I am God's Son, born to realize my Self beyond the mortal, fallible self I made. Perhaps in life the distinctions are not so simply seen and surmounted. The self I made has its persistence, as though it is almost inescapable. The Self God created, who is my reality, is almost unknowable. Knowledge must go beyond my conditioned memory. Remembrance of who I am is possible. *My name, O Father, still is known to you. I have forgotten it and do not know where I'm going, who I am, or what it is I do. Remind me, Father, now, for I am weary of the world I see. Reveal what you would have me see instead. ACIM Lesson #224.*

Ω

53.

A

My Self is beyond thought. I cannot be known in the conventional sense of intellectual understanding. A scripture like *A Course in Miracles* reveals specific testimony as to the Self. It makes clear that my imposed limitations must end. ***My thoughts do not mean anything. ACIM, Lesson #10,*** and ***Let me not see myself as limited. ACIM, Lesson # 250*** The emptiness of the mind is essential to knowing the Self. Who can be empty? Try it; it's not easy to silence thought; even this assessment is questioned. There is something tenacious having little to do with thought. The *Course* refers to determination. This does not mean just clear and persistent effort toward a goal. At times it may mean sustained effort. But could it be, in this case, that determination means more like some destiny bound to occur as though it had already been written to occur exactly how it happened. Determination could mean pre-destination. Life Forces have a very detailed and accurate script for my life to play out. I can accept my role in the larger drama of events and work toward coming to harmony with all people and events which seem to be inconsistent with peace and joy. By myself my situation is hopeless, but with the light of a true teacher, I can assess this hopelessness and totally let go. Without the aid of my Self, the Holy Spirit, I would die blind and lost. With assistance, I continue the long and arduous task of undoing the self I made so I may know my larger God created Self-Identity.

Ω

54.

A

It is high time to grow up. Looking for support outside myself is childish. It is a form of wanting attention from "mommy" and fearing retribution from "daddy," the whole time feeling guilty from a sense of false humility. It is time to cease doubting myself and be an adult. At fifty-one I can finally tell myself to grow up. *The real basis for doubt about the outcome of any problem that has been given to God's Teacher for resolution is always self-doubt. And that necessarily implies that trust has been placed in an illusory self, for only such a self can be doubted. This illusion can take many forms. Perhaps there is fear of weakness and vulnerability. Perhaps there is a fear of failure and shame associated with a sense of inadequacy. Perhaps there is a guilty embarrassment stemming from false humility. The form of the mistake is not important. What is important is only the recognition of a mistake as a mistake. ACIM, Manual for Teachers, Section 7* I can recognize my mistake and then move on. Being an adult is to accept responsibility. I have resources of my own to employ. Growing up means to accept my Self-sufficiency, accept what is as it is, to move on from mistakes, to pick up the salvageable pieces of my life and to discard what cannot be saved. To be an adult is to know my essence, know my Self, my true Self, and also to know fully the deceptive nature of my ego self and not fall for it. To be an adult is to be quietly happy.

Ω

55.

A "problem" is a memory replaying in the present because it represents a thought yet to be dissolved. The only thing to do with a problem is to forgive it and hand its dissolution over to God. A problem is an illusion because Reality is a state in which there are no problems. The teacher told his student, **There are no problems in life apart from the mind. (Krishnamurti to Tara Singh)** The mind, in this case being thought which is stored as memory, is the whole cause of the past. To be free is to be free of memory, of the past, of thought. Freedom is to be present, totally, unequivocally. Heaven and Presence are synonymous. These states of stillness were attainable in listening to the teacher's words. Step by step he would undo thought, rendering it dissolved. I would find myself in a moment of stillness, experiencing the present in its fullest. The greatest blessing in my life has been to have had these moments of freedom. It is the basis for meaning in my life. Without these moments my thought would not have been silenced enough to make contact with this peace. Life provides what is needed to one who wishes to outgrow the insanity of his world and be with the Will of his Creator. Life provided a teacher, a friend, a confidante, in the relationship I had with Tara Singh. There has been no greater gift in my life than to have been introduced directly to a state of mind in which there are no problems.

Ω

56.

A "problem" is a memory replaying in the present. How quickly can I completely let go? It takes no time to be still, just an intense quality of attention. Attention is absence of effort, of seeking, of designing an outcome. To be 100% responsible for the content of my mind and see the need to empty that mind is attention. It begins by observing how contradictory my thought is. Then there is invocation for correction, for sanity, for one-mindedness. This is a form of trust that within me is this mind of no thought. Thought's nature is one of opposites which seem to be in a constant state of conflict. I must release myself from thought's jurisdiction. It is a matter of vigilance of watching my thought and of constant invocation for release. This is the work of the day. To undo, I need but observe myself, my inner reactions, and let them go. They are not Reality. To arrive at my own Reality is a matter of seeing the unreality of my made-up self and refusing to live by its false values and ideas. At some point I must meet with my own falseness and not judge it. Only through non-judgment can anything be released and made whole. To judge is to keep alive conflict. I must accept and own my mistakes before I can begin the correction of them. There is a point, through practice, in which correction is involuntary because my thought process is handed over to Him who is in charge of correction, salvation, forgiveness.

Ω

57.

A

What are the discoveries of each day? If there are none, life becomes stagnant and routine. Certain repetitions are unavoidable. Eating, bathing, clothing, breathing are so closely part of living we seldom consider them apart from life itself. Without a breath, the body dies. Can I be grateful for each breath, and glad for an atmosphere which sustains my life and all life around me? Existence is immersion in the elements of earth, air, fire, water, and space. The body is mostly water and earth; air is needed for it to live; fire is an inner life force which generates crucial body heat; space is the reservoir of the body's occupation, and beyond the body everything's place ad infinitum. Honoring the body elemental is fitting, yet a higher truth is spoken in *ACIM*. ***I am not a body. I am free. Lesson #199*** This statement establishes another reality, one of pure Identity, pure spirit, pure peace. ***Spirit is in a state of grace forever. My reality is only spirit; therefore, I am in a state of grace forever. ACIM, Chapter 1, Section III*** Identifying myself with the body is an obvious interference to grace. It is I who must see myself doing this and invoke the help to cease identifying with the body, and rather identify with the Spirit. While in the body, I care for it, but to be with Who I am I need only see I am not my body, my experience, my personality. Pain and pleasure are transcended. *What is now—* is acceptable. I can be with the Spirit of who I am as Life created me in this very moment.

Ω

58.

A

Rest is in being Awake! To be Awake is to be fully aware of how I deceive myself. Deceptions, by their very nature, are unreal. For example, an opinion I have of another is mostly false. I don't see the other person as he really is but as an image I have made. This image produces conflict, suspicion and separation. By seeing it as such, I can let it go. Why would I hang on to the false? Better to say, "I don't know," and maintain no images than to be in the grip of my own illusions. The human being has a sense of aloneness. Life in a body has this quality of singularity. My body is not your body, though it is similar. I experience it as separate from other bodies. When I feed another's mind and body with the spirit of Truth I have received, or even with the food given to nourish the body, I diminish that sense of separation. Art's primary purpose is to touch the shared beauty of being— either touching a chord of harmonious sound and sight, or deeper insight, or the basic need of a good meal, or the forgiveness which absolves us from error. I may share another's pain. By my own choice of empathy, I may let pain and sorrow visit me so as not to be callous to the suffering of others. Suffering does not dissolve suffering, yet a stop along the way of ending suffering is to not to try to escape it. Can I suffer without desire to rid myself of suffering? In this state of non-desire, I find suffering dissolved by my neutral awareness of it.

Ω

59.

A

D. H. Lawrence brings me back to the flesh and blood reality of living. It is fine to ponder the spirit world, but here and now the body and our personal existence in it occupy our main attention and our whole attitude toward life. Are any of us truly alive in the flesh, incarnated fully to the degree physical existence is embraced as the palpable power of having been created? We seem to be dying, not living; all the rituals in which we engage to verify our existence become charades of living, substitutes for the real live ebb and flow of our own bodily force. I find myself on the verge of coming out of a long-living death, one in which I have not fully accepted that I am here in whatever form that takes. Where else could I be? Striving and searching for a more ideal state has done nothing but keep me from the full acceptance of my wholly living Self. Lawrence brings me back from the brooding doldrums of neurotic denial of my real flesh and blood. He calls to my "man alive" voice of camaraderie, one who understands the wounded nature of my psychic self, one who can infuse new life, almost even new breath into my wearied soul. Always the characters in his stories are grappling with the same issues I have, we all have, to come to my manhood incarnate, a responsible life of real Self-honesty, one that honors the insightful part of me, and the sensual part of me, and the disappointed part of me, but most of all, the completely Self-honest part of me.

Ω

60.

The holy instant requires my "little willingness" to bring my illusions to the truth and let them go. I don't know what I am to do, yet do I need to? To be grateful for what life brings is my responsibility. Thank you, Lord, to have these opportunities to be free. All encounters are opportunities to see what I need to let go. **Father, today I am Your Son again. ACIM Lesson #234** This lesson implies I have forgotten my Father, but today I will remember I am His Son. This remembrance is salvation. A remembrance overrides any self-judgment I maintain and dissolves it. A pang of insecurity or tinge of guilt is undone by this lesson. Anytime I invoke the attention of my Creator, there is a power to silence my thought. It is an invocation of the very Unknown, along with a trust that Higher Forces are benevolent when I am repentant of my misperceptions. Tara Singh, my teacher, would be direct in pointing out my shortcomings, but he would also pick me back up and acknowledge my strengths. A true teacher has nothing to add to my learning; his offering is one of dissolution of the false in me. He points out the relative and unreliable nature of my thought with which I identify. And by working with life, he awakens my heart. It is a remembrance of who I am. **Love created me like Itself. ACIM Lesson #67** In truth with this reality, the real teacher imparts something beyond words—*life for life* relationship.

Ω

61.

A

Something compels me to write. Perhaps it is the feel of the pen, the fingertips accustomed to a stick of sorts between them, and a listening to my thoughts which become recorded on paper like a trail of crumbs left behind for another, or myself, to find a way. It is best not to know what to say ahead of time, then what I write is free and spontaneous. By not knowing ahead, there is space to be silent, perhaps the most potent source from which something comes forth, like a first thought of new and unlikened energy, a revelation that beckons a new vision. Some people may prefer to be entertained by television or drink or some such pleasure. I am inclined to sit quietly and contemplate, to observe my impressions, to question my motives, to see atonement for my mistakes and give attention to an inner life. People come into play, but I do not need people in order to write. I may need them to have something to write about, but that need is tempered by the heat of my own observation, reactions, responses, and eventual acceptance of them and what I have to say about them. We are all in relationship in some form. Even a man marooned on an island is related to the elements of land, sea, sky, sun and stars. I may be on an island of solitude when I write, yet in my mind everyone I've ever met is there. It would follow I write about myself in relationship to these elements—be they animal, vegetable or mineral—in all my multitude of life encounters and relationships.

Ω

62.

A

After a day of physical labor, the body is tired. I sit in my chair. My chin falls to my chest and I awake to a start, having been asleep for who knows how long. My hands are nicked and rough as they are the principle tools in my repertoire of necessary implements. They take the brunt of abrasions from the objects and materials they maneuver. It is the common state of the body after intense labor, and it is intense because I take it seriously. When I am contracted to provide and install something in a house, the intensity of my focus is placed on that, and this physical intensity wears the body out. A person in this world needs money. By contracting I earn it, providing something necessary in the form of a door, a window, a bathroom, a kitchen, tile floor, etc. It's not too complicated although to someone unmechanical it would be. What is required is an ability to repeat the same task with consistency, to address new tasks with the similar manner of good craft. Even unfamiliar jobs, when given the same intensity of attention, come out just fine. It is the quality of my attention which makes this so. The material itself reveals how it should be done. I am able to adapt to a new situation with ingenuity that can construct what is needed. I don't know how to do it, but by merely doing it in the way I always do things—with acute attention to detail—the pieces fall into place. I am grateful to be good with my hands. It makes me independent of *working for another*.

Ω

63.

A

I am not a writer of fiction or stories, though my admiration flows toward a few writers such as D.H. Lawrence, Herman Melville, Ken Follet, Fyodor Dostoyevsky and Willa Cather who wrote fiction to reveal the depth and breadth of human character. These storytellers had a higher truth in mind: man's search for the Truth with a capital "T", his own particular truth in the concrete encounters of a life lived—lived through them and their fictional characters. One can say all art is autobiographical, drawing from the actual experience of the artist. Otherwise, it is speculation, fantasy, empty expression. A person goes through something in life—a challenge, a loss, an aspiration, relationships which work and those that don't, various types and amounts of work, times of productivity, times of laying fallow, healthy and happy times, times of illness and doubt—the whole human experience. Life and death walk hand in hand. All the stuff my body is made of has some expression a priori. It cannot be denied. A tree expresses itself as a tree. A lizard expresses a lizard. A man has a nature as well, but he also has an essence beyond nature, an awareness of a Source not limited by body, thought, physical presence, or expression. Being free, he must have awareness of this freedom. To be aware of freedom makes man unique, unlike animals that cannot perceive their identity beyond nature. Self-Identity is what makes man a human being.

Ω

64.

A

The power of forgiveness is greater than the power of vengeance. The world thinks the opposite, confusing forgiveness with weakness and vengeance with strength. When things go awry, and I am 100% responsible, it serves no one to think I am guilty; but to proceed with the invocation of forgiveness will do more to dissolve the situation. I may bear humiliation, but isn't that better than perpetuating the cycles of vengeance? And what is humiliation? Others may think badly of me, my reputation is soiled, my integrity brought into question. If I entrusted the untrustworthy within some part of my work, I am ultimately to sever my ties with my own irresponsibility. Sometimes an error bites me in the butt, coming from what appears to be out of nowhere. But I am responsible for heaven or hell. My subconscious still believes in hell and perpetuates that result. I can't seem to "help it." This is why forgiveness is so necessary and the admission I do not know why things unfold as difficulties. Am I willing to correct myself in the events gone awry by taking 100% responsibility? I must. What are my options? Blaming another is not viable. Attacking myself is stupid, as is attacking another. My thought is meaningless. Why perpetuate it? Forgiveness ends my thinking; this is my function. My function is to still my thought. It is my salvation which God has provided in my relationship with the wise. Self-responsibility is the only responsibility there is; it is unaffected by my mistakes, dramas, glitches, mis-steps, and errors.

Ω

65.

An action of grace has no judgment in it, nor does it defend itself. It may bear humiliation because it is certain of its innocence. Humiliation is but acceptance of another's judgment upon me and knowing judgment is meaningless, save the one of Love. Love does not judge. Someone asked the Christ how many times a person should be forgiven. "Seventy times seven," was his reply; in other words, with no limits. It is a simple principle. When I do not judge another, I will not be judged for the errors I have made. Release is certain to one who does not judge. When I feel I am being judged, this, too, is a thought to be released. Forgiveness is the only means of dissolving "guilt" at all levels of one's being. It becomes a constant vigilance to be in the spirit of forgiveness in which humiliation is transformed into humility. I may look a fool, and a mistake is not denied, but this does not lower me from the heights of true humility. I say heights because there is nothing depressingly low about accepting who I am as God created me. Mistakes are made at the thought level—intrinsically ridden by opposites. At the level of Identity mistakes are not possible. The desire to not make a mistake is vigilance to be ceaselessly aware of my Identity. From this awareness comes an extension of my Self. To be my Self is to extend goodness not as a deliberate act, but as a natural way of being and working in this world.

Ω

66.

A

Your task is not to seek for love, but merely to seek and find all of the barriers within yourself that you have built against it. It is not necessary to seek for what is true, but it is necessary to seek for what is false. **ACIM, Chapter 16, Section IV** If I am in conflict of any kind, then I have elevated my illusions to the status of a "truth." This cannot be. It is best to surrender my illusions to Him who can dissolve them. I do this by examining my thought. What are my opinions which are illusions? By looking carefully at my thought process, I may see conflict arise and begin to question the judgments that feed this internal conflict. Conflict always involves some form of guilt; either I have judged another "guilty" of some infraction or I have judged myself unworthy to be who I am as God's Son. Both are virtually the same mistake, yielding the same illusion of separation. Better to admit I do not fully know myself than to pretend I am aware of Him. The Self is in me. Why seek anywhere else? My thoughts do not issue forth from my Self; rather they come from fear, insecurity, and falseness of the ego. Better to say nothing than to speak with the forked tongue of pretense. Silence is the doorway to wisdom. Stillness is supreme action because it establishes the ending of thought, the emptying out of illusions from my Mind, the home of my true Self.

Ω

67.

A

The wise do not seek what is a priori, that which is predetermined and unchangeable. They are certain of that Presence. What they attend to is the false and temporal part of themselves in order to undo it. When illusions are erased, then it is obvious that only reality exists. The wise, then, deal primarily with our illusions, our errors, our misperceptions and develop a love for correction. He begins only with himself and stays focused on his own misperceptions. All "external" events around him are mere projections of what is going on inside of him. Therefore, nothing is judged by separation. The error is inside, not outside. If I am experiencing something painful or adverse, I am responsible for causing that consequence by my thought, my memory. I do not even need to know the particular thought of cause, just know that I am 100% responsible for it. Therefore, I am never a victim; and I have the means for correction through forgiveness. The steps for correction are thus quite simple: Identify the pain or error, invoke forgiveness by accepting responsibility, and trust Divine Forces' Power to set things right. Correction is an Action, beginning on the internal level but inspiring action on the external level as well . This is what is meant by "extension." A true Joy cannot be contained; it yearns to extend and share. By its extension is it made manifest. Correction is an extension as well. My internal correction brings order to the external situation around me.

Ω

68.

A

Think *once of 'Arunachala' and the ego will be rooted out. Sri Ramana Maharshi* The mountain, Arunachala, in southern India, is sacred. A place of pilgrimage. The sages revered it, and Sri Bhagavan in the early 20th century chose Arunachala as his home. Taraji and I travelled there in 2001 along with John McClure. It was an arduous journey as are all excursions to India, half-way around the world. Even by modern standards, the places in India which have an intense holy vibration are usually off the beaten track and require a special determination to get there. Tara Singh had a long-standing relationship with the people at Ramana's ashram. He was an honored guest. I had the good fortune to accompany him on one of his journeys to Arunachala, his last, and to be a witness to the remarkable places of his ancient homeland. India, in general, is a place of dust, heat, and poor hygiene. But in these remote outposts of spiritual intensity, cleanliness and order reign supreme. The people are very educated; most speak English, and the hospitality extended to the guest is incomparable to any in the West. There is a sense of communal helpfulness. Fear and suspicion do not exist. Simplicity is the order of the day. The regularity of a daily schedule of worship, meals, service, and silence form an actual balm to the soul. One is refreshed and renewed by the atmosphere and the spirit of Sri Bhagavan, ever present in the space around Arunachala, the holy mountain of his mission and calling.

Ω

69.

A

In India emphasis is placed on liberation from the ego self of man-made accumulations in favor of the real Self of God-created Spirit. Transcendence of the physical existence to the non-physical reality of being is one of the foremost themes of Indian thought. Ancient sages are revered who made this transcendence and brought its light to mankind. Teachers of this high caliber are worshipped, almost as God incarnate. Their premise is to serve humanity. "Truth-Simplicity-Love-Service" are the pillars of their philosophy. Not to lie, not to waste, to live within one's means, to share what you have with others, to treat another as you would be treated, to feed those who are hungry—these are implicit in "Truth-Simplicity-Love-and Service." The meaning of life is not defined by personal accomplishments, but by human relationships and the loving quality of those relationships. Internal obstacles to living a virtuous life are to be faced and dissolved. This is the meaning of being educated. If one is smart and also greedy, to what end is his intelligence? If one is generous but not also frugal, how far will his resources go? There are many issues of internal character which the sages dealt with in a practical manner. In this present society, focus is on external accomplishments which are used to define a person. This is meaningless. What matters is the quality of one's heart, capable of loving another. In India the sages mastered this inner intelligence of the heart.

Ω

70.

A

A novelist writes about people's lives. Characters are formed and described in detail; their relationships unfold in a story. The philosophy and power of observation of the novelist is apparent from what he writes. Like a painter, he describes what he sees through words that invoke mental images—concrete, palpable things and happenings. Character is foremost because people are the focus; their actions in particular settings under certain circumstances form the story. The story is the means for the novelist to express the heart of what he believes and holds dear. It could be a great tragedy but articulated in such a way that it rings true to the struggles, difficulties, and contradictions of life. Conflict may be the impetus of movement toward resolution, insight into a better world not only for the characters in the story, but for readers of the story whose lives are changed by this resolution. An observation is for the living and it is important to make note of the living. How else could meaning be real in our awareness except by observation that reveals the innermost workings of the human heart through the characters in the novel. Taken in conglomerate, all characters represent aspects of the novelist's own character, own mind. Psychology is formed by an unprecedented and free observation, without bounds, to examine what is inside of us, represented by the description of well-formed characters.

Ω

71.

A writer describes life; paints a picture in words of what he observes. The power of his observation goes beneath appearances and touches at the threshold of human nature universal. He describes people whose types are clear and distinct. The hero may be a person of common origin but with uncommon vitality for living. In Willa Cather's work there is usually a person like this, one from common roots with exceptional sensitivity and insight. Probably she herself was this. From the stoic necessity of pioneer life her people had grown firm in a righteous way of survival and practicality. Spiritual life was tied to the dictates of the land out of which their lives as farmers followed with a demanding rhythm and discipline. The trials of early settlers who moved west from the eastern states and immigrants from Europe who came to the new world with little but their own will, permeate the stories of Cather's writing and provide the seedbed for a few remarkable characters who possess an indomitable spirit and love of life, even amidst the gravest hardships. There is a great reverence for family, for the strengths and the limitations that a family possesses, and for the one lofty soul who rises above those limitations by a power to overcome his or her own internal struggle with the contradictions those limitations impose. This is her hero or heroine—he or she loves the family most by transcending its limitations.

Ω

72.

A

A novelist is a lover of people, of human character, of the art of description, of conversation, of action and events. A story is told through people and their relationships; therefore, the novelist is a lover and master of relationships. Why his work is called "fiction" is misleading because the best novelist writes after a truth—a truth of human nature or a truth of an observation of character, of traits, of nuances, of interest and interaction. Fiction implies "made up" or "fabricated from the imagination." The novelist who is worth his salt draws from actual experiences and from people he has known or wishes to know directly. The main reason he changes the names is to protect himself from the backlash of disapproval from those whose lives he exposes in his stories; to protect their innocence in a way, and to protect his own innocence in writing about them. Most people are unaware—unobservant of the remarkable people and events that pass before us either in clear exposure or by potential for something more extraordinary. Too satisfied by the routines of living we barely open our eyes and awaken our hearts. Who is really with it? A novelist is alert, probing himself for some account in human terms of his life and its vicissitudes. Who does he meet, with what vitality does he meet whoever? This vitality is the very energy of his own observation. Alive fully, he will actually see life happening inside himself.

Ω

73.

A

What are the aspects of the novel? What makes a good story, the parts of its structure which cannot be left out no matter what? There has to be a setting, like a stage, upon which the novel's drama may be played out. Although setting may not be as important as character, it is inevitably necessary. Character is the supreme element in the novel. The hero, or protagonist, is the key character around whom the other characters revolve and evolve. There is relationship between the characters, and the type of relationships that are described help to define the characters. Events and actions of the characters form the basis of the story. A character must "do something." Without action there is hardly a story. The action may be one of the character's own will or an event thrust upon the character by some act of fate or destiny. Once in the momentum of his destiny, the main character will show his character—his internal nature—by virtue of what he says and does. This action is of life and though it may not be verbatim from actual events, it must possess the veracity of actual events and characters. Without the feats of the mythic heroes, the heroes of actual life would be little inspired beyond the confines of their own conventions. Without the noble actions of real people, there would be no mythic heroes annotated. In this case, fiction feeds life and life feeds fiction in the most epic way. The novel gets to the core of living, so real people can empathize and identify with the characters of the story.

Ω

74.

A

There is only one end of the spiritual quest: to love my brother as myself. Without relationship—the love of one for another—life is a waste. The artist, the novelist, the writer after a truth must have this love within himself as the very motivation for his work. Without it the work is dead, not alive with real meaning. Without it the work is merely a technical feat, a rendering of empty form which has no real relationship to life. It is easy to confuse an ability to render form with artistry. Inspiration is something transcendent of this ability, imbuing what is shaped and formed into something living and breathing, something alive with love. Something alive, with empathy for another human being often means that the hardship and pain endured is actually felt and experienced by the one who is empathizing. The artist must have been through something traumatic and difficult in order to write about overcoming difficulty. One can endure and overcome hardship or cave into it. Character is strong to the extent I trust in a Power which wants only the best for me and helps me deal with pain and hardship and the circumstances of failure. Certain things in life are not subject to defeat. Love is one of these important life assets. Love is the fuel of the creative. Without it would all my gestures, words, deeds, actions be meaningless. Love redeems me from non-love. I can dwell in Its house forever.

Ω

75.

A

There are numerous branches in the road of life which, when taken, turn one's fate in very certain directions. It does no good to deliberate on the road not taken nor to pine over what could have been. The fact of what is must be acceptable in the end. What may have seemed like a sensible direction has come with difficulties and doubt—but who can say another would have been any less uncertain with fewer difficulties? A decision is made then the challenge to stick with it. To be with a teacher I often chose an action that depleted my finances, yet I was with him nevertheless. I always paid my bills and my own way. Now the teacher has passed but a Presence inside me remains, a Presence only he imparted as a gift from God of real relationship. Can I rise to give as much? This is yet to be seen. Did I give myself totally to him as he did to me? At times I did, but at times I held back for fear of being humiliated or made to do something I was unwilling to do, such as walk out of home life. The road I took was the familiar one of caring for the family I was already born and married into. Though I have never felt conventional about a family life, I could not totally leave it behind. Enlightenment must be possible within the structures of family and work already in place; the grass is not necessarily greener over the hill. I chose the road through familiar pastures, ones in which I am to find my Self amidst the grasses already growing.

Ω

76.

A

I have a wonderful room which is in a house built in the 1880s. There is a bay window with an archway over it, the source of effulgent light at most times of the day. As houses are close together in the city, most of my view is the neighbor's stucco wall, but this does not dim the light, rather the opposite effect occurs as the light is reflected off the white stucco intensifying the brightness of the day. In front of the three double long windows in the bay are three large terra cotta pots perched on small wooden stools, the homes of a half-dozen clivia plants with broad, long leaves arching off a central stalk at the base in a woven concentration. These plants are many years old—their ancestors coming with us 26 years ago from Cleveland. In their season of bloom, usually spring, they send up a shoot like an amaryllis which bursts into a spectacular multi-trumpeted bloom—an explosion of bright orange. Against the backdrop of the dark green leaves, the bloom stalk ascends from the middle of the woven base, for a time hidden in the thicket until tall enough to push its way above trajectories of the palm-like foliage. The room, painted a shade of chalky salmon, is aglow in the light, anticipating the coming of the clivia's bloom. I have my chair to the right of the bay, also expecting the coming of this annual offering of bright orange. It comes like a nectar of color and I am blessed by it every year when I least expect it.

Ω

77.

A

There is a blessing in not working for another. I am afforded space and time just to be. When I say just to be, I mean to be myself without dependence or motive, relying upon Divine Providence to meet my needs. I have space to write, paint, read, and be of service. The work I do with my hands is usually someone's necessity; I earn money by meeting another's need around their home—carpentry, tile work, painting, plumbing, etc. This keeps me financially responsible—not wealthy in terms of a big bank account, but wealthy in ways of satisfaction. I must work, but it is something I do on my own terms, not someone else's. Plenty of people find solace and security working for large corporations but I could never conform to the 9-to-5 lifestyle. My maternal grandfather was Self-employed and imparted the wisdom to work for myself and be Self-reliant always. It would come down to a matter of freedom which I found more secure than a regular paycheck. Things always came my way to do and I earned money with my sense of good craft, being adept with my hands. Having a background in the arts helped me speak with sensitivity toward aesthetic matters, relationships of materials, color, quality, and function. This sensitivity expanded to people. I learned about different personality types and could see when someone wanted to take advantage. My work has enriched my life and is always new in some respects; something energetic.

Ω

78.

A

There seems to be a great struggle for people striving for happiness. Success, often associated with happiness, may not bring a joy within. A joy within may not depend on worldly achievements and acquisitions. I am not a "billionaire man"; neither am I a "poor man." I have traveled abroad and much within my own vast country; I have seen the differences between the East and the West; I have been educated in universities; I have supported myself independently with my own faculties; I have been creative when I have felt like being creative. The wise have not eluded me. I have been with them directly. Even an introspective look at myself, with all its familiar traits, limitations, and strengths has not been without fruit and merit. With this experience, I see that happiness does not arise from a source of experience alone. Happiness is when all struggles end. Strife is no more and nothing more is sought. Sorrow and disappointments are past and cannot touch me. When I do not seek fulfillment through something external, how can there be disappointment or unfulfillment? The bigger issue is my inner life. How much do I love? What do I give? Am I at peace with myself? Happiness is an inside job. No one but I am responsible for it. It comes when I least expect it in the quiet and solitary moments of the day. When I am not preoccupied, I see my happiness is all there is, permeating everything.

Ω

79.

A

Why do people feel that paradise is something to enter after death while actual living is a trial and sometimes a hell? The notion of nirvana, heaven, or paradise is something projected as an opposite of what is not wanted now. Now is something "less than" heaven; therefore, "heaven" is something to enter into in the future—not now. That belief/projection keeps a person in hell. Whatever my state of mind is now is what I am responsible for. Heaven, a state free of conflict, of not wanting something to be different, is only now. If heaven exists at all it must be attainable now. For something to be real it must exist. Something that exists must exist now, otherwise it does not exist. My state of mind is either in heaven or it is not. My state of mind encompasses what exists; it shares in what is real. Heaven, existing now, must be encompassed by my mind. My state of mind, which is in the present, must encompass heaven, which is real, existing now. What I think is dual—I think of heaven and *not heaven* (hell). What exists and is real has no opposite. A mind which can see what just is, as it exists, has no conflict, no dualism. This mind does not involve itself with opposing factors. What I see really exists. When I witness moments in which I have no desire for anything to be different I have a state of mind that has rejected conflict as meaningless. Love has no opposite. It exists and forms what we call Heaven. Total awareness of Love is making contact with Heaven.

Ω

80.

Α

An action which brings joy is the only real action. It is often remedial because I find myself in a state far from joy, and it is an internal action of ceasing to expect, or to want something from external circumstances. As a visual artist this has often been difficult to comprehend, as much of my focus has been on appearances. Painting is concerned with visual elements but also with content, which is an internal matter. There is always something in concrete, physical terms related to the action. I paint or draw within a space; it is a physical application. I need not have what I paint refer to an object outside of itself—such as the traditional sense of depicting people, places, and things. The painting and its internal elements and relationships will be seen or not seen on its own terms. This is an action which brings me joy. The content unfolds as the painting progresses. I don't always know what the painting contains; what it contains are my actions and each addition or subtraction to the painting is purposeful and clean. If not, then what am I painting into it? I am responsible for the content of the painting, but this does not mean I am always fully aware of all its meaning. As long as each stroke, each line is pure at heart, then the end result will be pure as well. It is best not to know too much of what I'm doing. To be sure, to be responsible for one moment in a string of moments is enough.

Ω

81.

A

There is a vast universe inside a person, an ever-expansive space as particular as a new spring bud ready to burst into flower. Words only skirt around description by indicating a presence, a light, a vision, which transcends descriptions. It cannot be taught, yet an awareness of this presence is given one, awakened in one, perhaps by another, but perhaps mostly by a readiness inside, one which draws an encounter toward itself—an encounter of like minds. The mind which is aware of the vastness within exudes a particular atmosphere, an aura of unique difference, one of acute attention, super sensitive awareness of *what is* as it is fully. This mind looks and sees something beyond appearances, something deeply sacred without being pretentiously religious about it. It has emptied itself of judgments and opinions; filters of perception have been suspended so that what is perceived is whole and free to be itself. Much of our daily life is activity far afield from this rarefied perception—one expanded and emptied—because we are preoccupied with survival in a commercialized world. The real world may not resemble the dull state of our preoccupations. The universe within me requires leisure in which the mind can rest in observance of itself. In these moments of reflection and leisure, preoccupations are released, and the world in front of me, alive and whole, stands forgiven.

Ω

82.

A

My teacher, Tara Singh, has left these planes. His work was done, and he had no more reason to stay, having communicated all he had to say. Now I am "on my own," so to speak, to be with my internal Teacher, one, who without the help of Taraji, would have evaded me. On numerous occasions my instructions from Taraji led me toward an inner journey toward my Self. "The space is to be found within," he said. Stillness and silence are supreme; action is something natural and choiceless—like the action of a tree growing. I need but follow the next step, then the next, then the next, one at a time, passing like days. At the end of his life, Taraji gave me a great gift—to show me how little progress I had made toward realizing my Self. His helplessness was met with the conventional approach by the "professionals." I was cut out of the loop of his physical care, perhaps for good reason, but it gave me the opportunity to see how much of me was helpless too. Legal precedents were imposed, and my intervention would have brought criminal prosecution upon me. The ones in charge of his caretaking seemed in some way aloof and inconsiderate of his direct wishes, all the time acting in what they thought were his "best interests." Who can say? It all seemed ruthless to me, happening under the shroud of professional necessity, a form of polite hell. My contribution did not liberate him or me from suffering on the external plane. I have to forgive myself for the way things unfolded.

Ω

83.

A *Course in Miracles* has something to say about this inner Self, this reality which arises above the suffering of the world, even in the midst of pain and suffering. It lifts the mind into Divine Thought in which duality and uncertainty of change does not exist. "Where is my home" is a question *ACIM* answers. **There is a place in you where this whole world has been forgotten; where no memory of sin and of illusion linger still. There is a place in you which time has left, and echoes of eternity are heard. There is a resting place so still no sound except a hymn to heaven rises up to gladden God the Father and the Son. Where both abide are they remembered, both. And where they are is heaven and is peace. ACIM, Chapter 29, Section V** This "place" is inside of me. All beauty of the world is but a reflection of the beauty within of which this passage speaks. **Think not that you can change their dwelling place. For your Identity abides in them, and where they are, forever must you be. The changelessness of heaven is in you, so deep within that nothing in this world but passes by, unnoticed and unseen. The still infinity of endless peace surrounds you gently in its soft embrace, so strong and quiet, tranquil in the might of its Creator, nothing can intrude upon the Sacred Son of God within. ACIM, Chapter 29, Section V** My relationship with Taraji invokes the truth of these words to rise above all suffering.

Ω

84.

A

Beauty is inside of me first, otherwise I would not recognize it without in the offerings of the natural world. Beauty manifests in nature and in human relationships. It is not something transient. The manifestation may come and go but beauty itself, something so vast and all-pervasive, is not threatened by the erosions of time. Beauty is a stillness that does not judge; it merely observes. All things contain it; therefore, I am connected to all things through it. When I say something is ugly, I have judged it so, therefore beauty evades me. But when I observe the beauty within with no judgment without, nothing is ugly—it is just what it is. The great sage Ramakrishna spoke of enlightenment in one who could see beauty in the great Ganges River and in a ditch of dirty water the same. It is a state of being free of attachments, judgments, preferences and choices. The saint and the murderer both contain beauty and when I really see that, I am liberated. But we pretend to see and pretend to be free. Our judgments continue unchecked and we deem beauty to have an opposite. We often deem beauty in certain things we wish to possess, and once they are possessed, gradually the thing deteriorates from having that original attraction—its beauty is then fleeting. Beauty is not something here today and gone tomorrow. It is an acceptance of what is now, totally as it is now. Even those who do not see beauty are beautiful.

Ω

85.

A

Many stories are told, and much written material occurs every day. What makes my words true enough that reading them years from now would make them retain freshness and vitality? An artist is an artist of life first and foremost, and life is relationships. The relationships I have are the material from which I write. Most of my relationships now concern people who hire me to do work in their homes. I am a good craftsman and people sense this either from my initial meeting or from recommendations from others for whom I have already done work. I could call these relationships with customers, yet that would diminish the encounter to a kind of commercialized routine. I don't regard these people as customers or clients; neither are they necessarily "friends," although some may develop that way. They are who life sends to me to meet myself. I always meet myself, not only in offering the full extent of what I have to give, but also in them the mirror in which I see myself reflected in their response to me. The pretext of coming into their homes as a carpenter, mason, or craftsman has become a necessary pretext, one that utilizes who I am and what I have to extend. The quality of my attention sets me above the craft and my integrity makes the relationship motiveless. I charge a fee for what my time, efforts, and skills are worth, but the real encounter is the relationship. It is non-commercial.

Ω

86.

A day is given. Character is strong which meets it with newness and energy, not concluding a preconceived action, but not shirking the completion of those actions already set in motion. I am presently engaged in painting a kitchen for Mr. Hal Weinstein—a quiet man in his sixties who lives in a high-rise apartment building on the 21st floor overlooking the entire Fairmount Park, Center City Philadelphia, and the spectacular horizon line into New Jersey and beyond. Mr. Weinstein's vista is one unobstructed by other buildings; his apartment has a wrap-around balcony, floor-to-ceiling windows, an expansive living room that gives one the vantage point of being on a platform above the world. Being so high off the ground in one's living space is a kind of ascension of the body physical and has an effect as being an aid, a catalyst to pondering that ultimate ascension which connects us to the Gods. Mr. Weinstein is a sensitive soul who spent his life in business, did reasonably well, and now can coast off the fruits of his labors. He has a propensity for color and art though he actively admits he does not have any real education in these matters, but he can appreciate paintings and sculptures as indicated from the various artworks and interior design in his apartment. I am there not by accident. I am there to paint his kitchen with colors that will truly sing in the end.

Ω

87.

A

The rain has finally arrived, much to our need for spring moisture. It has a forceful but gentle sound, not the torrent of a storm with thunder and not the lighter sound of a mist or shower. So far it is steady. I hear the droplets hitting the rooves and gutters, some metallic surface is being drummed regularly. The wind is picking up as I can hear the water hitting the trees in the distance as the sound of rain comes to a crescendo. The small white dog comfortably stretched out on the carpet in her evening posture of relaxation, breathes heavily, almost a snore. I am quiet, listening, as I write to the various sounds that compose the evening symphony of common but extraordinary passages, all blending together, unbeknownst do these sounds blend except to the listener. Does the rain know that someone has perked his ears to take in its intensifying notes? But isn't that how nature seems; what it is, it is, not needing notice or acknowledgment to be. The real thing to notice is my own being relating to and from a definite part of nature. Isn't the wind and rain inside of me? How else would I know it's there in all its primordial force if I were not there as well from the very beginning? I was a rock, then a falling rain, then numerous plants, animals, and finally a human. The poet Kabir said, "What did I ever lose by dying?" I retain the identities of my former lives here and now in contemplation.

Ω

88.

A soul evolves; vital to the extent it has something to give, to share, to extend. It may not be adept at social niceties but to consider others is important and to consider one's Self in relationship to others is paramount. There are two forces in the psyche of humans, especially males. One is a need to acknowledge his position in the community, the other to stand stalwart alone, an independent man. John Donne expresses the former, "No man is an island." Rainer Maria Rilke expresses the latter, "We are solitary. We may delude ourselves and act as though this were not so. That is all. But how much better it is to realize that we are so, yes, even to begin by assuming it." The universe in its entirety exists in the mind of a man or woman. The mind is a reservoir for all that is. Intellect divides into parts; an action of the heart integrates and makes whole. A solitary being to which Rilke refers is more apt to have a sense of the whole because he sees all as a reflection of himself with no need to distinguish "this from that." What Donne says does not mean a man is a cog in the collective, it means he is empathetically connected with all life in all its joys and sorrows. Rilke states it in a different way; the individual is utterly alone as if existing on a plane in which his own psyche cannot be escaped. He is at once a solitary conduit through which a universe flows, needing no other people to complete himself.

Ω

89.

A

When still and quiet, there is little to say. The beauty of this state of mind seems to permeate all that I observe because stillness and beauty are already there and there is nothing to say. A slight ringing in the ears confirms this different quality of attention. I can sit quietly any time of the day or night and have this awareness of peace. Thought may ramble on involuntarily, but it does not affect the peace which is already there. After a short time, thought slows and the space of quietude becomes expanded. I owe this awareness to my Teacher, Tara Singh, who introduced me to this other state of being. Without him and *A Course in Miracles* he represented, I would have continued to give authority to my thought. Thought is never at peace. It has an agenda or grievance that keeps my mind preoccupied. Unwilling to accept, at odds, always insecure, it needs to "do something" to right the situation. What could thought possibly do? I see thought's inherent unwillingness to let go—let go of all it has accumulated and made. One could say self-improvement works; education gets one a better job, more money, affluence, etc. But does this "self" give us ultimate satisfaction or freedom? One can be "owned" by things which waste resources in maintaining. Simplification is not self-improvement. It requires I live with what is essential, not to waste but to save resources—physical and mental—through a contact with the spiritual. In quiet I make that contact.

Ω

90.

A

To be free of memory I have been given the process of *A Course in Miracles* and Ho'oponopono. Along with these come relationships with the wise: Tara Singh, Ihaleakala, Kamailelauli'i. This is a very sacred trust requiring a different reverence and application. If I am not with it—the process of inner correction—then I am caught in the sorrowful patterns of memory. And I would be wasting my life. The work to do is simple, yet the ego's tricks and unwillingness are strong. This is why constant vigilance and "ceaseless cleansing" are necessary. This amounts to a kind of remembrance, moment-to-moment, to say to myself, "I love you," or, "thank you," or, "nothing I see means anything." Whatever will take my mind to *empty* is the necessity of my attention. There is space in my day to be quiet and appreciate silence. What activity could be superior to peace? It is miraculous to observe my thought and to dissolve and erase problems. There is only one "problem," separation from Self-Identity. It is always there but I am absent when I am with the ego's memory. I don't even know how my mind distracts me, but it does. Therefore, my only function is to forgive myself. By forgiving myself, I can forgive others. Freeing myself first is what I need most. One in bondage cannot free another. Only a free man can bring others to the awareness of their own freedom, usually pointing out how our bondage is self-imposed.

Ω

91.

A friend can bear another's pain and difficulty with some response of help. There are simple things one can do. The basic needs of food, clothing, and shelter can be overseen. Someone who has been ill may not feel up to shopping, but I could do that. A real friend would. So do it! Don't just talk about it. Action is the only thing that means anything—one born out of love, concern, and caring. Life provides opportunities to respond. Be grateful that it does. Our lives, so lived in isolation even amongst people, rarely step out of our own self-centered concerns. To help a friend in need is probably one of the few actions in life in which self-centeredness ceases. It could be something as simple as buying a bag of groceries and taking them to the friend, unasked. An action of giving is superior to any acquisition; even the Taj Mahal can't compare with Mother Teresa feeding the poor. Each is beautiful, but in giving there is no self-aggrandizement. The Taj Mahal was built by Shah Jahan as a monument for his queen. In a sense it was a giving of architectural beauty and perfection for all future generations to appreciate, but the simple act of giving a bag of groceries to a sick friend may be equally beautiful to the human heart. We think in terms of grandiose wonders of the world when inside of us there is little comparison or caring. Intellectual ignorance keeps us isolated. Giving breaks this isolation.

Ω

92.

A

The impact that a person has upon his surroundings, including the people around him, depends on his inner qualities. There are basic issues of character that are natural. One who gives himself to others has mastered love and caring. His impact on his surroundings would be different than the impact of a greedy person. The difference has to do with life flow. A giving person is flowing and responding into the world he lives in—a kind of exchange takes place. A person who believes in lack is hanging on, grabbing, and hoarding. This kind of person is not flowing. The sacred pools of his being are stagnant. One who believes in the abundance of Creation which flows equally to all things at all times does not worry about having enough. A trust that Life takes care prevails; therefore, there is no need to stockpile and hoard. There is wisdom in frugality, saving, and not wasting, yet these are very different than the resulting behaviors of greed. To give sensibly may require a kind of "rationing" and egalitarianism. It may require a fast, or what looks like withholding, but in the end all needs are met. There is enough to go around in the whole human community without one single person going hungry. It is a matter of giving. When man is divided by such "have and have nots," the reasons for caring are shadowed by the thrill of personal gain.

Ω

93.

A

To the degree that what I write is true is the degree I live by my words. I could say "early to bed and early to rise," but I would be a liar. I like to read into the night, and I give myself the space to get up when I am inclined—sometimes early, sometimes not. The point is not to pressure myself or feel victimized by a schedule imposed by someone else or by myself. When there is someone to meet, I meet them on time. When there is a plane to catch, I catch it. But this common tendency to be locked into a nine-to-five straitjacket is something so foreign to the natural cycles of human wellbeing that I wonder why so many have fallen victim to it. Fear, I suppose, runs our life to the point we conform to the status quo of jobs. The employer is just as much a part of the jail, even though he is in charge of the lock and key. When others are exploited to do the bidding of a boss and people make their livelihoods off the labors of others, the boss is behind bars as well, always running roughshod over the employees, making sure his obligations are met and the wage slaves are doing the work. There needs to be more personal accountability for what I do and what I say. The wise person never says he will do what he cannot complete, nor will he engage himself in a venture that does not interest him. Freedom is a state of being now, not later, and it must be recognized as such and maintained with constant vigilance.

Ω

ALPHA OMEGA

94.

Α

A person is influenced by those around him, therefore the company he keeps primarily determines that influence. This is why going to school provides a company of people interested in education, in learning, in awakening their own excellence and goodness—a beneficial company. The reason is not primarily to learn "skills" that will be required to get jobs, although that may be one reason, but rather to awaken myself to be who I came to this planet *to be*. What are my real interests and abilities? What impact may I have upon the world, my local world of people I know and people with whom I have contact? The company I keep will contribute to who I am. This company of people exhibits a set of values. What do I value? What do the people I know value? What do we exchange that affects these values? Is there love for another? Do I give something? What do I give? I live in a city, in a house, and live by the work of my hands and my knowledge of the building arts. These arts are basic needs of life in a house: plumbing, carpentry, electrical, painting, masonry, and a certain amount of design sense. Knowing a craft does not make it an art. But without knowing the craft the art cannot adequately develop. Similarly, the company we keep can have an art. There is a social craft, but it is the rare artist who can love and contribute something real and enlightening to the whole of human endeavors.

Ω

95.

A

Philadelphia, or "City of Brotherly Love," was founded by a Quaker whose father was a military man. Quakers renounced all war unequivocally, seeing God in everyone, even their so-called enemies. William Penn had a different vision of city life. It was a holy experiment, one in which green space was considered vital to well-being, one in which Native Americans were treated fairly and humanely, one in which education and learning was seen as an elevating factor in a person's life and development, one in which industry needed the balance of agriculture, one in which large tracts of wilderness were preserved, one in which people could worship freely without intervention, one in which people had a hand in governing their own affairs. All these principles brought forth by William Penn remain the heritage of a vital place and the ideological backbone of what Philadelphia stands for. From these ideas sprang forth a new nation. It was here that words of destiny were uttered—"All men are created equal"—and here that the documents forming a union of United States committed to a democratic system of self-government were debated and given over to the people for ratification. It is here now that we must realize that all men still are the children of One Creator, equally loved, and therefore equally deserving of the best our city's legacy has to offer.

Ω

96.

A

The human brain holds all the goodness as well as all the evil mischief simultaneously. Its nature is dualistic, and perhaps this awareness is the "fruit" from the forbidden tree of knowledge from which we ate bringing about our expulsion from Eden. I am no moralist; neither am I a bad person who deserves condemnation. "He who is free of error cast the first stone." This wise rebuke would put most of us in our place of needing forgiveness, which is fortunately a viable option. Because what I give, I also receive; to pardon another is the most effective way to pardon myself—and pardon is always justified, even for what is perceived as the vilest crime. My view, and it is certainly not prevailing, is that true repentance is always a real and probable possibility when the possibility is on the table. We are so victimized by our own point of view, our very thinking has become distorted, locking us into predictably destructive results. We may not even see the violence of our ways, the selfishness of our motives, and the results of many problems due to our memories and thoughts. Fortunately, the mind is malleable, and it can be changed. This is why wise people exist, to rearrange the self-destructive thinking of others along different lines of life-affirming paradigms. New thinking yields new results; real forgiveness washes away our old destructive ways and means.

Ω

97.

A

The man who stands alone is more likely to be free of motives. Alone he is not subject to doing things for the approval of others. He needs a trade in order to pay his way, and he needs to be free of opinions of "good vs. bad." There are self-destructive patterns that are more important to recognize so they can be rooted out and overcome. Concerning a trade, right livelihood is providing something that is essential to live. The fair exchange of these provisions is called economy. Before money, it would have been goods and services rendered. These still are the basis for economy, but most goods and services are translated into numerical values and these comparative numbers are called money. Money is not actually the paper and metal discs. The goods and services of my trade are evaluated numerically, and this evaluation is the basis for exchange. When I value what I do more than the person receiving it does, no exchange happens. But when evaluations are similar, and I can provide the quality of goods and services assigned that value, then an economic exchange takes place. Providing what people need to live makes it right. Providing the unessential creates an imbalance, introducing waste of resources and superfluous exchange which may cause shortages in more essential areas. A man who stands alone can control what he exchanges and be free of the consequences of waste.

Ω

98.

A

The world has its own ways which are determined by thought, ways that are inherently dualistic. A "good" has a "bad." The good party is in its own view better than the bad party. The wise would observe the nature of thought itself contains the seeds of conflict, observable in personal, local, national, and international affairs. These conflicts are playing out according to someone's thinking or collective thinking. "Memory is replayed as problems," says the wise (Ihaleakala). Thought makes up our personality which makes up our world. The world is not separate from us. We formulate all of it according to our desires and wishes. In the event of war and killing, we are the sole culprits. It does not happen to us, rather we make it happen and justify it with thoughts of good vs. bad, usually placing ourselves on the side of the good. There are some who see the fallacy of an ideology, that thinking in terms of good vs. bad produces destructive results. My thought does this too. I am responsible for war, killing, the death of my own innocence. Without true repentance and forgiveness there is no escape from thought, therefore no escape from conflict. "Attack thoughts" are those that evaluate good vs. bad, or good guys vs. bad guys, or right vs. wrong. What is right in the true sense, is to step out of thought and see that it cannot make the same decision. Its very nature is fear which acts from vested interest which is inherently violent.

Ω

99.

A

Repentance, Forgiveness, Transmutation—the three active parts of Ho'oponopono come in the ancient Hawaiian form of wisdom, given by Morrnah Simeona originally, and maintained and disseminated by Ihaleakala and Kamailelauli'i. A process of problem solving, Ho'oponopono's promise is that problems are memories replaying, originating in the subconscious mind, showing up in our physical experience for which I am 100% responsible. It places control of the problems in the hands of the problem maker—myself. Through active repentance and invocation for forgiveness, the transcendental part of my mind can receive the assistance of Divine Intelligence to transmute the problem to zero. One cannot escape memory, most of which is submerged in the subconscious, actively producing results, often problems. The transmutation of thought producing ill effects is essential to living. Like any remedial process, it must be used to work. Attention is essential to a disciplined practice. Without moment-to-moment application, the mind is left open to problem-producing memory. The memory of God, or Love, though not obliterated by problems, is obscured. Defogging the mind is constantly necessary. Attention is the vigilance needed to "defog." When the mind is clear, inspiration can be in charge, replacing the memory of "hell" with one of Heaven.

Ω

100.

A

Notebooks are thoughts. Thoughts are either replayed memories (past) or inspirations (present). Inspiration's source is not the conscious mind. Inspiration's source is the Void, Zero, Infinity, Nothingness, Divine Intelligence. When the mind can be taken back to its Source, it is more likely to receive Inspiration. Problems need to be dissolved through repentance, forgiveness, and transmutation—in short, by miracles. The conscious mind cannot perform miracles, but it can initiate Ho'oponopono down through the subconscious mind in order to invoke my Self and Divine Intelligence to transmute memory of pain, sorrow, death, fear into neutrality—so Inspiration can breathe new life into me. Inspiration is from Divine Intelligence. Replayed memory of problems is from the subconscious mind. Engaging in thoughts of problems does not dissolve them. Ho'oponopono (repentance, forgiveness, transmutation) does. All problems are in me. There is nowhere else that problems occur. The mind of past thought (memory) is the storehouse of problems. Only miracles can dissolve them. A notebook contains thoughts. Are these memories or miracles? I write to free myself and anyone who reads these words from thoughts. My thoughts are meaningless. Real thoughts are those I think with Divine Intelligence. How rare are these. All one can do is petition to erase memory of errors, in order to reveal those thoughts of Divine Inspiration.

Ω

101.

Nature is always new. There is memory, such as an acorn remembers to grow into an oak tree, but there are no thoughts of conflict or desire to be something else. These conflicts seem peculiar to humans. All things are in a period of growth or decay. A huge boulder of granite, once formed, begins to slowly erode. A human grows into an adult body then begins to decline toward an end, according to the unconscious "death urge." Everything in Nature seems to have a birth, a life, and a death. For millennium man has been concerned with immortality amid the stage of his apparent mortal existence. He has attempted to improve that mortal existence with the affluence of beautiful possessions and wealth. With command over those less affluent, with notions of power and ideologies, men dominate over other men, even with a promise of an immortal afterlife for a reward of living an accepting life here in the mortal one. None of these notions are new. What is new is a present moment free of these notions. Nature is present and free. We are part of that freedom. The notion that our bodies will decline and die has to do with the thoughts we think now in the present. The future is an illusion. It exists mainly as a fear of dire possibilities. The past is gone, also an illusion. What exists now is the only reality because to be real is to be present. Great souls are known by their lofty thoughts which do not die. "All men are created equal" (by their Creator) will not die, though Jefferson no longer exists in a body.

Ω

102.

An action of life produces something; a truth which extends itself. An acorn is true, and it extends an oak tree. A man called Lincoln is true and he extends the end of slavery. In the course of human events there are beings who impact and change that course. A man called Gandhi brought freedom and dignity to India on the premise that its rulers, the British, were not bad people, but their policy was wrong. To colonize and exploit the people and resources of India, which it had done for hundreds of years, was wrong. Non-violently, that is non-militarily, Gandhi organized strikes and civil disobedience which brought the British to see that they could no longer rule that vast nation. When India achieved its freedom after WWII and the English went home to find their own nation devastated by war and plagued by shortages of the most basic goods, the Indians invited them back to help in the reformulation of a new government. Lord Mountbatten was appointed prime minister to show there were no hard feelings and that the British were appreciated for what they contributed to India in the form of law and order. Humanism on the grand scale of governments was instituted by the life action of one man, Gandhi. Every human being must ask, "what is the action of my life?" "What do I have to extend of my goodness?" Giving these questions attention is the impetus for a truly productive existence.

Ω

103.

A

Action and activity are two distinct movements; the first being of life and the second of projected thoughts, or to use Ihaleakala's terminology, the first is from Inspiration, the second from replayed memory. Action produces something new, vital, and necessary to life. Activity is a recapitulation of something old and worn out, usually done to maintain the status quo of self-interest. Activity is what the human brain knows and perpetuates for survival of the personal. Action, impersonal, always is concerned with the well-being of the whole. A tree does not protest when it is cut down to give its wood to the construction of a house. The bison did not migrate away when the plains Indians hunted them for meat and hide. Nature gives itself impersonally. The singing birds do not care if humans are listening; nevertheless, they still warble their songs. Ages and eons passed before I took birth in this lifetime; thousands of ages will come and go after I pass out of this lifetime. To be free and not attached to physicality I must empty my Self of thought, of memory. It is a process of erasure through repentance, forgiveness, and transmutation. What is there to erase? Attachment to physicality puts the conscious mind in charge, leading to endless bondage of activity. Letting go of this false control, placing my Self in the charge of Higher Mind in connection with Divine Intelligence, opens the possibility for Action.

Ω

104.

А

I am not one to shun physical work. Being adept with my hands, I am able to make things that are needed. On a strictly practical level I make bathrooms and kitchens; on the aesthetic level I make drawings and paintings; on the mental level I write down my impressions and thoughts; on the spiritual Self-Identity level I practice Ho'oponopono and *ACIM*. We must see that Truth comes in many forms, but in content it is One, it is Whole, it is Absolute—true in all space and in all time, everywhere, past, present, and future. Ho'oponopono/*ACIM* are processes of Atonement, or corrections which erase my false "self" so that my true Self-Identity can emerge and be seen. Vision is the gift of Truth brought about by vigilance, discipline, and practice to undo and erase problematic memories that recur and repeat. This process is a function of taking a birth—perhaps its only function—making the purpose of life freedom from all problems. Happiness is what is left when problems (non-happiness) have been dissolved. It is a tedious process because like the Hydra's many heads, once one problem is severed, two more seem to spring up in its place. Without determination and seeing, the conscious mind cannot accomplish liberation. I would get discouraged and give up. Determination is needed. It makes possible the virtually impossible.

Ω

105.

A

To be with the day and the concerns of that day I need not be too concerned about the future. Each day will have its task which presents itself naturally. And there is a wonderful lesson in *ACIM,* ***I place the future in the hands of God. ACIM Lesson #194*** When honored, this lesson takes away the anxiety of not knowing what the future will hold. Why would I think my needs would not be met? The present is all there is, and gratefulness must be always found in the present, even for events and conditions past. Each day is now, none like the rest. Will I meet it with that newness, or will I impose upon it some dead memory? There are repeating cycles which do not alter the newness. I can always wake up a little more into my Self. The day's newness depends on how much I am awake to see it. There is beauty to witness in the simplest of things, of event and encounters. I have a cherry wood trunk I made with my own hands. Over the years the color of the wood has deepened into a glowing reddish brown with darker grain of subtle burgundy. I think the tree would be approving of giving its body of wood to these ends; that it could now be admired and used and appreciated for its beauty from an aged patina. Life is there to notice. I would be dead not to notice, missing out on the elemental joys of Nature so vast and varied, so inexhaustible in the newness it presents to one who can see.

Ω

106.

A

The times contain solutions to "problems" manufactured by those who do not see clearly the problem, therefore do not really work as solutions. Problems are not external. Billions of dollars are spent on Homeland Security to make us safe from "terrorists." Insecurity is inside us. 9/11 was a symptom, not a cause of an arrogance and insecurity pervading American life. We rely on corporations to provide our every need and government to safeguard those corporations, some being larger in financial scope than the economies of small countries. Are markets ever secure? Government relies on its authority to enact and enforce laws that ensure security to its citizens. We have social security, a system meant to provide for the old. Can a government ever make a person secure? The external changes may bring about an insecure situation. Insecurity is the fuel that feeds our constant search, our very grasping for security. We cling to our possessions and our status quo of vested interests as though these are the source of our security. How we have misled our minds. Security comes not from a bigger military or a bigger stock portfolio. It is another kind of inner transformation resulting from questioning all I have valued. When I have undone my internal impurities then I can be secure with my Self. This Self is safe and unassailable, ever secure.

Ω

107.

A

Usually what one learns from another is put in the storehouse of memory then used to repeat that learning. Most of what we learn is not too useful. We learn to be greedy, or anxious, or self-indulgent. We learn skills, but the internal issues are seldom addressed, for if they were, our lives would not be full of problems and reactions to those problems. Most of our thinking is a reaction, or rather a collection of opposing factors. "I like this, but I don't like that." Then we have choices and by choosing we think we are in control of our lives. If choosing solved problems would there be war, starvation, murder, poverty? Our learning has fallen short of liberating us from problems because the conscious mind of thought and the subconscious mind of memory are incapable of solving problems. Seeing this is the first and most necessary step to invoking the Unknown, the Void, to its inherent capability to dissolve my problems, *which are thoughts*. **My thoughts do not mean anything. ACIM Lesson #10** To realize the truth of this statement would take a miracle—a transmutation of thought into inspiration. The breath is inspiring. I don't need to think about breathing any more than my heart beating, yet these two functions keep me alive in a body, involuntarily. Perhaps there is an involuntary Mind living apart from physicality which keeps me alive spiritually.

Ω

108.

A

The empty mind is enlightened, and so few arrive at such clarity. An incarnated soul is given a chance to undo memory, thought, the past. Seldom does he choose to come to empty because the process of undoing is long and tedious. Without the testaments of the undoing process, examples of quantum shift in perception from a problem to a solution, the student would become discouraged. The results of cleaning may not be observable. What is observable is that problems recur. The wise point out that the source of problems is a memory, a thought which has not been released. I can notice that problems are less frequent, there is more space for quiet, more inner peace. I feel discouragement sometimes; it is a form of ingratitude. Even feeling this in the face of discouragement, I choose to do the cleaning—repentance and forgiveness. Transmutation is in my Creator's Hands. I have little to do with that, nor do "expectations" amount to much. It is best to expect nothing and embrace *ACIM*/Ho'oponopono as the way of living. A practice is developed by repeated and vigilant attentions. To be empty of thought requires constant undoing. As long as I have existence—a memory—there is work to undo. Without Divine help and my acceptance of it, salvation is not possible. The help is to practice Ho'oponopono/*ACIM*.

Ω

109.

A

Vigilance is watching the mind, my mind, for what it contains. I have thoughts which are negative or positive, happy or sad—in short, relative thought. ACIM/Ho'oponopono would term these meaningless/memory thoughts. I need not look hard inside myself to find these. The wise point out there are billions of meaningless thoughts in me which I do not even know I have, residing in my subconscious. The issue of vigilance becomes the clearing of these thoughts to be with thought of a higher nature that is Absolute, non-relative, true in all space in all time. These Thoughts of God/Inspirations are in me as well. In order to access them I must first silence my relative thought. *ACIM* does this by stating **My meaningless thoughts are showing me a meaningless world. ACIM, Lesson #11** Ho'oponopono does this by process of erasure initiated by thought, but not completed by it. Conscious mind says to subconscious mind, "I'm sorry, please forgive me." Both minds admitting something is amiss but admitting they have no solution—this constitutes an Invocation to Higher Intelligence for the canceling out of thought. In the hands of transcendental Powers, the matter can be dissolved. *ACIM* calls this "a miracle," Ho'oponopono calls it "transmutation." They are the same. Now a mind is still and can receive inspiration from the Divine Creator which will always be whole and at peace.

Ω

110.

A

Memory is unwilling, for the most part, to let go. Thought, which is memory, wants to hang on to the hell it made because it is the one thing it has authority over. To give it up is a loss of authority, which brings fear to the mind. This fear manifests unwillingness in a myriad of forms—sickness, poverty, destructive emotions, sense of separation, etc. Thought believes it made itself, which it did, but in separation from Identity. Identity, on the other hand, knows it did not make itself, rather it was created by its Creator (Divinity) in its likeness of Love (Void). Its nature is Absolute Peace—Silence and Stillness. Identity has the power to co-create, to be the channel of its Source. It can only do this when thought/memory is taken to zero. Emptiness is the nature of Identity, in the beginning. There is a yearning to share its joy; a yearning to create. Divinity gives to Self-Identity an Inspiration to make manifest. A new creation is born in the likeness of its Source. "I am the I. I come forth from the Void into Light." Ho'oponopono Opening Prayer. Anything born of the I is synonymous to the I. This is why Jesus said, "I and my Father are One." He had completed his *ACIM*/Ho'oponopono process and entered into the Absolute Void, the Rock of Immortality; therefore, all he extended was in its likeness, Pure Love.

Ω

111.

Ω

Memory is the fact that *I see only the past. ACIM Lesson #7* That is how the body lives. It is a separated entity. The body is memory; thought is physical, though more rarified. It is like steam, water, and ice, being all of water. But a miracle is present in thought, one in which thought can see it is not whole or absolutely true. It can also see it has no means of its own for healing itself. This is why *ACIM*/Ho'oponopono is given. When thought realizes its limitation, its own conflict, it has one of two options: continue or stop (and enter the still mind, the Void). The system of Repentance-Forgiveness-Transmutation is needed to restore the mind to Oneness. I am Mind, unseparated with my Source, Divine Mind. Memory is a small part of Mind which erroneously thinks it is whole and happy when it is fragmented and miserable. When I am aware that I am "sick" and ask God to heal me, nothing happens. I remain sick because the "god" I invoke is an illusion of thought. I must face myself and see my error is inside of me, and the solution is inside of me as well. All sorrow is inside of me. This is what Jesus felt in Gethsemane. I must own my sorrow, my memory. By invoking my Mind, starting with my subconscious memory, admitting I don't know the problem or the solution, I open the door for the miracle to take place (even if I am unaware of its results of healing). Symptoms are merely a reminder to keep vigilant only for the kingdom of God.

Ω

112.

Discouragement is lack of courage. Why do I lack courage? Have I ever really faced my discouragement? It is a form of fear; wanting a situation to be different than what it is, then blaming Divinity for not bringing that "ideal" about. The ego wants to "seek but not to find" (*ACIM*); therefore, discouragement is a "tool" of the ego to keep me from being who I AM as God created me. A process of cancellation is needed to cancel out thought. Even "goals" need to be cancelled. A goal says, "I'm not perfect. I need to do something to get perfect." This is the root of desire, seeking from a premise of disappointment, and discouragement. I need to admit to myself, ***I do not know what anything is for. ACIM, Lesson #25,*** in order to void my memory. When I truly get this lesson, the mind is empty instantaneously. Hearing and realizing occur simultaneously. The ears to hear are grateful for the truth. What goal need I seek when I have heard the truth? Any seeking from that point would be a denial of the truth. Discouragement would be a grand denial. Why? I have courage to face my ignorance. What else do I need to face but myself with the light of forgiveness and non-condemnation which are given to me through *ACIM*/Ho'oponopono? What other needs are not met when the main one, my need for Liberation, is fully met. Holy relationship is a fact erasing all discouragement.

113.

A

We are so conditioned by our upbringing concerning what we put into ourselves in terms of food, experience, and ideas that we seldom stop to question what is best to consume. Consumption is unavoidable. Without breathing air, we would die in a few minutes. So, breath is the most essential function of life in our body. Have we given it the attention and reverence it deserves? Pranayama, the yogic practice of conscious, controlled breathing, purifies the breath so that the subtle energies, more rarified than even air—call them Life Forces—can be taken in, consumed. It is so simple, yet in modern systems of so-called health, so absent. We have a system of "health" which has become "disease management," because mankind in general has fallen into degenerate patterns and practices. Without correcting the basic relationship with consumption, we become polluted with toxins. Commonly seen pollution in our environment occurs because inside of us (me) is a form of pollution. Disease and ill practices are handed down through memory, much of which is lodged in our subconscious. Thoughts of separation from our Creator have produced illness and death. Breath is the first function to be clarified in order to return to balance, harmony, peace—our Self-Identity. Pranayama or HA (Ho'oponopono) are means toward wise consumption.

Ω

114.

A

Water is the second most essential element to sustain life; air, then water. Both are free flowing, having no inherent boundaries. Air, more rarified, will flow just about anywhere up or down. Water, denser, will flow side-to-side, but mostly downward being more affected by gravity. The consumption of water is more essential than eating solid food. A body can live on air for a while, and with air and water longer. Who knows how long I could sustain myself on just air and water in unlimited supply? Who has tried it in this age in this part of the world? Some yogis in India have been reported to live on only prana. Who knows if this is legend or fact? That we do not presently, in this society, have much of a conscious and profound relationship with prana or water is apparent. We consume but have little reverence nor true appreciation for that which we consume. Who pays respects to the air? Who treats water with reverence? Without a relationship with these most essential elements, how can anyone walk in a sacred manner? The cleansing properties of air and water are scarcely understood. Who knows what role they play in healing, not only healing the physical body, but healing the mental body as well. Earth, air, fire, water, space are the five categories of elements mentioned in the ancient original texts. Without a relationship with these, how can anyone pretend to know the sacred?

Ω

115.

A

Earth is the progenitor of food created by Divinity to sustain the physical body. It is a more gross level of existence than air or water, not so flowing unless molten hot. Most put earth before breath and drink, somewhat erroneously, because it moves awareness in the wrong direction, establishing false priorities. Look at junk food and the havoc it reeks on health. People want to identify with the densest part of themselves. Earth is an aspect of being here now, but it is certainly farther removed than air and water from Essence. Essence is Being, a non-physical state. Although air is not Essence, its properties resemble a relationship: air is to earth as spirit is to physicality. Not quite, because air is still physical, but prana is the bridge between Spirit and air. Prana is realized through the breath, not confined to the breath, being imbued in everything. This is how Self-Identity can be "one and all." Like a hologram, the Self is a replica of the Whole Universe. This is why Whitman said, "I contain universes." He had evolved into an awareness that the Self is very particular, as well as broad and all-inclusive, simultaneously. I accept my body and its needs while I am "in a body." Who am I to say how long I will stay in physical form? The real work is not to place a limit of time upon myself. By the same token, be vigilant that total enlightenment, Being, will be actually be realized in me.

Ω

116.

A

I have a concept of myself, an image composed of aspects of personality, thoughts; in short, my memory. When I cleanse this concept by looking closely at the contradictions, the pain, the sorrow and fear it contains, I cannot help but yearn for a purer Identity which is free of all conflict and sorrow. The fact that I am not this concept, this content of memory, that it can be cancelled out, is reassuring. It takes vigilance to do this. The wise point out a system. *ACIM*/Ho'oponopono are the processes given to me for this erasure. Their common bond is simply repentance-forgiveness-transmutation. The part I play is a discipline of constant observance of my mind. Memory is persistent in affecting my experience of myself. To be absolved of it is a relief and the way to be in the Present without smudge or blemish of the past. Some memory is necessary, obviously, without remembering the meaning of these words it would be impossible to communicate. The goal is to remove the "past" from memory. There is an ancient "memory" of the present, which is more like an attentiveness, a being now, in which my past thought is used, but it is cleansed and forgiven. When it really is cleansed, there is great beauty and joy. The Will of my Self-Identity is now consistent with the will of my Creator. I am the I. My Creator and I are One. This wholeness is always present, and I am more aware of accepting it.

Ω

117.

A

Man strives for perfection without seeing it in the present situation. "Self-improvement" comes in many forms, all starting from basically the same premise: I am not, I will become. With this premise there is never real fulfillment or acceptance of the perfection that is now. There is a difference between desire and receiving the given. Desire is a state of mind that does not have, therefore it wants what it does not have and seeks to get it. Receiving the given is a state of mind that recognizes all that it needs it already has. It is already "given." Therefore, there is something to give from this great reservoir of having. All things in creation are in a state of flow, a kind of exchange from one form to another. The air is given—it sustains Life. Water is given and the produce of the earth is given. More profoundly speaking, a teacher is given, the one who can liberate me from desire, from becoming, from false belief; the one who can dissolve my impurities or lead me in the direction that I may dissolve them myself. Deep in the memory is a sense of separation and, also, even deeper, a remembrance of wholeness, of Salvation. A true teacher will point out the extent to which I have fallen short of my own Being. There is a need for repentance or conversion (my choice to admit the mistake). Then the grace of restoration of my awareness of Who I AM as God created me, my Self-Identity, follows. Repentance and forgiveness are my sole responsibilities in order to realize my Self-Identity.

Ω

118.

A

"What has death and a thick body dances before what has no thick body and no death." These words were uttered by Kabir, a 15th Century Indian mystic poet, whose words were realized. We spend most of our lives identifying with the body, its needs and wants, and the personality "self" which goes with it. The day-to-day routines of work, acquiring money and possessions, entertaining ourselves, even taking ourselves seriously in some profession—all these—are the means of identifying with the body, with physicality. The dance of existence, no matter how highly successful or celebrated, has its own beginnings and endings. The body ages, and the things it could do before to impress and attain its desires, it may no longer do. It goes into decline and dies, unless the mind questions death—as in the philosophy, psychology and practice of Physical Immortality. In the case a transition, who am I? The poet states a fact, one he has deeply considered for a while, pondering the nature of Self-Identity. All physicality sees change: birth-life-death, beginning-middle-end. This is the dance of existence. In India it is symbolically represented by Shiva Nataraj—the dancing Lord Shiva whose countenance is still, even amidst movement, surrounded by a ring of fire. Lord Shiva plays out all manifestations that are predestined, but He does this in a state of total absorption into another state of being, one in which death has been transcended. Stillness is the silencer of all words and deeds, and death is but a passing whim.

Ω

119.

A

I am the Alpha and the Omega, the beginning and the end. I will give to the one who thirsts from the spring of the water of life without cost. (Revelations 21:6) The enlightened Being who comes awakens us to the First and the Last freedom. Created by a Life Force beyond our own understanding, we find ourselves in this Life pondering the purpose for being here. What is our function beyond the mere survival of the body, our jobs and our families? What is this "spring of the water of life" that is my natural inheritance, "without cost?" The Christ Consciousness, one totally aligned and in harmony with the Will of His Creator, is also our true consciousness. We ascend to the degree we embrace this True Self within us. It is our "first and last" freedom, our **Alpha Omega** at the base of our being giving us reason to be here. We thirst to know the Absolute—Divine Love and Joy—that transcends the thought of our egos. And the Christ "stands within" to aid us in this ascension. We rise up in Life, it seems, to embrace broader and deeper manifestations of the Truth. This is our first and last concern—to "know thyself," which is to know our Truth. Herein the namesake of this book and my inspiration's Source. I am its student and with the perennial challenge of living the words, and not just intellectually "knowing" them. Alpha and Omega—my BEGINNING and my END—will ultimately dissolve into that great unknowable Oneness we call God, as all my thoughts of separation are dissolved, and as I awaken my Identity to Love and be Loved.

Ω

120.

Α

The mind, having been introduced to the concepts of "good and evil," broods atop the fence between the two, pondering the nature of opposites. I am my mind containing both the good and the evil. How can I condemn the evil by thinking I am above it? Truth is an acceptance of what is both good and evil. In this acceptance they dissolve into one, no longer in conflict as true opposing forces. Gandhi said in the film *Water,* "I used to think that God is Truth, but now I am certain that Truth is God." The fact that I am a liar is the truth. I deceive myself and others in subtle ways when the ends are in my favor. My motives are very wily in getting what I want. My thought is always deceptive. When I accept this is the nature of my thought, everyone's thought, I am one step closer to silence. The nature of my thought contains both good and evil, joy and sorrow, right and wrong. There is a third factor available to me which transcends all opposites. The acceptance of darkness and light takes me out of the conflict of opposites, into the integrated field of truth. Limitations are only of my own making. When I accept the good and evil in me I am unlimited and at peace. There is no battle to be fought; there is no enemy to vilify; there is no "self" to condemn. My mind, having rid itself of attack thoughts, is now still and empty. As it is whole, now it is free.

Ω

121.

A

My first spiritual Love is for *A Course in Miracles*. My second spiritual Love is for Ho'oponopono. Thirdly—Babaji, the Divine Mother, and India have shaped my life. Above this Love is the direct guidance from the Masters—Jesus of *ACIM*, Babaji, and Ammachi as the Divine Mother. None of these are above the other in terms of a hierarchy. It happened that Life introduced me to *ACIM* first when Sondra Ray said, "It is the most important book written in 2000 years." She also introduced me to Babaji and Ho'oponopono, although it happened that she was not to be my main teacher for many years to come. Tara Singh, whom I met during Easter of 1989, would become my main teacher of *ACIM*. Dr. Ihaleakala Hew Len, whom I met around the same time, would become my mentor in Ho'oponopono. Both systems are designed to undo our thinking. Forgiveness is the key that binds *ACIM* and Ho'oponopono together. Although they are divergently different in form, they are essentially identical twins in content. I do not separate the two, nor do I place the people I met through one over the people I met from the other. I am just a pilgrim, and a not very pristine one at that, on that road of evolutionary progress toward realizing my ultimate God-created Self. No one can be more than that. It is the first and the last journey everyone must take to awaken their own Self-Identity. I rediscovered Babaji in 2008. My gratitude is due to *ACIM* and Ho'oponopono, as well as to the Divine Mother and Babaji, for all their guidance along the way.

Ω

122.

A

"I came from a long way down." Bob Dylan. There are men and women in this world who speak true words that come from a place of true humility. They can stop you in your tracks. There is not much difference between these people and the words they speak, because the life they live is consistent with what they say. To meet one of these men or women would transform one's whole life. I met such a man in Tara Singh. I came from a long way down and he lifted me to heights of my own being which otherwise I could not have reached; and even from that lofty vantage point, I could barely touch his feet. There are other great beings I have met: Sondra Ray, Morrnah Nalamaku Simeona, Dr. Ihaleakala Hew Len, yet Taraji, my teacher, my master, will always be first in the pantheon of my heart. He is the one who awakened me. He introduced me to who I am as God created me by undoing all self-concepts I thought I had. He began with undoing and he ended with gratefulness; the tumultuous first part never superseded the joys of the still and silent second part. In his presence I was not a body, not a personality of various problems. He brought me to emptiness where I will remain. His Love surrounds me, and that I extend. I began with him and I will end with him in that indefinable space beyond thought. In my *Alpha Omega*.

Ω

Epilogue

This is not the end. I am happy that you are here reading this. Endings are yet to be recognized as new beginnings. The contact we have made in *Alpha Omega* is an important encounter. I would like to hear from you, a part of my "ministry." When *A Course in Miracles* was given in 1976, I had little awareness then that 43 years later I would be accepting the fact, "I am among the ministers of God," Lesson #154. I also did not know—you, who are reading this book now, form an important part of this ministry. All the meanders of my life fade in importance—yet this one direct connection with you comes forth to matter. It could even be one hundred years from this day I am writing, yet always in the present of this real time of the Spirit. THANK YOU for coming on this epistolary journey with me, for whatever has inspired you has also inspired me in these writings. Could our minds be truly joined? I hope so. If the action of a spiritual awakening is to be worthy of my sustained attention, it would have to include you, my readers, in this action. A profound utterance from the top of a lonely mountain is diminished without sharing. So here I am in that act of exchange, with you. You decide what is useful, or not. And to the degree it is truly useful, helpful, and true, you decide also if it is profound. Time will tell if this books finds itself in the hands of readers into perpetuity. But for now it is enough that you are reading these words—*Alpha Omega*. With deep Love and Gratitude.

—Markus Ray—
65 years old today, 11/11/2109
Melbourne, Australia

Resources

The work of Markus Ray can be viewed on "Art Look—an art lover's companion." www.markusray.com You can also contact him there on that site, and sign up for his Art Look newsletter.

You can find Markus Ray's books on his Amazon Author's portal here: www.bit.ly/MarkusRay

Markus shares lectures, videos and commentary on *A Course in Miracles* with subscribers to "Miracles for You—1-Year Support Network" You can subscribe here: www.bit.ly/Miracles4You

Markus has a Facebook page at:
www.facebook.com/markus.ray.169

You can reach Markus directly at:
markus@markusray.com

Twitter: www.twitter.com/markusray1008

Instagram: www.instagram.com/markusray1008

To Have a Liberation Breathing Session or consultation with Sondra Ray & Markus Ray, book one here:
www.bit.ly/LBSession

MARKUS RAY'S Author's Portal :

<u>Bit.ly/MarkusRay</u>

SONDRA RAY'S Author's Portal :

<u>Bit.ly/SondraRay</u>

About the Author

Markus Ray received his training in the arts, holding a Bachelor's of Fine Arts Degree in printmaking and drawing from the Cleveland Institute of Art, and a Master's of Fine Arts Degree in painting from the Tyler School of Art, Temple University in Philadelphia, PA, USA. Also a writer and a poet, he brings spirituality and sensuality together in these mediums of expression. He is the author of a major work, *Odes To The Divine Mother*, which contains 365 prose poems in praise of the Divine Feminine Energy. Along with the Odes are his paintings and images of the Divine Mother created around the world in his mission with Sondra Ray.

Markus is a presenter of the profound modern psychological /spiritual scripture, *A Course In Miracles*. He studied with his Master, Tara Singh, for 17 years, in order to experience its truth directly. His spiritual quest has taken him to India many times with Tara Singh and Sondra Ray, where Muniraj, Babaji's foremost disciple, gave him the name Man Mohan, "The Poet who steals the hearts of the people". In all of his paintings, writings and lectures, Markus creates a quiet atmosphere of peace and clarity that is an invitation to go deeper into the realms of inner stillness, silence and beauty. He teaches, writes and paints alongside of Sondra Ray, and many have been touched by their demonstration of a holy relationship in action. His iconic paintings of the Masters can be viewed on www.MarkusRay.com which he often creates while his twin flame, Sondra Ray, is lecturing in seminars.

Markus also gives commentaries and lectures on *A Course in Miracles* in live seminars with Sondra Ray and in his Miracles for You program—bit.ly/Miracles4You.

BABAJI, JESUS & THE DIVINE MOTHER

Sondra Ray & Markus Ray are brought together by the grace of their Master, Maha Avatar Herakhan Babaji. Babaji Himself said, "Markus is my Humbleness. Sondra is my Voice. Together they are my Love." As Ambassadors for Him, their mission is to bring His teaching of "*Truth, Simplicity, Love and Service to Mankind*" along with the presence of the Divine Mother to the world. They do so through seminars like the New LRT®, the healing practice of Liberation Breathing®, and the study of *A Course in Miracles*. They are unfolding the plan of Babaji, Jesus and the Divine Mother, Who provide a spiritual foundation for their worldwide mission of service. Their relationship is a shining example of what is possible through deep ease and no conflict. They can take you to a higher realms of being, where Spiritual Intimacy©, miracles, and holy relationships can become a big part of everyday life. Their major book on relationships they wrote together is *Spiritual Intimacy: What You Really Want With A Mate*. They offer private Liberation Breathing sessions over Skype, Zoom and in person, and various Seminars and Sacred Quests around the world. They work with Liberation Breathing® to help people free themselves from limiting beliefs and negative thoughts. They encourage people to discover more profound levels of *DIVINE PRESENCE* in their lives, and awaken more awareness of Immortal Love, Peace and Joy in their hearts.

NOTES

NOTES

NOTES

www.ingramcontent.com/pod-product-compliance
Lightning Source LLC
Chambersburg PA
CBHW070732170426
43200CB00007B/506